The Spanish Language in the United States

The Spanish Language in the United States addresses the rootedness of Spanish in the United States, its racialization, and Spanish speakers' resistance against racialization. This novel approach challenges the "foreigner" status of Spanish and shows that racialization victims do not take their oppression meekly. It traces the rootedness of Spanish since the 1500s, when the Spanish empire began the settlement of the new land, till today, when 39 million U.S. Latinos speak Spanish at home. Authors show how whites categorize Spanish speaking in ways that denigrate the non-standard language habits of Spanish speakers—including in schools—highlighting ways of overcoming racism.

José A. Cobas is Professor Emeritus of Sociology at Arizona State University. Among his publications are (with Jorge Duany and Joe R. Feagin) *How the United States Racializes Latinos: White Hegemony and Its Consequences* (Paradigm 2009), (with Joe R. Feagin) *Latinos Facing Racism: Discrimination, Resistance, and Endurance* (Paradigm 2014), and (with Joe R. Feagin, Daniel J. Delgado, and Maria Chávez), *Latino Peoples in the New America: Racialization and Resistance* (Routledge 2019).

Bonnie Urciuoli is Professor Emerita of Anthropology at Hamilton College where she taught linguistic and semiotic anthropology. She has published on race/class ideologies of Spanish–English bilingualism in New York City, on the discursive production and marketing of "skills" in the United States, and on the construction and marketing of studenthood and diversity in U.S. higher education. Her books include *Exposing Prejudice: Puerto Rican Experiences of Language, Race, and Class* (1996), *Neoliberalizing Diversity in Liberal Arts College Life* (forthcoming), and an edited volume, *The Experience of Neoliberal Education* (2018).

Joe R. Feagin is Distinguished Professor of Sociology at Texas A&M University. He specializes in systemic racism studies. Among his books are *Latinos Facing Racism* (2014, with J. Cobas), *Racist America* (4th ed., Routledge 2019, with K. Ducey), *Rethinking Diversity Frameworks in Higher Education* (Routledge,

2020, with E. Chun), *The White Racial Frame* (3rd ed., Routledge 2020), and *Revealing Systemic British Racism* (Routledge 2021, with K. Ducey). He is the recipient of the American Association for Affirmative Action's Fletcher Lifetime Achievement Award and the American Sociological Association's W. E. B. Du Bois Career of Distinguished Scholarship Award, Cox-Johnson-Frazier Award, and Public Understanding of Sociology Award. He was the 1999–2000 president of the American Sociological Association.

Daniel J. Delgado is Associate Professor of Sociology at Texas A&M University in San Antonio. His research is focused on three areas: a Latino/a student's experiences in higher education, middle-class Latinx experiences with processes of racialization, and understanding how race and space intersect in the Southwest. He has published in several edited volumes and journals and is co-editor (with José A. Cobas and Joe R. Feagin) of *Latino Peoples in the New America: Racialization and Resistance* (Routledge 2019). He lives in his hometown of San Antonio, Texas.

New Critical Viewpoints on Society Series
Edited by Joe R. Feagin

For more information about this series, please visit
www.routledge.com/New-Critical-Viewpoints-on-Society/book-series/NCVS

The Spanish Language in the United States

Rootedness, Racialization, and Resistance

Edited by José A. Cobas,
Bonnie Urciuoli, Joe R. Feagin,
and Daniel J. Delgado

Routledge
Taylor & Francis Group

NEW YORK AND LONDON

Cover image: © Shutterstock

First published 2022
by Routledge
605 Third Avenue, New York, NY 10158

and by Routledge
4 Park Square, Milton Park, Abingdon, Oxon, OX14 4RN

Routledge is an imprint of the Taylor & Francis Group, an informa business

© 2022 Taylor & Francis

The right of José A. Cobas, Bonnie Urciuoli, Joe R. Feagin, and Daniel J. Delgado to be identified as the authors of the editorial material, and of the authors for their individual chapters, has been asserted in accordance with sections 77 and 78 of the Copyright, Designs and Patents Act 1988.

Library of Congress Cataloging-in-Publication Data
Names: Cobas, José A., editor. | Urciuoli, Bonnie, 1949- editor. |
    Feagin, Joe R., editor. | Delgado, Daniel J. (Daniel Justino), editor.
Title: The Spanish language in the United States: rootedness,
    racialization, and resistance/edited by José A. Cobas, Bonnie Urciuoli,
    Joe R. Feagin, and Daniel J. Delgado.
Description: New York, NY: Routledge, 2022. | Series: New critical
    viewpoints on society | Includes bibliographical references and index.
Identifiers: LCCN 2021037664 | ISBN 9781032190563 (hardback) |
    ISBN 9781032190556 (paperback) | ISBN 9781003257509 (ebook)
Subjects: LCSH: Spanish language—United States. | Spanish language—
    Social aspects—United States. | Sociolinguistics—United States. |
    Hispanic Americans—Languages. | Racism in language. | Race relations—
    United States. | LCGFT: Essays.
Classification: LCC PC4826.S656 2022 | DDC 467/.973—dc23
LC record available at https://lccn.loc.gov/2021037664

ISBN: 978-1-032-19056-3 (hbk)
ISBN: 978-1-032-19055-6 (pbk)
ISBN: 978-1-003-25750-9 (ebk)

DOI: 10.4324/9781003257509

Typeset in Garamond
by KnowledgeWorks Global Ltd.

Contents

Contributors

Kevin S. Alejandrez is a PhD Candidate in the University of Kentucky's Department of Sociology where he specializes in social inequalities with a focus on race. His current research analyzes social stratification and racial disparities among Latine farmworkers in the state of Oregon and how they have been affected by the COVID-19 pandemic and Oregon wildfires. His work also explores the ways in which such Latines interpret and respond to the inequalities they experience. Aside from his academic position, Kevin also serves as a community organizer for the Farmworker Service Center in Woodburn, Oregon.

Elizabeth Aranda is Professor of Sociology and Associate Dean in the College of Arts and Sciences at the University of South Florida. A native of Puerto Rico, she has dedicated herself to documenting the lived experience of migration and to share (im)migrants' stories through her research and teaching. Her research addresses migrants' emotional well-being and how they adapt to challenges posed by racial and ethnic inequalities and legal status. She is author of *Emotional Bridges to Puerto Rico: Migration, Return Migration and the Struggles of Incorporation* (Rowman & Littlefield, 2007) and (with S. Hughes and E. Sabogal) of *Making a Life in Multiethnic Miami* (Lynne Rienner, 2014).

José A. Cobas is Professor Emeritus of Sociology at Arizona State University. Among his publications are (with Jorge Duany and Joe R. Feagin) *How the United States Racializes Latinos: White Hegemony and Its Consequences* (Paradigm, 2009), (with Joe R. Feagin) *Latinos Facing Racism: Discrimination, Resistance, and Endurance* (Paradigm, 2014), and (with Joe R. Feagin, Daniel J. Delgado, and Maria Chávez), *Latino Peoples in the New America: Racialization and Resistance* (Routledge, 2019).

Daniel J. Delgado is Associate Professor of Sociology or at Texas A&M-University at San Antonio. His research is focused on three areas, Latino/a student experiences in higher education, middle-class Latinx experiences with processes of racialization, and understanding how race and space intersect in the Southwest. He has published in several edited volumes and journals and is co-editor (with José A. Cobas and Joe R. Feagin) of *Latino Peoples in the New America: Racialization and Resistance* (Routledge, 20190. He lives in his hometown of San Antonio, Texas.

Hilary Dotson is a Senior Researcher at Fors Marsh Group, leading research efforts in public health spaces. As a mixed-methods, applied sociologist, she is passionate about using data to increase social awareness, drive social policy, and improve people's lives. She earned a Ph.D. in Sociology at the University of South Florida and has published research in *Childhood, Deviant Behavior, Justice System Journal*, and *Journal of Poverty*. Her recent research supports federal agencies' suicide and sexual assault prevention initiatives.

Sharon Elise works as a Professor of Sociology at California State University San Marcos. She is currently working with Dr. Michelle Ramos Pellicia on a book on race, culture and identity in Puerto Rico pre and post Hurricanes Irma and María, the 2019 and 2020 earthquakes, and the current COVID-19 pandemic. Her work has appeared in *Journal of Diversity in Education, Thought and Action, Sociological Perspectives*, and *Western Journal of Black Studies*.

Joe R. Feagin is Distinguished Professor of Sociology at Texas A & M University. He specializes in systemic racism studies. Among his books are *Latinos Facing Racism* (Paradigm 2014, with J. Cobas); *Racist America* (4th ed., Routledge 2019, with K. Ducey); *Rethinking Diversity Frameworks in Higher Education* (Routledge, 2020, with E. Chun); *The White Racial Frame* (3rd ed., Routledge 2020); and *Revealing Systemic British Racism* (Routledge, 2021, with K. Ducey). He is the recipient of the American Association for Affirmative Action's Fletcher Lifetime Achievement Award and the American Sociological Association's W. E. B. Du Bois Career of Distinguished Scholarship Award, Cox-Johnson-Frazier Award, and Public Understanding of Sociology Award. He was 1999–2000 president of the American Sociological Association.

José Angel Gutiérrez, Professor Emeritus, Department of Political Science, University of Texas-Arlington, has authored over 17 peer-reviewed books and over two dozen articles plus three children's books. In contract negotiations he has three additional manuscripts and a fiction novel; his first such endeavor. He owns a Dallas-based law firm and is a practicing attorney in Texas and several federal jurisdictions. He is the President and CEO of the Greater Dallas Legal and Community Development Foundation, a legal services organization. Most recently, he was a Fellow at Stanford University's Center for Advance Studies in the Behavioral Sciences.

Ana S.Q. Liberato is an Associate Professor of Sociology at the University of Kentucky. Her research interests include inequalities based on race, ethnicity, gender, and class and their interplay with migration, mobility, and political identities and attitudes. She is the author of *Joaquín Balaguer, Memory and Diaspora: The Lasting Political Legacies of an American Protégé* (Lexington Books, 2013). Her work appears in journals, such as *Ethnic and Racial Studies, World Development, Social Indicators Research, International Journal of Modern Sociology,* and *African American Studies.*

Rosina Lozano is an Associate Professor in the History Department at Princeton University, where she teaches courses on Latina/o/x history and Comparative Race and Ethnicity. She is the author of An American Language: The History of Spanish in the United States (University of California, 2018).

Daniel Mamani is a second-year PhD student in the applied demography program at the University of Texas at San Antonio. He obtained his bachelor's degree from Schreiner University and a master's degree in health and kinesiology from UTSA. His research interests include biodemography, health disparities, and health behaviors.

Mike Mena is a PhD candidate in linguistic anthropology at The Graduate Center (NY). In 2021, he was awarded the NAEd/Spencer Dissertation Fellowship to fund his longitudinal ethnographic research that analyzes the neoliberalization of higher education in the United States. He has published in *Language in Society* as well as contributed to various public-facing education projects, including podcasts and visual essay collaborations. Mena produces the award-winning educational YouTube channel named *The Social Life of Language,* which continues to receive national and international recognition for its multi-modal pedagogical l approach and as intellectually informed public activism.

Michelle Ramos Pellicia is Associate Professor at California State University San Marcos. She is currently working with Sharon Elise on a book on race, culture and identity in Puerto Rico pre and post Hurricanes Irma and María, the 2019 and 2020 earthquakes, and the current COVID-19 pandemic. She is the author of *Language Contact and Dialect Contact: Crossgenerational Phonological Variation in a Puerto Rican Community in the Midwest of the United States* (VDM Verlag, 2009), and (with Patricia Gubitosi) *The Linguistic Landscape in the Spanish-speaking World* (John Benjamins, in press) and has published in *Latino Studies, International Journal of the Linguistic Association of the Southwest, Confluencias,* and *Modern Language Journal.*

Alessandra Rosa (she, her, hers) is a sociocultural anthropologist, professor, researcher, activist, public speaker, and consultant. Currently, she is a Postdoctoral Scholar in the Department of Sociology at the University of South Florida (USF). Prior, she was an Assistant Professor at Lynn University and a Visiting Instructor at Florida International University.

As a transnational feminist scholar, she has dedicated her teaching, research, and service to fostering diversity, equity, and justice. Her work has been published in academic journals, e-journals, book chapters, as well as non-academic outlets. Her book manuscript is soon to be published by the University of Nebraska Press.

Rogelio Sáenz is a Professor in the Department of Demography at the University of Texas at San Antonio. He has written extensively in the areas of demography, Latina/os, race, inequality, immigration, public policy, and social justice. Sáenz is co-author of *Latinos in the United States: Diversity and Change* (Polity, 2015) and co-editor of the *International Handbook of the Demography of Race and Ethnicity* (Springer, 2015). He regularly writes op-ed essays and research briefs for a variety of media and academic outlets throughout the country. Sáenz received the 2020 Saber es Poder Academic Excellence Award from the University of Arizona's Department of Mexican American Studies.

Bonnie Urciuoli is professor emerita of anthropology at Hamilton College where she taught linguistic and semiotic anthropology. She has published on race/class ideologies of Spanish–English bilingualism in New York City, on the discursive production and marketing of 'skills' in the U.S., and on the construction and marketing of studenthood and diversity in U.S. higher education. Books include *Exposing Prejudice: Puerto Rican Experiences of Language, Race, and Class* (1996, Westview), *Neoliberalizing Diversity in Liberal Arts College Life* (forthcoming, Berghahn), and an edited volume *The Experience of Neoliberal Education* (2018, Berghahn).

Section I

Language, Race, and Power

Introduction

Language, Racialization, and Power

Bonnie Urciuoli, José A. Cobas,
Joe R. Feagin, and Daniel J. Delgado

Focusing primarily on the consequences of U.S. relations with Mexico and Puerto Rico, this book examines how those relations played out in the United States colonial viewpoint that came to racialize the use of Spanish in the United States. The chapters in this book provide sociological and semiotic-linguistic perspectives on the experience of Mexican American and Puerto Rican Spanish speakers. The semiotic-linguistic analyses build on the sociological: discourse is meaningful social behavior only because discursive events are anchored in the structures and processes of social life (Silverstein 1976) in turn shaped by history. Although U.S. Spanish speakers are from all over Latin America (as well as the Philippines and Spain), the U.S. racialization of Spanish speakers has been semiotically ordered by its political, economic, and social relations with Mexico and Puerto Rico. The subsequent racialization of Spanish fits in with other U.S. markers of non-whiteness.

As the extensive literature on racialization (see, e.g., Omi and Winant 2015, Feagin and Ducey 2019) makes clear, racialization is a sociohistorical process that takes place when a social group maintains a position of structural dominance (social, legal, political) over another group or groups on the basis of supposedly natural and inherited signs of inferiority. Such signs of difference may be physically visible (skin, hair, facial features), non-visible but assumed (intelligence, character), behavioral (language), and so on; in that sense, such signs of difference are racialized. Once race is assumed, any such signs may be imputed; indeed, racialized people are often assumed, in the absence of material evidence, to have a darker skin tone or a foreign accent. The privileged group uses such signs and their imputed meaning to justify the denial of belonging or participation, oppressing and containing people displaying such signs especially through the use of force. In the United States, those claiming racial privilege have defined themselves as white and have defined the racially unprivileged in terms of the conditions through which the privileged came into contact with them: as slaves and slave descendants, indigenous people, inhabitants of what had been Spanish colonies, indentured and exploited labor. Hence the classifications of non-whiteness are now known as African American, Native American, Latino American, and Asian American. In this

DOI: 10.4324/9781003257509-2

way, U.S. history and society are framed by a white Weltanschauung, termed the White Racial Frame by Feagin (2010:10–11), in which whites supposedly possess such superior traits as an attractive phenotype, superior language, high morality, intelligence, work ethic, and restrained sexuality and fertility while subordinate racial groups have opposite and inferior traits.

Whiteness then is much more than skin color. It is the exercise of racial privilege in a social position safe for those exercising it. People claim that position by pointing to *only* that 'inheritance.' White privilege rests on the bright lines that clarify the oppositions (often violently reinforced) between markers of whiteness and non-whiteness. Thus, as Harrison (1995) and many others have shown, whiteness and non-whiteness are interdependent constructs, maintained for centuries through white-dominated economic, social, legal, scientific, and educational institutions, claims, and practices. Whiteness also saturates the public space of language in the United States (Hill 2008).

English as a sign of whiteness is intertwined with U.S. histories of territorial conquest, white settler colonialism, slavery and black suppression, and exploited migrant labor (Urciuoli 2020). The ways in which language is racialized point to the terms of racialization. The racialization of Spanish in the United States is most associated with the two historical sites of U.S. political domination of the Spanish-speaking world most associated with Spanish-speaking migration to the United States: Mexico and Puerto Rico. U.S. seizures of Mexican territory after the Mexican-American war resulted in an extensive U.S.-Mexican border (with Mexican Americans representing the "other side" of the border), and the United States took over Puerto Rico after the Spanish-American war. At both these sites, the 'other' was racialized as non-white. The Anglo-Saxon (to use the 19th-century term) opposition to Spanish-speaking non-white otherness came into focus in that history and shaped the racializing of the rest of the non-Anglo non-white Western Hemisphere.

When any marker of difference, including language, is racialized, it is no longer simply a thing in and of itself. Semiotically, racialization is structured as an opposition: on one side unmarked (normative or modal) and on the other marked (non-modal, not fitting in in a way imagined as inherent or natural) and associated with natural properties that are seen to define the marked as innately inferior. Racialized markers are thus semiotically charged, trailing the histories of these racialized oppositions. As Brekhus (1998) makes clear, it is most important to maintain the analytic focus on the process of marking through which the relation of unmarked to marked emerges. If the focus is limited to the signs of markedness themselves, those signs all too easily come to essentialize the marked group so that what makes the unmarked group unmarked is analytically ignored. Since those who are unmarked generally take for granted their own semiotic transparency, the point of analysis is to show why and how they do so, as Sasson-Levy (2013) does in her analysis of Ashkenazi 'invisibility' in Israel.

Following that lead, this book shows historical specifics and social processes through which English became the invisible background and racialized Spanish became the visibly marked foreground figure. The origin of the issues discussed in this book lies in 15th-century European colonial expansion and its involvement in the African slave trade. The oppositions originating then have persisted through centuries: (white) European masters versus (non-white) indigenous and enslaved people, and eventually (white) U.S. expansionists versus descendants of the people colonized by the Spanish (who also became non-white). All the associated oppositions of physical 'inheritance' and language were based on assumptions about social belonging and maintained by legal, business, scientific, and other social structures that reinforced the bright line between whiteness and racial otherness.

The 'normal' state of belonging in U.S. society privileges European, especially Northern and Western, 'heritage.' Such 'normality' also intersectionally privileges straight male and Protestant social positions, as shown in Carter's (2007) account of the 1880–1940 historical co-emergence of Anglo-Saxon whiteness and gender/sex normativity. The archetypal situation for the United States and other countries with histories of African slavery and settler colonialism is the opposition of whiteness and non-whiteness, non-whiteness being ascribed to those whose land, resources, and labor were appropriated. For the United States, that appropriation, with its concomitant racialization, was extended to Mexicans and Puerto Ricans, the descendants of Spanish colonizers whose land, resources, and labor were most directly exploited by the United States in the form of white politicians, ranchers, corporations and smaller business owners, and so on. Even without those colonial projects, the United States would have found ways to racialize the non-Anglo-Canadian Western Hemisphere; after all, by around 1900, the United States was using legal, political, scientific, educational, and other rationalizations to racialize many people in southern and eastern Europe and pretty much the rest of the world. But what the Mexican and Puerto Rican colonial projects did was set the terms for how that displacement and its subsequent racialization took place: that speakers of Spanish are foreign, dangerous, and invasive, and so is Spanish.

The mismatch of historical and social reality on the one hand and powerfully held naturalized assumptions on the other is what racialization is all about. It operates not only through bright lines but also through misrecognitions and loose alignments, ignoring some things and exaggerating or inventing others, pulling them together in affective associations that routinely overpower facts that are under people's noses. Realities lose definition and disappear before sets of associations in which the racist gaze seeks a coherence that validates its assumption of power. If the markedness of blackness echoes a past of slavery, in which African-descended people were regarded only as appropriated labor, the markedness of colonized Puerto Ricans and Mexicans (and by extension other Western hemisphere descendants of Spanish settlement) were marked as inhabitants of extensive real estate acquired through conquest, the proper function of which was the enhancement of white U.S. wealth. Similarly, indigenous Americans were regarded as primarily an obstruction to white Anglo-Saxon control of the Western Hemisphere's land and resources, a control seen as "manifest destiny" (Horsman 1981). In this picture, Puerto Ricans and Mexicans occupy a position of oppressed markedness just short of blackness, and by association so generally do Spanish speakers and Spanish. The realities of their former situation, the events that brought them into the U.S. orbit, the nature of their current lives, and the varieties of Spanish that they speak disappear in the face of whites' racialized fantasies of language that play out in multiple ways including as public performance by self-styled language police (on which more shortly).

U.S. colonization builds in part on Spanish colonization. One of the great ironies of the white American racialization of Spanish is that it obscures the legacy of Spanish itself as originally a colonial language, becoming as well an indigenous and an immigrant language, a legacy addressed by Lozano (2018; see also Lozano this volume, Chapter 1). It is therefore important to remember that the colonizing role of English addressed in this volume does build on a centuries-long colonial base established by Spain. The U.S. colonization of former Mexican and Spanish territories was the second round of colonization they experienced, their first round being the Spanish colonization, including language, of indigenous people; Vélez-Ibañez (2017) provides an extensive treatment of the establishment of Spanish and later English linguistic hegemonies in the Southwest region of North America, starting in 1540. And the United States, like Spain before it, assumed the moral right to exercise power, however much the historical details differ. The assumption of that moral right to power was certainly exercised by all European-origin settlers in the new world through their use of the African slave trade, which fueled centuries-long processes of racialization. The assumption of the right to power and the capacity to exercise it was also manifested in the language policies that informed colonial government and settlement, such as the enforced imposition of European languages on indigenous people especially through religion and schooling, or the severing of enslaved people's connections to their native African languages.

Bourdieu's (1991) concept of linguistic capital examines the contemporary market principles that order manifestations of power through language practices and policies, an approach also developed by Gal (1989) and Irvine (1989). The economic and political principles that maintain and justify how power and the concomitant place of language are ordered can shift over time: power once exercised through church and crown is now exercised through markets. What remains constant is that there are ordering principles that people internalize and act on as their "natural" right. We see this in the essays throughout this collection, most explicitly in the lead chapter by José Cobas and Joe Feagin, "Language Oppression and Resistance: The Case of Middle-class Latinos in the United States." Using Bourdieu's frame to analyze in-depth interviews with middle-class U.S. Spanish speakers, Cobas and Feagin examine the social dynamics through which the place of Spanish is kept firmly subordinate to English, manifested in the strategies through which linguistic practices of native Spanish speakers are controlled and silenced by Anglos in public situations. Anglos do so assuming they have the right to do so while exercising power in ways almost never challenged except by the Spanish speakers they target. Such Anglo power thus becomes invisible, hiding behind an ideology of language standardization (Spanish accents are a particular target) that thinly disguises a racialized equivalence of Spanish and native Spanish speakers. (See Feagin and Cobas 2014 for expanded treatment of these points.)

The question of rootedness is outlined in the next section, which takes up the historical, sociological, and language realities of Spanish in the U.S. Rosina Lozano's chapter, "The Early Political History of Spanish in the United States," addresses the colonial, indigenous, and immigrant spaces occupied by Spanish, showing how different the social and historical realities are from white racialized fantasies. Far from being foreign or invasive, Spanish has been in the United States practically since its inception, longer than English in some regions, and was once positively viewed and deeply integrated into the politics, legislation, and newspapers of the territories, states, and cities of the Southwest where it now is likely to be demonized. In fact, Spanish (becoming effectively indigenous after displacing local indigenous languages) was instrumental in the residents of these territories learning to participate in the white U.S. political order and was for a long time the language preferred for negotiation and trade by indigenous people. In "The demography of Latino Spanish speakers in the United States," Rogelio Sáenz and David Mamani lay out quantitative evidence for structural inequalities affecting Spanish speakers. Pointing out the sheer (and still growing) size of the U.S. Spanish-speaking population and noting their diverse nations of origin, they draw a detailed picture of social and geographical factors shaping Spanish rootedness and retention. They examine patterns of Spanish and English at home and note a general rise over decades in English dominance among both U.S. and foreign born. They note the earnings inequality affecting Latinos generally, especially those born outside the United States and those not English dominant. This shows the structural consequences of racialization that affect even fluent English speakers. Ironically, the authors point out, Spanish language abilities disvalued in native speakers of Spanish are valued in white non-native Spanish speakers, now for generations.

The problem of racialization – in which those realities of rootedness are ignored, reconstructed, or vociferously denied – is taken up in the next section. In "What anti-Spanish Prejudice Tells Us About Whiteness," Bonnie Urciuoli examines the racialized imagining of Spanish from the perspective of U.S. whiteness and what that says about white beliefs about race and language. Americans routinely imagine language as "naturally" a system that must be kept logical, correct, and "unmixed" for accurate reference. This provides a rationale for mapping race from biology onto language: since individuals "should" take control of their language habits, which includes using only English in public, people who set themselves up as language police feel licensed to publicly denigrate Spanish and by extension its speakers (or perhaps any foreign language, but certainly those spoken by non-whites). Once a group of speakers is imagined, they are slotted as an undifferentiated mass into a hierarchy of what the imaginer values.

In "A Language-elsewhere: A Friendlier Linguistic Terrorism," Michael Mena details a peculiarly neoliberal form of higher education denial of racialized realities at the University of Texas – Rio Grande Valley. Mena contrasts the institutional "linguistic terrorism" long experienced by students from immigrant Mexican backgrounds (of their Spanish as deficient, wrong, etc.) with a "friendlier" terrorism in which Spanish is aligned with language as a neoliberal skillset disconnected from indexes of students' own social realities and only obtainable through the university. This reframed Spanish, located anywhere but in students' lives, is standardized and raceless and takes on institutional worth through its (skill-like) economic value, fitting the "neoliberal diversity" fantasy that masks the realities of white racism in so many colleges, universities, corporations, and organizations generally. The experience and nature of racialization projected onto Spanish speakers is explored by Alessandra Rosa, Elizabeth Aranda, and Hilary Dotson in their chapter, "'You are not Allowed to Speak Spanish! This is an American Hospital!': Puerto Ricans' Experiences with Linguistic Discrimination and in Central Florida." People report unfair treatment due to language accent correlating with darker skin tones, level of higher education, marital status, and place of birth. Such characteristics converge in a racialized perception of English pronunciation ("accent"), all of which is not only a judgment of language but of speakers themselves. People describe being explicitly called outsiders from an undifferentiated place of racialized otherness where they should have stayed and whose language they have no right to use in U.S. white public space. The final chapter in this section takes an ethnographic turn shifting the critical gaze from English to Spanish. Michelle Ramos Pelicia and Sharon Elise, in "Black Spanish, White Leanings, Trigueño Mythologies in Puerto Rico," deploy a critical sociolinguistic approach that illustrates Spanish's own European colonial legacy, showing uses of Puerto Rican Spanish discourse that can bring into being and naturalize the social category of blackness. Puerto Rican racial ideology rests on an assumption of a tri-racial past – Spanish, African, and *indio* (Taíno). The latter, assumed to be extinct, masks the (Spanish) white and (African) black opposition by playing into a racial ideology that asserts all Puerto Ricans share all three heritages, making them racially "the same"; however, individual appearance may vary. This ideology is undercut by the everyday language of blackness found in referring expressions and habits of use, all of which reinforce white value.

The final section documents strategies of resistance to the racialization of Spanish. Kevin Alejandrez and Ana S.Q. Liberato, in "The Enchantment of Language Resistance in Puerto Rico," trace the policies and legislation through which American colonial administrators from 1898 sought to instantiate

English in Puerto Rican institutional life as a mechanism of control and sign of loyalty. Efforts were particularly directed toward establishing a school curriculum (and required English) based on U.S. models to make Puerto Rico bilingual, while Puerto Rican educators pushed back hard against English-only instruction in public schools. Despite elite pockets of English (through private education), Puerto Rico remains Spanish speaking. However practical many Puerto Ricans find English, Spanish remains overwhelmingly valued as a sign of Puerto Rican historical and cultural distinction and ideological opposition to U.S. domination. In "Subtracting Spanish and Forcing English: My Lived Experience in Texas Public Schools," José Angel Gutiérrez provides a personal history of racialization growing up and going to school in Crystal City Texas, or as Mexican American residents call it, Cristal, an important site of Mexican American activism and home of the La Raza Unida political party which Gutiérrez co-founded. He recounts growing up in a segregated school system in which Spanish and every other aspect of being from Mexico was systematically and often punitively disvalued by whites. He also recounts the powerful consciousness learned from his parents through which he came to recognize, value, and build politically on the same signs, starting with language, so disvalued in Anglo eyes. His account demonstrates the possibility of political pushback, as well as its cost in social labor and sheer knowledge.

To summarize, the essays in this book bring together sociological, linguistic, anthropological, and semiotic perspectives, with accordingly varied works of literature, that cumulatively illustrate the situation of Spanish and Spanish speakers in white public space and how that space makes itself felt through language: "if you are not white, you're here on our terms, we decide what's acceptable, and we will let you know what is not." We see this in the present contrast with an older history of public-sphere Spanish provided by Lozano and in the damage to present-day Spanish speakers described by Sáenz and Mamani and in Rosa, Aranda, and Dotson's account of Puerto Ricans in central Florida targeted for white discrimination by speaking Spanish in public spaces. We see it very clearly in Gutiérrez's description of his language experience in Texas public schools. We see it in Urciuoli's analysis of attacks on the public use of Spanish (and other racialized languages) in the United States, and more subtly in Mena's account of a "friendlier" linguistic terrorism, in which a neoliberalized promotion of Spanish displaces its connection to home and family. In Puerto Rico we see it in Alejandrez and Liberato's account of (ultimately unsuccessful) U.S. colonial policies aimed at displacing the official value of Spanish in Puerto Rico and we see it more unexpectedly in the account by Ramos Pelicia and Elise of Spanish language discourse that reinforces whiteness by othering African racial heritage in Puerto Rico. These two chapters illustrate the contradictions of whiteness in Puerto Rico: Spanish ideologized as a sign of resistance to English-speaking whiteness while used in ways that reinforce the opposition of Puerto Rican whiteness and blackness born in Spanish colonial history.

Throughout these chapters we see how racialized language ideologies (like other ideologies of race) depend on loosely affiliated notions that reinforce the perspective of privileged whites: the affiliation of Spanish with racialized outsiders assumed to be uneducated and poor, and thence with invasion and danger to (white) "America." These affiliations constitute a master narrative played out in attacks on Spanish speakers by individuals, in oppressive business and educational policies, and even neoliberally disguised as university promotion of a Spanish from nowhere with nothing to do with those outsiders. All these affiliations are remarkably resistant to correction by historical or social realities. Nor is this surprising: the function of white racialization is the establishment of an us/them polarity of superiority/inferiority, which has nothing to do with facts.

We close this introduction with an observation. On May 25, 2021, the Pew Research Center published figures comparing polls of Republicans and Democrats in 2016 and 2020, responding to the question of whether "being truly American" means it is "very or somewhat important" to "speak English," "share U.S. customs and traditions," "be a Christian," and "have been born in the U.S." Of all four criteria, speaking English scored highest among Republicans and Democrats both years: Republicans responded at 96% in 2016 and 89% in 2020; Democrats responded at 87% in 2016 and 65% in 2020. Those are very high numbers. What lies beneath them is a belief implicitly equating language with something deeply American. Of the other three aspects of being American on which people were polled, the one whose numbers came closest to speaking English was "share U.S. customs and traditions": Republicans responded at 89% in 2016 and 86% in 2020, Democrats at 79% in 2016 and 59% in 2020. By contrast, 63% of Republicans in 2016 and 48% in 2020 responded that "be a Christian" was important, with Democrats at 41% in 2016 and 25% in 2020; 60% of Republicans in 2016 and 46% in 2020 responded that "have been born in the U.S." was important, with Democrats at 50% in 2016 and 25% in 2020 (Connaughton 2021). What these figures suggest is that Americans, especially those defining themselves as the right of center, have a clear image of an ideal American who speaks English and shares U.S. customs and tradition, whatever their religion and wherever they were born. What drives this investment in speaking English (and practicing "American customs and traditions") is that English (along with the right social attitude) so easily stands in for whiteness for the reasons examined in this introduction. The implication is that even if one were not born white, one can learn to act white, not do those things that point to racial otherness, and thus reaffirm the United States race-language order.

References

Bourdieu, Pierre. 1991. *Language and Symbolic Power*. Cambridge MA: Harvard University Press.

Brekhus Wayne. 1998. "A Sociology of the Unmarked: Redirecting Our Focus." *Sociological Theory* 16(1):34–51.

Carter, Julian B. 2007. *The Heart of Whiteness: Normal Sexuality and Race in America, 1880–1940*. Durham NC: Duke University Press.

Connaughton, Aidan. 2021. "In both parties, fewer now say being Christian or being born in U.S. is important to being 'truly American.'" Pew Research Center. Retrieved July 6, 2021. (https://www.pewresearch.org/fact-tank/2021/05/25/in-both-parties-fewer-now-say-being-christian-or-being-born-in-u-s-is-important-to-being-truly-american/)

Harrison, Faye. 1995. "The Persistent Power of 'Race' in the Cultural and Political Economy of Racism." *Annual Review of Anthropology* 24: 47–74.

Feagin, Joe R. 2010. *The White Racial Frame: Centuries of Racial Framing and Counter Framing*. New York: Routledge.

Feagin, Joe R. and José A. Cobas. 2014. *Latinos Facing Racism: Discrimination, Resistance, and Endurance*. Boulder CO: Paradigm Publishers.

Feagin, Joe R. and Kimberley Ducey. 2019. *Racist America: Roots, Current Realities, and Future Reparations*. Fourth Edition. New York and London: Routledge.

Gal, Susan. 1989. "Language and Political Economy." *Annual Review of Anthropology* 18:345–67.

Hill, Jane. 2008. *The Everyday Language of White Racism*. Malden MA: Wiley-Blackwell.

Horsman, Reginald. 1981. *Race and Manifest Destiny: The Origins of American Racial Anglo-Saxonism*. Cambridge MA: Harvard University Press.

Irvine, Judith. 1989. "When Talk Isn't Cheap: Language and Political Economy." *American Ethnologist* 16(2):248–267.

Lozano, Rosina. 2018. *An American Language: The History of Spanish in the United States*. Oakland CA: University of California Press.

Omi, Michael and Howard Winant. 2015. *Racial Formation in the United State*. Third Edition. New York: Routledge.

Sasson-Levy, Orna. 2013. "A Different Kind of Whiteness: Marking and Unmarking of Social Boundaries in the Construction of Hegemonic Ethnicity." *Sociological Forum* 28:27–50.

Silverstein, Michael. 1976. "Shifters, Linguistic Categories and Cultural Description." Pp. 11–55 in Keith Basso and Henry Selby (eds.), *Meaning in Anthropology*. Albuquerque NM: University of New Mexico Press.

Urciuoli, Bonnie. 2020. "Racializing, Ethnicizing, and Diversity Discourses: The Forms May Change but the Pragmatics Stay Remarkably the Same." Pp. 108–127 in H. Samy Alim, Angela Reyes, and Paul Kroskrity (eds.), *The Oxford Handbook of Language and Race*. NY and Oxford: Oxford University Press.

Vélez-Ibañez, Carlos. 2017. *Hegemonies of Language and Their Discontents: The Southwest North American Region since 1540*. Tucson AZ: University of Arizona Press.

Chapter 1

Language Oppression and Resistance

The Case of Middle-Class Latinos in the United States[1]

José A. Cobas and Joe R. Feagin

The population of US Latinos has increased steadily, and they now constitute 13.7% of the population (US Bureau of the Census, 2004). This steady growth, 'the browning of America,' is viewed with alarm by many whites, who often view such immigrants as a threat to 'American values' and the US 'core culture' (Cornelius, 2002).

Language lies within that core, and the dramatic growth of US Latinos is viewed by many whites as a threat to the survivability of English, often termed by them 'the official language of the country.' As recently as 1987, most people in one national poll thought that the US constitution had already made English the official language (Crawford, 1992), and thus they saw no real threat. This benign perception has changed. For example, the influential Harvard professor Samuel Huntington (2004), who has served as advisor to government officials, has articulated strong anti-Latino sentiments in this stereotype of US immigration. Like many prominent white officials and executives (Feagin and O'Brien, 2003), Huntington worries greatly that the United States will become aggressively able to comprehend each other's languages and values.

Our Conceptual Approach

When the first English settlers arrived in North America, they saw themselves as bringing 'civilization' meant English language and culture. American Indians, viewed as 'savages,' were a serious barrier to their plans (Fischer, 1989). German immigrants represented another obstacle; Benjamin Franklin established a school in Pennsylvania to educate them. Franklin feared these immigrants could 'Germinanize us instead of us Anglifying them' (Conklin and Lourie, 1983: 69).

By the mid-nineteenth century the civilized-savage polarity was replaced by a racist *Weltanschauung* that played up the achievements of the 'Anglo-Saxon race' against the shortcomings of inferior 'others.' A common element in both the English-other and the white-other conceptions was that the dominant group viewed the language of the 'others' with suspicion and often sought to eliminate it. In the aftermath of the 1848 Mexican-American War, the

DOI: 10.4324/9781003257509-3

eradication of the Spanish language became an important US goal. This objective was pursued in the schools of the southwest (Gonzalez, 1990).

Efforts to squelch Spanish and other languages persist today. In 1986, California enacted legislation to make English the state's official language. Since then about two dozen states have enacted similar provisions (Navarrette, 2005). Many contemporary Spanish speakers feel in their daily lives the pressure to give up their mother tongue in favor of English (Montoya, 1998). One might argue that whites' attempts to prevent Latinos from using Spanish do not involve negative racial attitudes. Yet, this is a difficult position to sustain in light of many negative stereotypes about Latinos' language and accents. In whites' stereotypical accounts, the Latino speech is said to reveal low intelligence and untrustworthiness (Urciuoli, 1996; Santa Ana, 2002). Interference with Latino speech occurs regularly, and the interlocutor is often well educated. Such acts seem to derive from strong emotions in a country that Silverstein characterizes as having a 'culture of monoglot standardization' (1996: 284).

Pierre Bourdieu (1991) identified as socially significant a group's linguistic capital (e.g., a prestigious language dialect). The linguistic capital of Parisian French is higher than that of French in the countryside. According to Bourdieu (1977: 652), when individuals are in the linguistic market, the price of their speech depends on the status of the speaker. The outcome of linguistic exchange is contingent on the speaker's choice of language, such as in situations of bilingualism, when one of the languages has a lower status. A group can strive for an advantage in the linguistic market in order to bring about political and material gains. One way to achieve this end is by promoting the language it commands. Yet, the efforts of a group to achieve linguistic dominance are often met with resistance (Bordieu, 1991: 95–96). Although some classes, for example, the members of the bourgeoisie in post-Revolution France, operate from an advantageous position, the linguistic ascendancy of a class is the result of a struggle in the language market that is seldom permanently resolved. Achievement of language dominance does not necessarily mean that other languages disappear. Nonetheless, the dominant language becomes 'the norm against which the (linguistic) prices of the other modes of expression … are defined' (Bourdieu, 1977: 652). Drawing in part on these ideas, we view white efforts to delimit or suppress Spanish as a thrust to protect or enhance the reach and power of English speakers *vis-à-vis* Spanish speakers.

The mechanisms used by US economic and political elites to establish English ascendancy over Spanish vary, as well, will be demonstrated. Language subordination of Latinos in the United States includes the idea that English is superior to Spanish (Santa Ana, 2002). A second method is the denigration of Spanish-accented English. Other foreign accents are not judged in the same harsh terms:

> It is crucial to remember that not all foreign accents, but only accent linked to skin that isn't white, or which signals a third-world homeland,

that evokes ... negative reactions. There are no documented cases of native speakers of Swedish or Dutch or Gaelic being turned away from jobs because of communicative difficulties, although these adult speakers face the same challenge as native speakers of Spanish.

(Lippi-Green, 1997: 238–239)

Another form of language denigration is ignoring speakers of Spanish even when they have a command of English. They are ignored by some whites as groups of people not worth listening to, as if their knowledge of their mother tongue renders their message meaningless and undeserving of attention (Lippi-Green, 1997: 201). The process of linguistic denigration of non-whites also includes another component: the expression of skepticism or surprise when people of color evidence command of standard English. Non-whites' linguistic abilities were so contaminated that when they show their abilities in writing or speaking unaccented English, some whites are unprepared to believe what they see or hear (Essed, 1991: 202).

Oppressed groups typically defend themselves to the best of their ability against effort to denigrate their language or erect barriers against their use. Some examples are the Basque, Catalan, Occitan, and Bosnian peoples (Shafir, 1995; Siguan, 2002; Wood, 2005). Cultural groups struggle to keep their language because it is fundamental to social life and expresses the understandings of its associated culture in both overt and subtle ways (Fishman, 1989: 470). Many Latinos prefer to use Spanish because it affords them a richer form of communication. Other US racial groups struggle to protect their languages (cf. Horton, 1995: 211).

Although Latinos are disadvantaged in the language market, because of the power of whites, they often resist attempts to squelch their language. When told to stop speaking Spanish on the grounds that Spanish is out of place, Latinos often respond by asserting the legitimacy of their mother tongue. At a deeper level, this may be seen as a disagreement in which the white side is trying to disparage Latinos' language and the Latinos are making efforts to counter that image. In other instances, the Latino persists against prohibitions on speaking Spanish through different means. In a celebrated US court case, Héctor García was employed as a salesperson by Gloor Lumber and Supply, Inc., of Amarillo, Texas. Gloor Lumber allowed its employees to communicate in Spanish on the job only if there were Spanish-speaking customers. García broke company policy by speaking Spanish with Latino coworkers. He was fired, sued, and he lost (Gonzalez, 2000). García insisted on his *right* to speak Spanish.

In this chapter, we demonstrate a number of different techniques that are perceived by our subjects as attempts by whites to undermine the status of Spanish speakers and discourage the language's everyday use. We also examine forms of Latino resistance to this linguistic restriction and oppression.

Our Data

In this exploratory analysis of linguistic barriers and resistance, we employ new data from 72 in-depth interviews of mostly middle-class Latinos carried out in 2003–2005 in numerous states with a substantial Latino population.

For this pioneering research (the first of its kind, so far as we can tell), we intentionally chose middle-class respondents for two reasons. First, they are the ones most likely to have substantial contacts with white Americans in their daily rounds and are thus more likely to encounter racial barriers from whites and to feel the greatest pressures to give up language and cultural heritage. Second, they are the ones who are considered, especially by the white-controlled mass media and by middle-class white Americans generally, to be the most successful members of their group and thus to face little discrimination in what is presented as a non-racist United States. Thus, ever since the social scientist Nathan Glazer's (1975) book *Affirmative Discrimination* was published, a great many US scholars have argued that there is little or no racial discrimination left in US society and that, in particular, middle-class people of color face no significant racial or ethnic barriers. The first extensive qualitative fieldwork on the life experiences of contemporary African Americans – conducted in the late 1980s and early 1990s – took this approach, and in this research project we have followed much of the rationale and research guidelines for that prize-winning research (Essed, 1991; Feagin and Sikes, 1994; Feagin, Vera, and Imani, 1996).

In this innovative research we intentionally focus on those Latinos generally considered middle class and economically successful, such as teachers, small business owners, office workers, and mid-level government administrators. More than 90% of the respondents have at least some college work, and 58% have completed at least a college degree. A small business minority hold clerical or manual jobs. Using the qualitative methods of researchers studying everyday racial experiences (Essed, 1991; Feagin and Sikes, 1994), we used a carefully crafted snowball sampling design with more than two dozen different starting points in seven states to ensure diversity in the sample. Initial respondents were referred by colleagues across the country. As we proceeded, participants suggested others for interviews. Few respondents are part of the same network as others in the sample.

The respondents are mainly from the key Latino states of Arizona, California, Florida, Illinois, New Jersey, New York, and Texas. In total, 60% of our respondents are Mexican-American; 18% are Cuban-American; 13% are Puerto Rican; and the remaining 9% are other from Latin American countries. This distribution is roughly similar to that of the US Latino population. Altogether, 64% of the respondents are women and 36% are men.[2]

Language Control Stratagems and Resistance Responses

We examine relationships between whites, the most powerful US racial groups, and Latinos, a group that whites usually define racially as 'not white' (Feagin and Dirks, 2006). One reason for this focus is their central importance for the position of Latinos in US society. Another is that there are very few accounts in our Latino interviews of other Americans of color attempting to discriminate against Latino respondents on language grounds. One reason for this, we venture, is that non-Latino people of color are usually not in a position to complain loudly about the Spanish language even if they wish to, because they do not have significant power in US institutions.

As we observe below, even those whites not in the middle class, as much recent research has demonstrated (see Feagin and Sikes, 1994), feel great power as whites to assert the privileges of whiteness versus people of color. As we will observe constantly in our accounts, Anglo whites in the upper-middle, middle, and working classes feel powerful over middle-class Latinos. In most accounts, the white discriminators are of equal or higher socioeconomic status than those Latinos targeted for discrimination.

The common goal in the language-control methods of whites is to disparage the language of Latinos. The methods follow a variety of strategies. Some are aimed at Latinos' use of English: asking participants to stop speaking Spanish, because 'English' is the language of the land or because the white interlocutors want to know 'what's going on,' and ignoring Latinos who speak Spanish. Other forms of control are deriding Latinos' accents, raising questions about their proficiency in English when Latinos demonstrate skills. Whites define Latino speech as tainted in two senses. First, when Latinos speak Spanish, they are using a language that 'does not belong' in the United States and may be saying things behind whites' backs. Second, when they speak English, their accent is inferior and does not belong. Whites see themselves as the authorities to adjudicate language use. Attempts to control Latinos' language or disparage it often provoke responses from the Latinos involved in the interaction or witnessing it. The discussion that follows is organized around the different types of language control and denigration stratagems.

Silencing Spanish Speakers

One language control strategy is 'silencing.' It is a stratagem most frequently mentioned by respondents. Silencing is straightforward: it consists of a command from members of the white group to Latinos to stop speaking Spanish. It carries the supposition that whites can interfere in the Spanish conversations of Latinos to stop them from speaking Spanish. The command is usually based on the explicit or implied assumption by the interlocutor that 'We only speak English in America.'

A Cuban-American attorney remembers this story from her childhood a few decades back. It shows a classic case of silencing.

> We were in a [supermarket] ... It was during the Mariel Boatlift situation ... there was a whole bunch of negative media out towards Cubans 'cause ... many of the people that were coming over were ex-cons or what-not ... And so my mother was speaking to us in Spanish ... and this [white] woman passed by my mother and said ... "Speak English, you stupid Cuban!" ... And then my mother turned around, and purposefully, in broken English, because she speaks pretty good English ... said, "I beg your pardon?" ... [The woman] repeated the statement.

The Cuban interlocutor's response in quite assertive:

> And my mother ... asked her if she was a native American Indian. And when the lady responded "No ... I'm Polish" ... my mother responded ... "Well, you're stupid fuckin' refugee just like me ..." And the lady, I don't know what she said, but my mother said, "Do you know why I'm here, in this country? ... I'm here [which was not true] because I just came in the ...[Mariel Boatlift] and the reason ... was because I killed two in Cuba, [and] one more here will make no difference" ... And so then [the woman] thought my mom was being serious and left there really quickly.

When she asks the white interlocutor, most likely a middle-class shopper, about her Indian ancestry, the respondent reposts by saying in essence that she and her language are as American as a white Polish woman's.

In the next account, the attempt at silencing is indirect. A white Anglo post office employee, who is probably working class or lower middle class, complains to the postmaster, a Latino, that two fellow workers are speaking Spanish on the job and asks the boss to make them stop. The postmaster refuses to comply:

> I had that situation when I was working for the post office. I had two Chicanos that were talking in Spanish. There was an Anglo carrier right in the middle and she approached me and told me that I should keep them from speaking Spanish. I said, "You know both of them are Vietnam veterans and I think that they fought for the right to talk any language they want to."

The postmaster's response attributes legitimacy to the Latinos speaking any language they choose because they are veterans who fought in Vietnam and are Americans entitled to any language they please.

A Latino respondent in a southwestern city was trying to help a Mexican immigrant at a convenience store. Their conversation was in Spanish. As they talked, a white interlocutor interrupted and voiced his displeasure at their use of Spanish, first by the indirect means of complaining about the supposed loudness and then more directly by suggesting the immigrant should leave the country.

> [This] farm worker ... is Mexican. I was speaking to him [in Spanish] ... and this [white] individual asked us if I had to speak so loud. "Can you guys lower your voice?" ... *Were you guys talking out in the street?* No, there is a Circle K [near work]. We were standing right by [the counter]. *Did you respond to this man?*
> I very politely explained to him and he was shocked [at the quality of the English] when I looked at him and I said, "Pardon me sir, I am speaking to him in Spanish ... because he doesn't speak English." His response then was, "maybe he should move out". I said to him ... "if he moves out then why don't you go pick the stuff out in the field?" *What did he say to that?* He just turned around and walked away.

The response from someone who may have been a fellow shopper says, in essence, that the Mexican immigrant is performing a useful function in the United States, doing necessary work that the white interlocutor and many other whites apparently are not willing to do. At the very least, the respondent appears to say he has a right to communicate in his mother tongue.

In the next episode, a successful executive related an incident that happened when he was on vacation with his family and visiting a famous amusement park. He and his wife came to the United States at an early age, and they have advanced English proficiency. Yet they decided to often speak to their children in Spanish while they were young so that they would learn the Spanish language. He provided this account:

> I had a really bad experience at Disneyworld ... My son at the time was ... three ... He jumped the line and went straight to where there was Pluto or Mickey Mouse or something and I said, "[Son's name], come back," in Spanish and ... ran after him. And I heard behind me somebody say, "It would be a fucking spic that would cut the line." Now my wife saw who said it, and I said, "Who said that?" in English and nobody said a word. And I said [to my wife], "Point him out, I want to know who said that." And she refused. I was like, "Who was the motherfucker who said that?" I said, "Be brave enough to say it to my face because I'm going to kill you." You can see me I'm 6'3', 275 [pounds]. Nobody volunteered ... *So nobody stepped up?* No, no and there was a bunch of guys there, and I would have thrown down two or three of them; I wouldn't have had a problem.

The executive's response was clear, to the point, and came from the heart: his child was insulted by (probably middle class) white visitors to this expensive theme park. He was deeply offended for his family. Clearly his strong reaction could have led to further serious consequences, yet he was willing to take this risk by responding aggressively to the ultimate racist slur for Latinos.

In these accounts, whites who are attacking or discriminating vary in social status. Sometimes, they are of higher socioeconomic status than our respondents, and at other times they are of equal or lower status. Yet, all whites seem to feel the power to hurl racist commentaries at Latinos who are attempting to live out normal lives.

Practices silencing Spanish speakers reveal the asymmetric statuses of the English and Spanish languages. It would be inconceivable for a Latino to ask a white Anglo to stop speaking English in any Latino neighborhood. Such reciprocity in action would suggest a language equality that does not exist, and Latinos are well aware of this societal situation. We asked a South American respondent the following question, 'Sometimes ... I ask people I interview ... "Have you ever seen a Mexican at a grocery store turn to [white person] and say, 'Please do not speak English?' Have you seen this happen?" She laughed, "No, no!"

Despite attempts at the imposition of barriers, Spanish-speaking respondents frequently answer back, softly or aggressively, thereby insisting on their right to use their native language.

Voicing Suspicion: Fear of Spanish-Speaking Americans

In the everyday worlds of Latinos, whites' language-suspicion actions differ from language silencing acts in that the latter emanate from a conviction that English is the only acceptable language in the United States. Language-suspicion actions generally involve less confrontation.

Whereas silencing actions derive from a strongly held notion about what should be the dominant language, language-suspicion actions are likely to reveal a notion that Spanish speakers need to be watched, that they are perfidious or sneaky (Urciuoli, 1996). Silencing draws from a type of an ethnocentric discourse, one that goes back to eighteenth-century Anglo-American fears of German immigrants and their language (Feagin, 1997: 18). The suspicion response is rooted in anti-Latino stereotypes. There is a common substratum of racialized thinking: when Latinos speak Spanish, they are not playing by the 'right' rules as envisioned and asserted by whites.

A major difference between silencing and voicing suspicion is that some of the white interlocutors who object to Spanish on the grounds that they are excluded express, at least on the surface, a desire to be included in the interaction. This inclusion is, however, one that is seen and defined in white terms, for the conversation must be in the white person's language.

Another respondent provided an example of suspiciousness on the part of a more senior white manager who did not want her workers speaking Spanish:

> Most of the coworkers and the supervisors or managers are bilingual ...
> but ... my manager was only unilingual ... She does not understand ...
> that we were not talking about her ... We were talking about our business
> ... and personal stuff, but she doesn't have to know what we were talking
> because we don't need for her to give us her ... point of view. If we need
> for her to talk we are going to ask her in English, not in Spanish ... [She
> said] "I don't want you speaking Spanish" and I told her "I do not agree
> with you because this is not right". *And what did she say?* She said "Well,
> it's not right; it doesn't matter". And I said, "Yes, it does matter and you're
> not going to stop me from speaking my first language."

The interviewee's response is an unequivocal statement about her right to speak her first language. It resonates with the theme so frequently seen in the ripostes given by other respondents: "I'm" entitled to speak my language.'

A male respondent reported on a situation where he was speaking in Spanish with another Latino in a bank, when a white stranger broke into their private conversation:

> On one occasion we were at a Bank of ... branch ... We were talking
> [in Spanish] and all of a sudden this [white] lady comes and asks us [in
> English] what we were talking about. *What did you reply?* We told her we
> were talking about our business.

Although we do not know what the white woman in this affluent setting had in mind when she interfered in the conversation, her action suggests the recurring concern of many whites that those not speaking in English may be plotting something contrary to white interests. There is no doubt that she took it for granted that she was entitled to interrupt. The Latino's response is matter-of-fact and seems to convey the notion that in his mind what he and his friend were doing was legitimate.

Another respondent reported that she was hired to work at a store in a US town near the Mexican border so that she could help the numerous Spanish-speaking customers who crossed from Mexico to go to the store. Yet she faced a significant problem when she tried to do her job: she could not speak to customers in Spanish if white customers were present. It seems that the store owners were less concerned with causing difficulties for their Mexican customers than with offending the white ones:

> In a store where I worked ... I [saw a] lot of discrimination [against] the
> people that were coming from across the line [frontier] to shop here ... If
> I [spoke] English [to them] they'd feel discriminated because they couldn't

understand me. Or if I spoke Spanish and there was an English patron shopping they'd feel that I was speaking against them or saying and I should be speaking [English] … How could I do this when I had English speaking people and Spanish speaking people but the one I was directly addressing was Spanish speaking and non-English speaking person? Yet I was felt made to feel that I should be speaking English because I was in America.

Even though she was upset at the unreasonable situation in which she was placed, there was little the respondent could do short of quitting her job.

Another respondent, a female manager in a public agency, was also asked if 'Anglo whites ever object to your speaking Spanish at work?' She replied:

Yes. They are like, could you please speak English because we don't understand what you are saying … Even the supervisor tells us sometimes that we should talk in English because there are some people that don't know Spanish. But you know what, I feel better speaking Spanish … because that's my primary language. There is a lady that actually, that's always complaining … There are times that … she just feels like left out of the conversation. She's like, I want to know what's going on, but there are times that she's kind of rude, so. *How do you usually respond to her?* I'm like, well, you need to learn Spanish.

The middle-class respondent asserted the legitimacy of her Spanish use in a different form by suggesting that those fellow workers, middle-class white here, who wanted to partake in her Spanish-language conversations learn Spanish. Such a request may seem ludicrous only if one believes that English is the only language worth speaking in the United States. Even when languages have been granted official status, individuals are not forbidden to use other tongues in setting like work.

Suspicion of Latinos speaking Spanish constitutes another instance of attempts on the part of whites to regulate Latinos' speech. In this instance, the reason given is that Latinos are talking about them. The justification for white attempts reveals a view that whites should be included in interactions with Latinos on the whites' terms. Despite whites' objections, the typical Latino responds by asserting his/her right to use their mother tongue.

Doubting English Proficiency of Latinos

Since anti-Latino rhetoric places such a heavy emphasis on Latinos abandoning their heritage language, one would expect that when Latinos ventured into the world of English they would receive encouragement from white. This is often not the case. There is white obstinacy here: Latinos speak Spanish, an inferior language, and thus they are apparently presumed to be tainted by their heritage language then they speak or write English, even when there is evidence to the contrary. In some cases, their English is assumed to be 'too perfect' (cf. Essed, 1991: 202).

One example comes from the college experience of a Chicana professional. She was born in a mining town in the Southwest, and her English did not have the accent many whites consider undesirable. She reported on an instructor who questioned her integrity:

> [A professor] in college refused to believe that I had written an essay ... because she assumed that Mexicans don't write very well and so therefore I couldn't have written this paper. *Did she tell you that?* Yes she did ... And so she asked that I write it over again ... *So what did you do?* I rewrote the assignment and she still didn't believe that it was my own ... She still refused to believe that it was my handwriting or my writing because she still felt that Mexicans could not express themselves well in English ... *Did she use those words?* Yes she did.

This woman explained that she came from a mining town where labor unions had helped Mexicans gains access to schools, so she had good English skills. The well-educated white instructor felt substantial power to impose her views: Mexicans cannot express themselves well in English. We see here an active countering response. The respondent stood up to the instructor but was unable to change her mind. Here again, we observe whites of higher social status or in more powerful positions discriminating against our Latino respondents.

Another Latina had a different experience. Asked whether whites have ever acted rudely after they heard her Spanish accent, she answered in the negative and discussed 'left-handed compliments' she receives:

> No. In fact people go out of their way to tell me that I don't have an accent.
> *Is that a compliment?* I think so ... *Tell me in more detail.* Well you know, they begin to ask me, well where are you from? Am I from Arizona? No I am not from Arizona ... I'm from Texas. And then their comment is that you don't have an accent. And I'm like what kind of accent are you talking about? I don't have a Texas accent, the twang. And then I'll say, no and I don't have a Spanish accent. I speak both languages. And they are like, well wow, you don't have an accent. Never fails ...

White interlocutors in her immediate environment express surprise at her apparently unaccented English. The astonishment expressed by whites is reflective of stereotypes concerning some Latinos' English proficiency. In such settings, whites assume *they* have the right to determine which accented dialect of English is prized. English has many dialects, all with distinctive accents, yet most US whites (unlike many European whites) are monolingual and do not view their own prized versions of English as accented.

In the excerpt, a woman from Latin America relates her experience with a paper she wrote. She had problems with contractions in English and had her paper checked by a campus facility that helped students. The center's staff found no mistakes. Nonetheless, the Latina's highly educated white male instructor did not approve of how she used contractions, and even though he did not take off points from her grade, he made some comments to the class about foreign students:

> I wrote a paper and I used some contractions and most of the time I have some problems with contractions ... I took my paper to the English writing center and nobody corrected anything. And so when I got my paper back [from the write instructor] and all the contractions were corrected and so I didn't say anything, but I took the paper back [to the writing center] and they explained to me that there was not any specific reason to have changed them ... *Did you get a bad grade on the paper?* No, but the teacher made a comment in class about foreign students and that we were in graduate school and we should write free of mistakes ... I said to myself that if I had been an American student using these words he would not have changed it ... It was because there was nothing else to correct on the paper. *He just was looking for something to correct, that's what you are saying?* Yes.

This respondent did not confront her middle-class instructor directly, but, in going back to the writing center, she refused to accept the definition on her abilities that he attempted to impose on her and expressed her anger at the language-linked discrimination (on a similar problem for African Americans, see Essed, 1991: 232).

Intended or not, whites' skepticism toward Latinos' demonstrated proficiency in English is part of the denigration of Latinos. Although it is not a direct attack on Spanish, it reflects notions of language deficiency among the mass of Latinos – based, ironically, on the deviation of Latino interlocutors from stereotypical expectations.

Denigrating the Accent

Another method of undervaluing Latinos' English proficiency is by mocking those who have an accent that whites consider undesirable. When they speak English, Latinos frequently experience close monitoring by whites, and, if some sign of a certain accent is detected, they risk getting ridiculed. In business or government settings white customers sometimes even refuse to deal with Latino personnel because their accent is 'not American.' Indeed, some Latinos feel so self-conscious that speaking English becomes difficult (Hill, 1999).

Consider this account from a highly educated Latino who went to a computer store. In response to our question, 'has a white Anglo ... acted abruptly after he heard your accent?' he replied:

> Oh, that has happened several times. I have had *owners* of a store imitate my accent. *To your face?* In my face, yeah. I went to buy a printer ... I said, I'm here to buy a printer and the owner imitated my accent, back ... *Did you buy the printer?* No, I did not ... I felt that I was growing red in the face ... And I said, "You know what, just forget it I'll buy it somewhere else," and I turned around and left.

Something as simple as buying a printer turned into a humiliation, in this case from upper-middle-class whites. Having the experience of someone powerful imitating his accent was not an isolated instance. Indeed, we see in several respondents' quotes this cumulative reality of discrimination; many forms of discrimination take place on a recurring basis in the lives of Latinos. In refusing to purchase, the respondent resisted the discrimination and registered displeasure.

Another middle-class Latino who works in the customer service department of a retail store gave this example:

> There was one time that I answered [the telephone] at my work currently, I had this lady ... and she goes, "I don't want to talk to you, you have an accent!" I was like, "you don't want to talk to me?" she goes, "yeah, I want to talk to an American." I was like "ok, well I'm sorry you're gonna have to redial to speak to someone that you want." She goes, "well go ahead and transfer me over." I was like, "I'm sorry, I'm not going to be able to transfer you over. I have to take the call. I'm here to help you if you need anything." She goes, "well I don't understand you". And I just kept going, "well if there's anything I can do for you, I'm here." So she finally gave me her number and we went over the account and at the end she goes, "I'm really sorry that I was too rude to you at the beginning."

The white caller assumed that the individual answering the telephone could not be 'an American' because she had a Spanish accent and went on to say that she wanted to deal with 'an American,' suggesting that the Latina could not offer the same level of service. The Latina insisted that she was able to help and the white shopper at the end gave the service representative a chance to help her.

A South American doctor, who works as a medical assistant while she attempts to validate her medical credential in the United States, told us about her problems when dealing with patients. One in particular was very rude:

> There is a white female patient who has not come out and said it, but lets me know that my accent bothers her ... I called another patient, an elderly

woman who was a little ways from me, and she did not hear me. The first patient, in a rather aggressive way, said to me, "Who is going to understand you with that accent of yours?" *What did you say?* I called the elderly patient again ... *Do you prefer to remain quiet?* I don't like to get in trouble over things that don't matter that much.

This white patient took it upon herself to intervene where it did not concern her and used the opportunity to make a scornful comment, which served no purpose other than to demean the doctor's accent. Note again the repertoire of responses. Here the Latina did not respond aggressively but dismissed the patient's behavior and kept her professional demeanor.

For another woman, her accent was a cause of discomfort while dealing with white clerks. She replied to the question, has 'a white Anglo store clerk acted abruptly after he heard your accent?' this way:

All the time ... They tend to say, "What?" And in rude way ... Always it is this "What?" ... Yes, it is never "Oh, I am sorry I couldn't hear you" ... They are gesticulating ... this non-verbal behavior that is telling you ... "who are you" or "I can't understand you" or "Why are you even here?" ... you get all these messages ... [they are all] very negative.

This respondent's accent evoked unwelcoming behavior from whites who may have been of lower social status than the respondent. In many instances, as we have seen, the whites who discriminate are of equal or higher status than the respondents. In other settings, they are of lower status, yet most whites of either status seem to feel the power to discriminate in this fashion. The respondent clearly felt that the legitimacy of her status in the country was being questioned. We see here the way in which language attacks can literally crash into a person's everyday life when least expected.

Language mocking can affect a person's emotions, as the next account illustrates. The perpetrator of an attack was a dear friend who evidently thought she was just joking:

Anybody ever approach you about your accent? Yeah, all the time, all the time ... I had a very ... bad experience with somebody I love very much. I was in ... in nursing school and I had this friend and we're very, very close. I mean we went through the nursing school together and we were great friends and I adored my friend, but she would always make fun of my accent. Because there's still a lot of words, I still can't say some words, a few words. She would always make fun of either the way the word sounded or whatever and I would never say anything because that's the type of person I am. I just take everything in and I don't verbalize my feelings most of the time. But that's me. So when we were graduating from the program I wrote her a letter and I told her that I love her very much and I wanted to continue to be her friend, but that if my accent bothered her that much that it was ok with me not to be friends anymore. And that I felt very uncomfortable with the way she criticized me with my accent. *She was a non-Latino?* She was Italian.

The Latina's educated Italian American friend evidently did not know the pain her mocking was inflicting. Our respondent endured the pain as long as she could but eventually decided that if taking the mocking was the price of the friendship, she could dispense with it. She was gentle but stood up for herself.

In her interview a Mexican American with a master's degree sounded apologetic about being US born yet possibly having an 'accent.' She noted that some white middle-class coworkers had been supportive, but others had made fun of her:

English is my first language, so I really don't know if I have an accent, but there are sometimes where some words come out different and that does get recognized by some people that I work with. And I don't think it's an intentional making fun of [it], but it's noticeable and you know they kind of make a slight joke off it. But I'd have to say I work around both types of people, [some] that have been really supportive despite some other people which you know they really look at you as not knowing as much [as whites].

Self-consciousness about a certain Spanish-linked accent is common among Latinos (Urciuoli, 1996), including those who are US born. In a related vein, Bourdieu (1991: 77) discusses the 'self-censorship' experienced by speakers who anticipate a low price for their speech in the linguistic market. This causes a certain demeanor (tension, embarrassment) which reinforces the market's verdict.

The denigration of Spanish and Spanish accents, whether in joking or more serious commentaries, is generally insidious and thus part of the social 'woodwork' in the United States. In contrast, whites rarely denigrate the many accents of fellow white English speakers in such routine and caustic ways.

Most of our respondents resist through an array of strategies. At work sometimes they refuse to go along with demands that they do not speak Spanish. There are other instances, such as when they work with the public, when the targets of mocking are in no position to resist. In other circumstances, as when they are customers in a store, they can express their displeasure at the way they are being treated, such as by discontinuing their shopping.

Ignoring Spanish Speakers

Many Latinos report that whites dismiss them as not being worthy of attention after hearing them speaking Spanish. Unlike silencing, deriding Spanish accents, or voicing suspicion, ignoring Spanish speakers is a passive form of expressing disapproval toward the use of Spanish.

The case reported by the following interviewee occurred at a high-end resort in Arizona. She and her family went for drinks:

In the last five years have you been mistreated in restaurants by whites because of your race, ethnicity, speaking Spanish or accent? Yeah, we went to [resort restaurant] and we tried to order some drinks, but the lady kept passing and passing and said that she would come, but never came to ask what we want to drink I think because she heard us speaking Spanish ... *And was the server, the person white?* She was white and we told her, we called her and told her if she wasn't going to take our order or what because why that discrimination? We asked her a few times to come nicely and she kept saying, "I will be back, I will be back" and so she apologized and excused herself of course "cause if not we were going to make a proble *Then you told her that you felt discriminated?* Yeah." *And you say "we", with whom were you at the hotel?* My mom and her husband and other friends. *And you were speaking Spanish?* Yeah. *And so the lady then came and ...?* And she kind of apologized and we said "if not we want to talk to your managers". *Did she change her attitude?* Yeah.

After repeated attempts, the respondent and family members said they felt discriminated against, and it appears that this caused the white server to change her attitude. In this case, the white person was clearly of lower social status than the Latino family members yet still felt she could discriminate in the provision of service.

Conclusion

The so-called 'browning of America' has raised fears among many whites at all class levels. The reason typically given is that Latinos represent a threat to the US way of life, with the English language as a major symbol of that way of life. Many whites have responded in part by racializing Latinos and their language and attempting to demean its importance.

Efforts at squelching Spanish at an interpersonal level takes various forms: outright commands to Spanish speakers to speak English, protestations that when they speak Spanish Latinos are talking about whites, skepticism about English proficiency of Latinos despite evidence to the contrary, and mocking Latinos' 'accents' and ignoring Spanish speakers. Latinos often resist these incursions into their heritage language, but their resources are usually limited when compared to those at the disposal of most of their white antagonists.

Latinos often resist this mistreatment – a formidable task in light of the white establishment's resources. Today, Spanish is ridiculed by influential whites, who often call for much stricter government control over Latin American immigrants. Ideological elements emanating from the dominant culture may mask for some Latinos the structural basis of their victimization and thus interfere with their ability to see the systemic structure of their oppression, yet there are no signs of surrender to whites' anti-Latino discrimination.

The xenophobic discourse aimed at Latinos relies heavily on the notion that they and their culture are sounding the death knell for English culture. This white discourse is heavy in rhetoric and short on evidence. Indeed, many English-language programs for immigrants have long waiting lists. Facility in multiple languages is a valuable cultural resource for US society. There is a widespread belief among our study's respondents that there should be more tolerance toward languages other than English. Asked about attempts to ban Spanish in US society, one respondent's answer was typical:

> I think the more languages you speak, the more cultures you have, the more educated you are. We're in a global society, I mean Spanish is the number two spoken language of the Americans. Is it ok with you to use Spanish in ballots or other official documents? You know this is the United States and English should be the number one language but, if they are U.S. citizens and they are paying U.S. taxes, then they should have Spanish ballots.

Interestingly, not one of our 72 respondents argued that language tolerance should be limited only to Spanish. Not one advocated that Spanish should replace English as the language inside or outside Latino communities. Analysts like Huntington (2004) accuse Latinos of being a threat to democracy and the 'American way of life,' which for them means Anglo-Saxon ways of doing things. Upon close examination, this is a peculiar accusation because most Latinos are accenting the virtues of language and other cultural diversity that the official US ideology accents in its omnipresent 'melting pot' imagery. The struggles between Latinos and whites over language do not take place on a level playing field. As Barth has put it, the interaction between the majority group and the minority group 'takes place entirely within the framework of the dominant, majority group's statuses and institutions' (1969: 31). Given their position in the racial hierarchy of US society, whites have tremendous resources at their disposal in the worlds of politics, business, finance, mass media, and education. Powerful white elites control much of the normative structure (Gramsci, 1988), as well as much of the dominant thinking about what is right and proper in society. In this white-dominated milieu, Latinos struggle to preserve their heritage language as best they can, but it remains a difficult task.

Notes

1. This chapter first appeared in Ethnic and Racial Studies Vol. 31 No. 2 February 2008, pp. 390–410, Taylor & Francis Online: Peer-reviewed Journals (tandfonline.com), and is reprinted by permission.

2. Totally, 88% of the interviews were done in person, the remaining 12% by telephone. All but two were carried out by Latino interviews, six in Spanish, and the remaining ones in English.

References

Barth, Fredrik. 1969. *Ethnic Groups and Boundaries: The Social Organization of Culture Difference.* Boston, MA: Waveland Press.

Bourdieu, Pierre. 1977. "The Economics of Linguistic Exchanges." Social Science Information 16:645–668.

Conklin, Nancy F. and Margaret A. Lourie. 1983. *A Host of Tongues.* New York, NY: The Free Press.

Cornelius, Wayne. 2002. "Ambivalent Reception: Mass Public Responses to the 'New' Latino Immigration to the United States." pp. 165–189 in Marcelo M. Suárez-Orozco and Mariela M. Páez (eds), *Latinos: Remaking America*, Berkeley, CA: University of California Press.

Crawford, James. 1992. "Editor's Introduction." pp. i–ii in *Language Loyalties: A Source Book on the Official English Controversy*, Chicago, IL: University of Chicago Press.

Essed, Philomena. 1991. *Understanding Everyday Racism.* Newbury Park, CA: Sage Publishers.

Feagin, Joe R. 1997. "Old Poison in the New Bottles: The Deep Roots of Modern Nativism." pp.13–43 in Juan F. Perea (ed.), *Immigrants Out! The New Nativism and the Anti-Immigrant Impulse in the United States*, New York, NY: New York University Press.

Feagin, Joe R. and Danielle Dirks. 2006. "Who Is White." Unpublished research paper, Texas, USA: A&M University.

Feagin, Joe R. and Eileen O'Brien. 2003. *White Men on Race.* Boston, MA: Beacon Press.

Feagin, Joe R. and Melvin P. Sikes. 1994. *Living with Racism.* Boston, MA: Beacon Press.

Feagin, Joe R., Hernan Vera and Nikitah Imani. 1996. *The Agony of Education.* New York, NY: Routledge.

Fischer, David Hackett. 1989. *Albion's Seed: Four British Folkways in America.* New York, NY: Oxford University Press.

Fishman, Joshua A. 1989. *Language and Ethnicity in Minority Sociolinguistic Perspective.* Cleveland, OH: Multilingual Matters LTD.

Glazer, Nathan. 1975. *Affirmative Discrimination.* New York, NY: Basic Books.

Gonzalez, Gilbert G. 1990. *Chicano Education the Era of Segregation.* Philadelphia, PA: The Balch Institute Press.

Gonzalez, Juan. 2000. *Harvest of Empire.* New York, NY: Viking Press.

Gramsci, Antonio. 1988. *The Antonio Gramsci Reader: Selected Writing 1916–1935*, David Forgacs (ed.). London: Lawrence & Wishart Publishers.

Hill, Jane. 1999. "Language, Race and White Public Space." American Anthropologist 100:680–689.

Horton, John. 1995. *The Politics of Language Diversity: Immigration, Resistance, and Change in Monterey Park, California.* Philadelphia, PA: Temple University Press.

Huntington, Samuel P. 2004. *Who Are We? The Challenges to America's National Identity.* New York, NY: Simon & Schuster Publishers.

Lippi-Green, Rosina. 1997. *English with an Accent: Language, Ideology, and Discrimination in the United States.* London: Routledge Publishers.

Montoya, Margaret E. 1998. "Law and Language(s)." pp 574–578 in Richard Delgado and Jean Stefancic (eds), *The Latino/a Condition: A Critical Reader*, New York, NY: New York University Press.

Navarrette Jr., Ruben. 2005. "The ways we deal with language." P. G-3. *The San Diego Union-Tribune*, 17 April.

Santa Ana, Otto. 2002. *Brown Tide Rising: Metaphors of Latinos in Contemporary American Public Discourse*. Austin, TX: University of Texas Press.

Shafir, Gershon. 1995. *Immigrants and Nationalists: Ethnic Conflict and Accommodation in Catalonia, the Basque Country, Latvia, and Estonia*. Albany, New York: State University of New York Press.

Silverstein, Michael. 1996. "Monoglot 'Standard' in America: Standardization and Metaphors of Linguistic Hegemony." pp. 284–306 in Donald Brenneis and Ronald K. S. Macaulay (eds), *The Matrix of Language: Contemporary Linguistic Anthropology*, Boulder, CO: Westview Press.

Siguan, Miquel. 2002. Europe and the Languages. [originally published in Catalan in 1995 as L'Europa de les llengües, Barcelona: Edicions 62] http://www.gksdesign.com/atotos/ebooks/siguan/europe.htm

Urciuoli, Bonnie. 1996. *Exposing Prejudice: Puerto Rican Experience of Language, Race, and Class*. Boulder, CO: Westview Press.

US Bureau of the Census. 2004. *Annual Estimates of the Population by Sex, Race, and Hispanic or Latino Origin for the United States: April 1, 2000 to July 1, 2003*, Washington, DC: Population Division, US Census Bureau, Table 3.

Wood, Nicholas. 2005. "In the old dialect, a Balkan region regains its identity." P. A4. *The New York Times*. 24 February.

Section II

Rootedness

Chapter 2

The Early Political History of Spanish in the United States

Rosina Lozano

Amid the current disputes over immigration to the United States, perhaps no subject is less well-informed historically—or more hotly contested—than the conflict over the place of Spanish in the nation.[1] Most tend to agree that Spanish is simply a language of recent immigrants. Some celebrate the spread of Spanish speakers as part of the nation's multicultural transformation. Others resist its use, fearing the debasement of an American culture that they view as built upon English as the nation's common tongue.

Spanish is far more than an immigrant language; cultural battles have been fought over it for more than a century and a half. Today, the importance of Spanish to Latino identity and national politics is palpable and extends nation-wide. But the origins of these conflicts lie deep in the history of the nation. Spanish played an essential role in the creation of U.S. political institutions in the newly claimed U.S. Southwest, setting the stage for later national discussions about bilingualism. Indeed, it became a central component of U.S. political and legal citizenship in the U.S. Southwest and, more recently, in places like Miami. Far from being exotic or foreign, Spanish is a thoroughly American language.

Sociolinguists assign languages to three major categories: colonial, indigenous, and immigrant (Macías, 2001:333–34). The Spanish language in the United States is all three due to its centuries-long presence on the land that has become the current nation. This chapter will explain each of these three stages as they pertain to the use of the Spanish language in politics and in society. The first section uncovers the ways in which Spanish operated as a colonial language. All of the lands that became the United States were populated by Indigenous peoples whose vast array of mutually distinct Indigenous languages had predominated in the soundscape for centuries, often millennia. First travelers and later settlers from Spain and Latin America brought *castellano*, their most preferred language of government, to Indigenous lands that would become the present-day United States as they colonized the region. Spanish was the first European language spoken in many parts of what became the United States, especially in the southern half of the nation.

DOI: 10.4324/9781003257509-5

The second section describes how Spanish became an Indigenous language over the centuries of colonialism that preceded the takeover of the lands that expanded the United States. When the United States took half of Mexico at the conclusion of the U.S.-Mexican War in 1848, tens of thousands of former Mexican citizens tenuously held portions of the newly created U.S. Southwest in the face of Indigenous nations who exerted their strength and dominance by regularly raiding Mexican settlements as a way to bound their territories and to gain resources (DeLay, 2008). The U.S. government saw Spanish as the original language of government in the region and encouraged its use in politics to help extend the nation's influence over the region. Indigenous peoples in the region also used the language for diplomacy and trade for centuries and continued to prefer it for decades after the U.S. claimed the lands.

The concluding section turns to the closing years of the nineteenth century and the start of the twentieth century, when the nation expanded into various non-contiguous Spanish-speaking territories. Puerto Rico, the Philippines, Guam, and Cuba all had very different relationships with the United States, but all had experience running their governments in Spanish. As more migrants from Puerto Rico and Cuba in particular entered the United States, Spanish became a language of (im)migrants across the East Coast. In the face of Porfirian policies and the Mexican Revolution, the early decades of the twentieth century saw the rise of Mexican immigration, which resulted in Spanish being increasingly viewed as a language of foreigners. The more than a million new migrants entering during those decades often overshadowed Spanish-speaking citizens, even though the latter continued to reside in the Southwest, especially in New Mexico and in the southern parts of Texas, Arizona, and Colorado.

Early Uses of Spanish in the Future United States, 1565–1848

The United States first had a non–European language landscape. The speakers of European languages first arrived as outsiders traveling unbidden but sometimes welcomed onto Indigenous lands. The earliest groups of expeditions were made up of members of the Spanish Empire. Speaking Spanish as they trekked over the land, these travelers often claimed and renamed natural points of interests—mountains, rivers, and geological treasures—with Spanish names. Through the Doctrine of Discovery, they believed they had a political right to take over lands inhabited by non-Christians. These travelers included men like Ponce de León, who in 1519 was the first European to set foot in what is currently the United States. He famously searched current-day Florida for the fountain of youth. Other expeditions observed and shared their geographical findings of what they called the Americas with Europe, including Alonso Álvarez de Pineda (who reported that the Gulf of Mexico was enclosed), Hernando de Soto (who told Europeans of the Appalachians and Mississippi

River), and Francisco Vásquez de Coronado (who visited the Rocky Mountains, Grand Canyon, and Great Plains).

The influence of Spanish expeditions remains throughout much of the country, with Spanish-language place names for states like Nevada, Colorado, and Montana in regions that had few permanent settlements during the Spanish colonial period and were still inhabited by Indigenous peoples. In the southeast part of Utah, the Escalante Mountains are named for Silvestre Vélez de Escalante, who helped lead the Dominguez–Escalante Expedition of 1776, which had traveled through the region (Blackhawk, 2006:88). The remaining Spanish-language names are a political act of colonialism that erased the Indigenous names from the region and favored the Spanish expeditions as the European discoverers of the land. Many of the Spanish names were later supplanted by English names as Anglo-American settlers moved West, though many remained or were added by Anglos as a way to give the lands a European origin story (Lozano, 2018:84–86).

Indigenous peoples, of course, knew all of these regions well long before these expeditions. These Spanish visitors were followed by Spanish settlers who moved into the lands in part to control and claim them for the Spanish crown. The small and insufficient number of settlers meant that for centuries the Spanish settlers and missionaries worked in a largely Indigenous world of tribute, diplomacy, and dependence on local Indigenous peoples. These realities existed alongside Spanish attempts to control or conquer Indigenous communities with violence. The Spanish expected Indigenous peoples who lived near them to provide them with labor, convert to Christianity, and offer tribute (Barr, 2007; Blackhawk, 2006; Hämäläinen, 2008; Hoffman, 2001). The Spanish taught and expected their language to be adopted by the Indigenous peoples. Over centuries, Spanish became a language of trade and communication among Indigenous peoples too. It was, of course, also used in politics and the administration of the territories by officials and settlers of the Spanish Empire.

The first European settlement in what became the United States— St. Augustine, Florida, in 1565—included Spanish-speaking soldiers. Its population during the Spanish colonial period was small: the 1790 census placed the settlers (including Anglo ones) at fewer than 4,000 people. Florida remained a land populated largely by Indigenous peoples. While some missionaries came to instruct Indigenous·populations in Spanish, the settlers who came hailed largely from the island of Minorca and spoke Minorcan, a dialect of Catalan, rather than *castellano* (Rasico, 1990:96–98). After decades of ignoring the Spanish past in Florida, it was not until the late nineteenth and early twentieth century that St. Augustine began to embrace its Spanish beginnings. It did so amidst a larger "Spanish craze" led by non–Spanish speakers that began in the 1880s and peaked in the 1920s. Visitors to the city are now treated as residents boasting about its Spanish architecture and past. But city authorities only did so after the state had lost all of its publicly displayed Spanish cultural celebrations and well after the Spanish language was no longer heard publicly or in Florida politics (Kagan, 2014:194–95). While St. Augustine's initial administration operated the politics of the territory in *castellano*, Florida would have to wait until the mid-twentieth century for Spanish to truly operate as a political language of some influence in the state.

A similar story can be told for much of the former Spanish territories. In Louisiana, small pockets of Spanish-speaking settlers lived in the northwestern part of the state in places like St. Bernard Parish, where they spoke the Isleño dialect. Most of the settlers in St. Bernard were originally from the Canary Islands. Their Spanish-language use remained isolated for centuries, as the community remained in swamps, which were largely geographically separate from other Louisiana settlers. This meant that these Spanish speakers had little sway in the larger politics of Louisiana under France and the United States (Lipski, 2008:209–12).

The use of Spanish did hold significant political power in one future region of the United States, however. In the region that became the U.S. Southwest, Spanish settlers operated a robust colonial system in the Spanish language. The use of the Spanish language remained there in politics even after this region became part of the growing nation. The territories of New Mexico, Texas, and California geographically looked significantly different from the U.S. states that bear their name today and encompassed many other future states. While the Spanish only settled and controlled certain portions of the territory, in New Mexico, in particular, they had continuously resided on the land since 1692.[2] The Spanish repeatedly had to reinforce their claims to their borders with force. They were largely unsuccessful during the colonial period at expanding through the entire territory due to the incredible strength of the Indigenous population, a lack of effort on the part of Spanish authorities, and a dearth of interest in moving settlers and soldiers into its furthest northern region. Indigenous peoples like the Navajo, Comanche, Apache, and Utes successfully controlled their lands, but Spanish settlements remained. Spanish settlers and, later, Mexicans successfully set up politics in these northern regions. (DeLay, 2008; Blackhawk, 2006; Hämäläinen, 2008).

Despite the challenges of Indigenous raids and the threat of being pushed off their settlements, the settlers in New Mexico and Texas, called *nuevomexicanos* and *tejanos*, created their own societies and their politics operated entirely in the Spanish language. Raúl Coronado has offered an astute examination of print sources written and distributed in Texas across the colonial and Mexican national period. His research has demonstrated the ways in which these territories, often considered historically as simply future parts of the United States, played a major role in challenging the understanding of Latin American conceptions such as liberty, revolution, and the Enlightenment for the entire Spanish-controlled continent (Coronado, 2013:10). By considering more carefully the Catholic-inspired approaches to these concepts by *tejanos*, rather than the Anglo-Americans or French, Coronado revolutionizes the ways in which

Spanish-language politics in the last decades of the Spanish period should be considered (8–9, 19–20, 28). For example, Texas was the first province in New Spain to defeat royalist forces (32). The discourse of the written documents of *tejanos* spoke of placing self over God and King, a revolutionary way of thinking about how politics should operate in New Spain (33). Coronado's work exhibits the great possibilities and the importance of studying Spanish-language political and personal texts in the often-neglected northern provinces of New Spain.

There were fewer settlers in California. Until the Mexican period, the major institution of political power in the territory was the Catholic Church, which controlled vast tracts of land on their missions and used Indigenous labor to survive (Hackel, 2005). Indigenous peoples in the mission system learned the Spanish language and used it for worship and as a lingua franca between coastal Indigenous peoples (Haas, 2014:50). As the mission period came to a close with secularization in 1833, California turned more toward a ranch society. Monterey, the capital of California prior to United States control, housed a governor. Especially during the Mexican period, this leader's role included the distribution of land grants to former soldiers in payment for their services as well as to other Spanish settlers and Indigenous peoples (Hackel, 2005: 369–74).

It was into this Spanish-speaking political world that the United States forcefully entered, first through economics and trade and then, in the 1840s, through war and acquisition (Reséndez, 2005; Hyde, 2011). The nation formed its Southwest out of Mexico's North and entered a region where *californios* and *nuevomexicanos*—Mexican settlers living in California and New Mexico, respectively—were the political leaders, owned the land, and knew its settlers. The United States permitted and at times funded the use of the Spanish language in politics, which after centuries was a native language of the politics of the territory. They did so to help create and implement United States institutions and political systems.

Spanish in the Politics of the Southwest, 1848–1898

The history of Spanish-language politics in the United States began in earnest with the takeover of former Spanish lands.[3] The most significant moment came in 1848 at the close of the U.S.-Mexican War. The Treaty of Guadalupe Hidalgo, which ended the war, recognized not just the land itself but also the people who lived on the land. These Mexicans were settlers on territory the United States now claimed but did not control due to the presence of autonomous Indians who raided newly arriving Anglos and long-standing Mexican settlers alike. Efforts to control the land required collusion between U.S. officials and the Spanish-speaking settlers who became elected officials and created the state and territorial systems bilingually or, in some cases, almost exclusively in Spanish. Joined increasingly by Anglos, the former Mexicans made up a demographically significant segment of the polity, which excluded American Indians from citizenship and suffrage. This reality encouraged the use of Spanish in politics in the absence of any federal intervention or regulatory prohibitions.

I use the term "treaty citizens" to unite these former Mexican nationals annexed with California and New Mexico. Article IX of the Treaty of Guadalupe Hidalgo granted U.S. citizenship to the Mexican citizens residing in the ceded territory. In a single bold stroke, the treaty extended U.S. citizenship to approximately 56,000 individuals born in California and New Mexico, without a proviso regarding race or language.[4] Although the treaty claimed to accept all Mexican citizens as U.S. citizens, Indigenous citizens of Mexico from California and New Mexico were not treaty citizens. The Mexican government recognized the Pueblos as citizens, but the United States did not, and Pueblos who lived in settlements near Mexican villages and towns in New Mexico found the treaty's promises especially hollow. *Californios* and *nuevomexicanos* became U.S. citizens who proved crucial to the initial creation of U.S. political institutions throughout the Southwest. Treaty citizens' origin point for citizenship also differed from that of the other major Mexican territory to join the United States in the 1840s—Texas. When Texas became a state in 1845, it already had an overwhelmingly Anglo population who controlled the state government and kept Spanish from becoming a language of politics. Language and citizenship together united treaty citizens.

Never before had the U.S. government offered so much power to people who did not speak English or whose whiteness was in question. With the end of the U.S.-Mexican War, the United States acquired 525,000 square miles encompassing deserts, mountains, and canyons and populated largely by autonomous Indians. In New Mexico, *nuevomexicanos* comprised almost the entire settler population. In Northern California, *californios* found themselves overrun by Anglo settlers, whereas in Southern California, they made up most of the settler population. The United States needed these treaty citizens to maintain control of the vast new territories it had acquired. These conditions permitted treaty citizens to establish social and political institutions that operated in Spanish—sometimes exclusively so.

Language concessions provided one culturally acceptable way for advocates for California statehood to gain *californio* support. That priority emerged at the 1849 state constitutional convention, which took up the task of governing in two languages. Anglo convention members accepted the delegacy of *californios* as white state-builders and supported their participation by requesting adequate translations prior to calling for a vote.[5] The convention made numerous attempts to support bilingual proceedings by endorsing generous interpreter wages and rejecting possible constitutional models that had not been translated.[6] At the end of the convention, delegates voted overwhelmingly to publish their proceedings in both English and Spanish and authorized a translator-certified Spanish version of the constitution.[7]

Notwithstanding efforts to get Spanish translations to its constituents, California was never a fully bilingual state. The tardy and inaccurate state translations thwarted day-to-day local interactions between the different language groups in local settings. Native Spanish speakers brought up missing translations on several occasions. In 1851 the legislature created an incomplete list of laws with Spanish translations.[8] During the ninth session, a committee compiled an extensive list of translated laws still in effect. They hoped to create one comprehensive bound volume of laws in Spanish. Andrés Pico, the committee chairman, complained (1858) about the quality of the translations, which included many discrepancies and errors and which he found at times almost "enteramente ininteligibles" (completely unintelligible). He described the use of translations in legal proceedings and emphasized their pivotal rather than ceremonial role. Pico explained that Spanish speakers worldwide would read the translations "que haya habido tanta causa para criticar" (for which there are many reasons to criticize). These concerns about quality and completeness implicate the legislature in failing the constitution's translation promises. The constitution adopted in 1879 completely dismantled all Spanish-language privileges throughout the state.

By contrast, the legislative branch of the territorial government of New Mexico stands out as operating almost exclusively in Spanish during the first decades of U.S. rule. In 1850, it attempted to create a translator position with a $2,000 annual salary paid by the U.S. Congress, with the option to employ a clerk. Given that this was the first bill that the territorial government listed in its first submission to Congress, the office of the translator clearly held a prominent place in the minds of the legislators, as it had in California during its first session.[9] But unlike California, where, as a state, the legislators had the power to create as many government positions as they could pay for, the New Mexico territorial legislators found that Congress limited their powers. As the comptroller for the U.S. Treasury, Elisha Whittlesey, explained in 1851, only Congress could create a permanent position in New Mexico, despite the fact that there could "be no question of the necessity of printing the laws and journals and bills also in both languages and of having a translator." The territorial legislators could only make temporary appointments.[10] Within a few years, however, Congress recognized translation as an indispensable service that allowed the territorial government to function. In March 1853, it authorized the employment of "a translator and interpreter, and two clerks" in each house. In addition, Congress required two clerks "qualified to write" in each language.[11]

Further hints of how Spanish operated in New Mexico's territorial government are available in the incomplete, English-language-dominated executive branch papers. These indicate that both the governor and the secretary of the territory (almost always Anglos from outside of New Mexico) adjusted to the Spanish-language environment. Some early legislative documents bear the markings of a "Translator's Office," signaling that they arrived at the executive branch having been translated from the original Spanish.[12] The executive branch received Spanish-language resolutions and letters from the legislature in the first decades and occasionally responded with engraved letterhead from the "Departamento de ejecutivo."[13] Governors often released proclamations in both languages in the same document.[14] Some governors chose at times to use the Spanish equivalent of their names on official documents—Henry Connelly became Enrique and William A. Pile, Guillermo.[15]

The United States held no other colonial possessions during this period, making the discussions surrounding *nuevomexicano* use of language and retention of culture a precursor for later ones in Puerto Rico, the Philippines, and other territories. From 1851 to 1870, the territory regularly printed its session laws with English on one side and Spanish on the opposing page, permitting easy comparison.[16] The continued dominance of Spanish throughout the territory appears in legislative journal orders for "doscientos en inglés y ochocientos en castellano/800 in Spanish and 200 in English" in 1861.[17] As late as 1867, a legislative memorial to Congress requested printed copies of the U.S. Constitution and Organic Law of New Mexico in Spanish. The Council and the House explained this was necessary because 80% of the members of the legislature only spoke and wrote in Spanish.[18] The legislature approved the printing of 2,000 copies of the governor's message, with 500 copies in English and 1,500 in Spanish, and continued to request either an equal number of copies of various territorial reports in both languages or more copies in Spanish until 1893.[19]

Office-seekers acknowledged and respected the reality of New Mexico's Spanish-language environment. Voting in the territory could not have begun or been implemented with any kind of legitimacy without Spanish. Scrolls from Valencia County show how the process with Spanish-language voters, candidates, and election officials worked. The records detail the election of "4 del mes de Septiembre de Mil ochocientos sesenta y cinco" (September 4, 1865) for the representative to Congress and the territorial senator and other major territorial positions. The *secretarios* (secretaries) and *jueses de la mesa* (precinct captains) stood by the results in their final tally—"certificamos que lo de arriba es legal" (we certify that the above is legal)—before sending them to the territorial government.[20] The precinct's ninety-inch roster tallied each of the votes cast by the 241 voters, alongside their names. The rolls include just ten non-Spanish surnames; they stand out for their distinct handwriting, suggesting that they were recorded in the voters' hands. Other "Libro[s] de Matricula de Eleccion" (election or poll books) submitted by Valencia County during the 1860s also appeared to have been kept in Spanish and showed Spanish-surnamed voters overwhelmingly.[21] Though few rosters survive for other precincts across the territory, there is no reason to think that Valencia County's experiences were atypical.

In New Mexico, Spanish-surnamed individuals filled the lists of territory-appointed positions, including justice of the peace, postmaster, notary public, census collector, sheriff, state senator, and jury members (Gonzales, 2016: 6–7).[22] While other states began requiring English literacy to hold office, New

Mexico's legislature opted in 1889 to permit officeholders to demonstrate literacy in either Spanish or English.[23] They established generous per diem rates for court interpreters and encouraged all citizens to serve on juries regardless of their facility in English. This occasionally required the use of interpreters at grand juries as well as the district courts.[24] Some local courts operated solely in Spanish (Gómez, 2000:1130, 1139, 1192).

The transition from Spanish to English as the working language of the legislature seems to have happened fairly quickly in the period between 1874 and 1878. In 1874, the legislature determined that official law was the one voted upon, whether it was published in English or Spanish.[25] Until 1876 almost every English version of the session laws is marked as a translation; in 1876, the number of English and Spanish laws was almost evenly split.[26] From 1878 on, however, most of the official territorial laws are listed in English. Spanish remained a reality in the territorial legislature even as official laws were increasingly those written originally in English. The persistence of monolingual legislators is apparent from the legislature's continued employment of a translator, an interpreter, and, as more Anglos entered the territory, an assistant translator.[27]

Territorial officials agreed that *nuevomexicanos* had rights irrespective of what language they spoke, and they defended attacks on Spanish. Few complained about the prevalence of Spanish, given Spanish-speaking citizens' continued political power and their role in the origin of territorial politics. Long-standing settlers saw language concessions as the norm, whereas new settlers—particularly those who arrived after the 1880s—had to grow accustomed to them. As calls for statehood increased, however, New Mexicans found that their preference for Spanish placed them at a disadvantage. Federal authorities consistently cited the presence of so many monolingual Spanish speakers as a reason to reject the territory's bid for statehood. The prospect of statehood was not universally endorsed by New Mexicans.

Access to the Spanish language is one measurable index of treaty citizens' incorporation in the U.S. polity. Whether in California, Colorado, Arizona, or New Mexico, treaty citizens throughout the Southwest largely accepted the form of the U.S. political system, with its parties and expectations of electoral participation, but they participated in these institutions primarily in Spanish. For treaty citizens, Spanish became a negotiated right. *Nuevomexicanos* benefited from Spanish-language policies that eased them into their lives as U.S. citizens. Even as political support for translations declined, it continued into the twentieth century. Those *nuevomexicanos* who lived in the portions of the territory that split off to create the territories of Colorado and Arizona in the 1860s, however, lost their Spanish-language privileges much sooner.

The federal government unwittingly endorsed the use of Spanish in New Mexican territorial affairs by permitting its people to elect monolingual Spanish speakers, which in turn made the Spanish language a normal part of the territorial political process. When New Mexico became a state in 1912, it included constitutional protections for the Spanish language in its new state constitution.[28] The types of language concessions and language politics occurring in New Mexico in the nineteenth and early twentieth centuries was prescient. In 1996, UNESCO's *Declaration of Linguistic Rights* included "minority language rights" that protected the right for minority language members to be recognized, the right to use the language in both public and private settings, the right to teach the language in educational settings, the right to preserve the language, and the allowance of the language in media and official spaces (UNESCO, Art. 3.1). Spanish speakers in New Mexico and parts of the Southwest pushed for these language rights over a century before UNESCO promised these rights. Their successes, the recognition of their language rights, and the need for Spanish-language translations by the federal government was significant. Having retained political positions, and therefore power, *nuevomexicanos* considered themselves an integral part of the territory and, by extension, the United States. This equal footing allowed *nuevomexicanos* to develop a more limited understanding of the role of the English language in U.S. identity than developed in the rest of the country.

The pervasiveness of the Spanish language, along with the concessions made for its speakers, challenge the idea that American institutions or culture are all-encompassing—especially in territorial spaces. Ironically, remaining in a quasi-colonial condition resulted in a more fiercely held and enduring attachment to the Spanish language that allowed Spanish speakers to become interwoven into the fabric of the political processes of the United States. Isolated rural regions, especially in the vast territory of New Mexico, maintained a cultural continuity that privileged the use of the Spanish language with little interaction with the federal government. The United States' continental territories received more autonomy and less policy-driven funding for the "Americanization" of its residents, and in this respect differed from later territories such as Puerto Rico and the Philippines.

Early Spanish-Speaking Migrants, 1890–1898

For most of the United States, Spanish was not the language of long-standing settlers who had created the original political systems of power but of those who were instead migrants to the land. A very small but very famous group of Spanish speakers in the United States resided in New York City in the last third of the nineteenth century. They included members from many different Spanish-speaking countries across Latin America and Spain. The largest subgroup of these early Latino communities hailed from the Caribbean, from Puerto Rico and Cuba, though some Dominicans also resided in New York City during this period (Hoffnung-Garskof, 2020; Pérez, 2018; Mirabal, 2017).

One larger-than-life figure from this group was the writer José Martí, an often-quoted and very respected figure whose work was published across Latin America. He was also a poet, translated novels into Spanish, and edited a Cuban independence newspaper, *Patria-Fatherland*. As a U.S. correspondent between 1881 and 1895, he shared many of the racial realities in the United States in the nineteenth century with Latin American nations such as Mexico, Guatemala, Venezuela, and Argentina. He also wrote his defining call for "Nuestra América," which promoted the creation of a larger hemispheric identity of Spanish speakers. Thus, the political implications of writings produced in Spanish in the United States had a transnational reach due to Martí and other exile writers. Martí died in 1895 during a failed invasion that hoped to gain independence for Cuba from Spain, but his departure was not the end of Spanish-language politics in New York (Pérez, 2018:270–99).

The Spanish language, the major colonial language of Latin America, was a major unifier as the Latin American nation-states were being formed and as some Spanish colonies sought their independence. New York City offered a place for these exiles to imagine this future. The city was, after all, the first place that the Cuban flag was displayed publicly, on May 11, 1850 (Pérez, 2018:53). The city was an important site of transnational economic gains and an enabler of political transformation in the Caribbean. Aside from writers, the use of the Spanish language took on a very important political purpose there that had little to do with extending the language rights of its speakers in the city itself. It included activism on the part of *tabaqueros* (tobacco rollers) and the formation of a strong working-class consciousness. It also included many people whom we would now call Afro-Latinos, who, alongside other Spanish-speaking Caribbean migrants, mobilized to obtain independence from Spain on the island. Their newspapers and writings were published in Havana and San Juan and influenced the political thinking of those on the islands (Hoffnung-Garskof, 2020; Pérez, 2018). While major concessions would not be given to Spanish speakers politically until the mid-twentieth century, politics in Spanish made a difference on a more transnational level decades before this group became a major demographic presence in the city.

Looking Forward: A Kaleidoscope of Political Meanings of Spanish, 1898–1920

Spanish remained a language of politics in small pockets of the United States into the twentieth century, especially in New Mexico. Aside from the official use of the Spanish language in politics for Spanish speakers, Spanish culture began to be increasingly used to erase Indigenous ties to the land in the U.S. Southwest and to forge ties with a Spanish fantasy past. This so-called craze for all things Spanish in the last decades of the nineteenth century and the first of the twentieth resulted in an increased desire for Spanish speakers to identify with Spain rather than Latin America. By participating in the Spanish fantasy past, some Spanish-speaking families, especially those in higher classes, found a way to be more accepted and assimilated into the larger culture of the nation (Deverell, 2004; Brown-Coronel, 2011; Kagan, 2019). Identifying as Spanish rather than as Latin American also permitted these Spanish speakers to distance themselves from the growing colonial population of Spanish speakers who forcefully became a part of the nation after the Spanish-American War and from the immigrants from Mexico that would soon follow in response to the revolution (Nieto-Phillips, 2008).

In 1898, the relationship between the United States and the Spanish language changed forever. At the conclusion of the brief Spanish-American War, the United States claimed colonial territories whose residents used the Spanish language. The largest by far was the island of Puerto Rico, which had around one million inhabitants (U.S. War, 1900:40). While the islands of Guam and the archipelago of the Philippines did not speak Spanish widely in everyday life, after hundreds of years under Spanish colonialism, *castellano* was the language of the elite and politics (Kramer, 2006:39–43, 61–67; Rogers, 2011:108–19; 221–26). The United States allowed Cuba to remain independent but initially made it a protectorate. With these acquisitions, the United States no longer had just an internal community of Spanish speakers but a larger colonial population. Whether to impose the English language or permit the Spanish language to be used to impart American culture and customs became a major policy decision of U.S. military and colonial officials, especially in the public schools. Being members of the largest Spanish-speaking population, Puerto Rican students and local educators found themselves in a revolving door of changing language policies throughout the first four decades of the twentieth century (Osuna, 1949; Gutiérrez, 1987; Clampitt-Dunlap, 2000).

Spanish-language networks grew far beyond treaty citizen families in the Southwest during this time and extended to the new colonies and new immigrants. The violence of the Mexican Revolution and earlier government policies in agrarian Mexico under the decades-long dictatorship of Porfirio Díaz led unprecedented numbers of Mexicans to migrate to the United States, dwarfing the previously dominant population of treaty citizen families throughout most of the Southwest (Sánchez, 1993:20–29; Monroy, 1999:75–95). By 1920, the Mexican-born population in the United States had grown to 651,596 (Ngai, 2004:52). These immigrants worked in Arizona mines, on Kansas railroads, in Colorado beet fields, in Chicago slaughterhouses, and in agricultural fields all across the country, but especially in Texas and California.

These new migrants faced a very different language reality than treaty citizens in New Mexico, California, and other portions of the former Mexican nation had in the 1840s. Their lack of language rights and the viewing of the population as foreign and inferior people became a more standard approach to Spanish-speaking laborers in the first third of the twentieth century. After operating as an indigenous language after centuries of Spanish colonization, the Spanish language was now also viewed as an immigrant or foreign language as Puerto Ricans and Mexicans arrived in increasing numbers. As the twentieth century wore on, the Spanish language came to have innumerable political meanings and purposes that largely obscured its long history in the United States.

Notes

1. This edited chapter has been written using materials from my previous scholarship. I am grateful to the University of California Press and Oxford University Press, who permitted me to use the material in this chapter from the following published works: Rosina Lozano, *An American Language: The History of Spanish in the United States* (Oakland: University of California Press, 2018); Rosina Lozano, "The Politics of the Spanish Language," in *The Oxford Research Encyclopedia of American History* (June 2018). doi: 10.1093/acrefore/9780199329175.013.368.
2. Santa Fe was first formed in 1610, but the Pueblo Revolt of 1680 removed the Spanish from the town for a dozen years until the reconquest of 1692 (Silverberg, 1994).
3. This section is excerpted mostly from Chapter 2 of *An American Language* but includes excerpts from the Introduction and Chapter 4.
4. This estimate does not include Texas or those eligible for citizenship but born in Mexico (U.S. Census Bureau, 1853:996, 972).
5. For translation requests, see California, 1850:25, 31, 218–19, 331. They considered taxed California Indians as voters because of *californio* Pablo de la Guerra's efforts (305–7). The decision to be counted as white contrasted with the treatment of Blacks (Almaguer, 2008:35–38).
6. Considered at $16 per diem and ending at $28, the interpreter's salary was equal only to the secretary's (California, 1850:95, 107, 25).
7. Ibid., 163–64, 398.
8. Cal. Leg. Journal, 2nd sess. (1851), 1449–52; Cal. Leg. Journal, 7th sess. (1856), 152.
9. H. Misc. 4, 32nd Cong, 1st sess., §§1, 4–5, pp. 5–6.
10. Elisha Whittlesey to William S. Allen, 11 September 1851, RI 451, box 8, William G Ritch Collection, mssRI, The Huntington Library, San Marino, CA (Hereafter RC).
11. W. W. H. Davis to Elisha Whittlesey, 15 January 1855, Territorial Archive of New Mexico, reel 27, frames 97–98 (hereafter TANM).
12. E.g., Legislative Assembly, Joint Resolution [from Translator's Office], 20 July 1851, RI 441, box 8, RC.
13. E.g., Resolution of the New Mexico Legislative Assembly, 13 December 1851, RI 472, box 9, RC; Facundo Pino to James S. Calhoun, 10 December 1851, RI 471, box 9, RC; Enrique Connelly to Diego Archuleta, 4 February 1864, RI 1308, box 21, RC; New Mexico Act, 23 December 1863, RI 1545, box 21, RC.
14. A sampling: James S. Calhoun, "Proclamation," 18 March 1851, No. 2, Rare book 49545, The Huntington Library, San Marino, CA (hereafter 49545); Lewis Wallace, "Proclamation by the Governor, 13 December 1878, No. 12, 49545.
15. Henry Connelly, "Proclamation by the Governor," 9 September 1861, nos. 3, 4; William A. Pile, "Governor's Proclamation," 8 September 1869, No. 6, 49545.
16. The 1868 N.M. Laws are an exception.
17. 1863 N.M. Laws 113–14.
18. 1867 N.M. Laws 179–80.
19. 1870 N.M. Laws 193–94; 1869 N.M. Laws Joint Resolution 1; 1893 N.M. Laws 32.
20. Election Roll for Valencia County, 4 September 1865, RI 2269, RC.
21. Election Rolls for Valencia County, 4 September 1865. More examples from Valencia County exist in the RC.
22. W. G. Ritch to Lew Wallace, 7 December 1878, reel 25, TANM.
23. 1889 N.M. Laws 18.
24. 1882 N.M. Laws 40; 1889 N.M. Laws 276.
25. By contrast, in Lower Canada, the bilingual legislature voted on both French and English texts (1874 N.M. Laws 17; Sheppard, 1971:59–61).
26. See, e.g., 1861 N.M. Laws 118.

27. See, e.g., 1887 N.M. Laws 18; 1889 N.M. Laws 9; 1891 N.M. Laws 245; 1893 N.M. Laws 151.
28. N.M. Const., art. VII, §3, art. XX, §12, art. XII, §8, 10.

References

Almaguer, Tomás. 2008. *Racial Fault Lines: The Historical Origins of White Supremacy in California*. Berkeley: University of California Press.

Barr, Juliana. 2007. *Peace Came in the Form of a Woman: Indians and Spaniards in the Texas Borderlands*. Chapel Hill: University of North Carolina Press.

Blackhawk, Ned. 2006. *Violence over the Land: Indians and Empires in the Early American West*. Cambridge: Harvard University Press.

Brown-Coronel, Margie. 2011. "Beyond the Rancho: Four Generations of del Valle Women in Southern California, 1830–1940." PhD diss., University of California, Irvine.

California. 1850. *Report of the Debates in the Convention of California on the Formation of the State Constitution, in September and October 1849*. Washington: J. T. Towers.

Clampitt-Dunlap, Sharon. 2000. "Nationalism and Native-Language Maintenance in Puerto Rico." *International Journal of the Sociology of Language* 142:25–34.

Coronado, Raúl. 2013. *A World Not to Come: A History of Latino Writing and Print Culture*. Cambridge: Harvard University Press.

DeLay, Brian. 2008. *War of a Thousand Deserts: Indian Raids and the U.S. Mexican War*. New Haven, CT: Yale University Press.

Deverell, William. 2004. *Whitewashed Adobe: The Rise of Los Angeles and the Remaking of Its Mexican Past*. Berkeley: University of California Press.

Gómez, Laura. 2000. "Race, Colonialism, and Criminal Law: Mexicans and the American Criminal Justice System in Territorial New Mexico." *Law & Society Review* 34:1129–1202.

Gonzales, Philip. 2016. *Política: Nuevomexicanos and American Political Incorporation, 1821–1920*. Lincoln: University of Nebraska Press.

Gutiérrez, Edith Algren de. 1987. *Movement against Teaching English in Schools of Puerto Rico*. Lanham: University Press of America.

Haas, Lisbeth. 2014. *Saints and Citizens: Indigenous Histories of Colonial Missions and Mexican California*. Berkeley: University of California Press.

Hackel, Steven W. 2005. *Children of Coyote, Missionaries of Saint Francis: Indian-Spanish Relations in Colonial California, 1769–1850*. Chapel Hill: University of North Carolina Press.

Hämäläinen, Pekka. 2008. *The Comanche Empire*. New Haven, CT: Yale University Press.

Hoffman, Paul E. 2001. *Florida's Frontiers*. Bloomington: Indiana University Press.

Hoffnung-Garskof, Jesse. 2020. *Racial Migration: New York City and the Revolutionary Politics of the Spanish Caribbean*. Princeton, NJ: Princeton University Press.

Hyde, Anne. 2011. *Empires, Nations, and Families: A History of the North American West, 1800–1860*. Lincoln: University of Nebraska Press.

Kagan, Richard L. 2014. "The Old World in the New: Florida Discovers the Arts of Spain, 1885–1930." Pp. 192–208 in Viviana Díaz Balsera and Rachel A. May (eds.), *La Florida: Five Hundred Years of Hispanic Presence*. Gainesville: University Press of Florida.

Kagan, Richard L. 2019. *The Spanish Craze: America's Fascination with the Hispanic World, 1779–1939*. Lincoln: University of Nebraska Press.

Kramer, Paul. 2006. *The Blood of Government: Race, Empire, the United States and the Philippines*. Chapel Hill: University of North Carolina Press.

Lipski, John M. 2008. *Varieties of Spanish in the United States.* Washington, DC: Georgetown University Press.

Lozano, Rosina. 2018. *An American Language: The History of Spanish in the United States.* Oakland: University of California Press.

Macías, Reynaldo. 2001. "Minority Languages in the United States, with a Focus on Spanish in California." Pp. 331–354 in Dürk Gorter and Guus Extra (eds.), *The Other Languages of Europe: Demographic, Sociolinguistic, and Educational Perspective.* Buffalo: Multilingual Matters.

Mirabal, Nancy Raquel. 2017. *Suspect Freedoms: The Racial and Sexual Politics of Cubanidad in New York, 1823–1957.* New York: New York University Press.

Monroy, Douglas. 1999. *Rebirth: Mexican Los Angeles from the Great Migration to the Great Depression.* Berkeley: University of California Press.

Ngai, Mae. 2004. *Impossible Subjects: Illegal Aliens and the Making of Modern America.* Princeton, NJ: Princeton University Press.

Nieto-Phillips, John M. 2008. *The Language of Blood: The Making of Spanish-American Identity in New Mexico, 1880s–1930s.* Albuquerque: University of New Mexico Press.

Osuna, Juan José. 1949. *A History of Education in Puerto Rico.* Río Piedras: Editorial de la Universidad de Puerto Rico.

Pérez, Lisandro. 2018. *Sugar, Cigars, and Revolution: The Making of Cuban New York.* New York: New York University Press.

Pico, Andrés. 1858. "Discurso de Don Andrés Pico." *El Clamor Público,* April 10, 1858.

Rasico, Philip D. 1990. *The Minorcans of Florida: Their History, Language, and Culture.* New Smyrna Beach, FL: Luthers.

Reséndez, Andrés. 2005. *Changing National Identities at the Frontier: Texas and New Mexico, 1800–1850.* New York: Cambridge University Press.

Rogers, Robert F. 2011. *Destiny's Landfall: A History of Guam.* Rev. Ed. Honolulu: University of Hawaii Press.

Sánchez, George. 1993. *Becoming Mexican American: Ethnicity, Culture, and Identity, 1900–1945.* New York: Oxford University Press, 1993.

Sheppard, Claude Armand. 1971. *The Law of Languages in Canada.* Ottawa: Information Canada.

Silverberg, Robert. 1994. *The Pueblo Revolt.* Lincoln: University of Nebraska Press.

UNESCO. 1998. *Declaration of Linguistic Rights,* http://culturalrights.net/descargas/drets_culturals389.pdf.

U.S. Census Bureau. 1853. *The Seventh Census of the United States: 1850.* Washington: Robert Armstrong.

U.S. War Department. 1900. *Report on the Census of Porto Rico 1899* (Washington: Government Printing Office, 1900). https://archive.org/stream/reportoncensusof00unitiala#page/n5/mode/2up.

Chapter 3

The Demography of the Latino Spanish Speakers in the United States

Rogelio Sáenz and Daniel Mamani

Approximately 39.1 million Latinos in the United States speak Spanish at home. If U.S. Spanish-speaking Latinos were a country, it would be the world's fourth most populous nation of Spanish speakers behind Mexico, Spain, and Argentina. Overall, aside from English, Spanish represents the language most spoken in U.S. homes with 41.7 million persons in 2019, nearly 12 times as many Spanish speakers compared to the second language—Chinese—most often spoken at home. In addition, Spanish is the most popular non-English language spoken in 47 states and the District of Columbia. With the growth of the Latino population over the last four decades, the number of Latino Spanish speakers has grown tremendously, soaring from 3.2 million in 1980 to 39.1 million in 2019. In addition, there have also been significant shifts in the English fluency of Latino Spanish speakers over this time.

Despite the Spanish language's deep roots in the United States in much of the southwestern portion of the country, land that once belonged to Mexico, there has been great hostility against the use of Spanish in public (Cobas et al., 2016; Feagin and Cobas, 2014). Social media posts regularly show white self-appointed language police belittling Latinos for speaking Spanish, telling them that they are in the United States where English is spoken, informing them to go back to the country they came from, and evoking stereotypes about the socioeconomic status and welfare use among Spanish speakers. Research has also demonstrated economic costs associated with speaking Spanish with an accent (Davila et al., 1993).

This chapter has four objectives. First, we assess the Spanish-language retention of Latinos over five periods of time (1980, 1990, 2000, 2010, and 2019). Second, we examine variations in Spanish-language retention across geographic and individual characteristics in 2019. Third, we overview shifts in language use involving Spanish use at home and English fluency over the five time periods. Fourth, we examine earnings inequality among Latinos on the basis of their language use (English dominant, Spanish dominant, and bilingual speakers) and how they fare compared to whites in 2019. Before conducting the analysis, we start off with a brief overview of the literature concerning Latino Spanish speakers.

DOI: 10.4324/9781003257509-6

Literature Overview

The Spanish language has deep roots of historical significance within the United States and has shaped and contextualized the United States since before the country's foundation and up to the present day. Spanish was one of the first European languages to arrive in the Americas and subsequently spread throughout geographical areas influenced by Spanish colonialism. Portions of these areas in North America were annexed by the United States, primarily through warfare (Acuña, 2019; Alvarez, 1973). Large sections of these areas, specifically the southwestern United States, have maintained significant Spanish-speaking populations to this day.

One of the most prominent features of the Latino population is its heterogeneity with Latinos varying tremendously with respect to national origin, generational status, socioeconomic status, and other attributes (Sáenz and Morales, 2015). Immigration from Latin America throughout the 20th and 21st centuries has helped in the growth and maintenance of the Spanish language among the Latino community and the nation as a whole. Still, there are major intergenerational shifts in Spanish maintenance among Latinos over their history in this country. Indeed, increased English proficiency among U.S.-born Latinos has coincided with their declining Spanish maintenance (Krogstad et al., 2015). This shift to English monolingualism seems to happen gradually over generations. Children of Spanish-speaking immigrants often have Spanish passed down from their parents in the home setting, while they learn English in institutional settings, usually school, resulting in a bilingual second generation (Mora et al., 2006). The third generation likely is where patterns of lower Spanish maintenance emerge (Veltman, 1988). Partial explanations of this transition include internal factors like intergenerational differences in attitudes toward Spanish (Guglani, 2016; Pease-Alvarez, 1993), along with external factors like the cultural environment, discrimination, and racism that can place pressures on families to learn and transition to English.

Discrimination as a reaction to changing racial/ethnic and language demographics has serious implications for Latinos, especially immigrants with limited English proficiency. Anti-immigrant sentiment has been a historical component of the United States with racist undertones (Cobas et al., 2016; Feagin and Cobas, 2014; Sáenz and Douglas, 2015). Along with physical characteristics, Spanish use words as a racial identifier that nativists utilize to identify "outsiders" or "foreign" individuals regardless of their actual nativity. Latinos have reported feeling singled out, discriminated against, or labeled by whites as "others" based on their language (Benner and Graham, 2011; Davis and Moore, 2014). Policies shaped within the context of race relations impact Latinos within institutional settings as well. In schools, immigrant children with limited English proficiency are often held back academically because of required English as a Secondary Language (ESL) courses and stigmatized because they speak a foreign language (Portes and Salas, 2010). Discrimination and racism negatively shape the Latino population and have implications for the socioeconomic outcomes of Latinos.

Language appears to play a role in determining earnings among Latinos. Early reports on this topic have suggested that income differentials between Spanish speakers (mono or bilingual) and English speakers exist, and that language attributes impact wages and explain differences in earnings between Latinos and non-Latinos (Bloom and Grenier, 1993; Grenier, 1984). More recent research on the durability of this English fluency earnings penalty shows that this feature remains in place with similar magnitude when comparing regions close to the U.S.-Mexico border with larger Spanish-speaking populations in the rest of the country (Dávila and Mora, 2000). These income differentials highlight the influence of language on economic outcomes for Latinos.

This overview of the literature concerning Spanish language use among Latinos provides a useful context for the analysis to be undertaken below.

Data and Methodology

Census microdata are used to conduct the analysis. In particular, we use data from the 1980, 1990, and 2000 Public-Use Microdata Samples and the 2010 and 2019 American Community Survey 1-Year Estimates public-use files. These data were extracted from the Integrated Public Use Microdata Series located at the University of Minnesota (Ruggles et al., 2021).

The primary data analysis is based on Latinos five years of age and older concerning the language that they speak at home and their fluency in English. We first determine the language people speak at home: (1) Spanish, (2) English, and (3) other languages besides Spanish and English. In 2019, 70.4% of Latinos spoke Spanish at home, 29.1% spoke English, and 0.5% spoke another language at home. We compute the Spanish-language retention rate (SLRR) by dividing the number of Latinos five and older who speak Spanish at home by the total Latino population five and older. In addition, we use information concerning the language spoken at home and the fluency of English among persons who speak Spanish at home to construct a measure on the language use among Latinos who speak either English or Spanish at home: (1) English-dominant speakers (persons who speak English at home), (2) bilingual (persons who speak Spanish at home and who speak English "well" or "very well"), and (3) Spanish-dominant speakers (persons who speak Spanish at home and who speak English "not well" or "not at all"). Note that Latinos who speak a language other than Spanish or English at home are not included in this part of the analysis.

The first part of the analysis examines the Spanish-language retention rate of Latinos five and older across five time periods (1980, 1990, 2000, 2010, and 2019) to assess trends in the use of Spanish among Latinos over time. This is done for the total Latino population as well as for the native- and foreign-born Latino populations as Spanish-language retention and language use varies greatly on the basis of nativity status. Subsequently, we use data for

2019 to assess the relationship between the Spanish-language retention rate and selected geographic and individual characteristics. The geographic measures include five variables, one based on the state of residence of Latinos and the other four based on the Public Use Microdata Area (PUMA) where Latinos reside. PUMAs are state-specific geographic areas that may be geographically as small as a particular area within a large city to as wide as numerous sparsely populated counties that contain an adequate number of individuals living in the particular PUMA to provide a geographic description of the PUMA without compromising confidentiality. In 2019, the PUMAs averaged 139,617 inhabitants regardless of race or ethnicity with a range of 88,540 to 293,328.

The five geographic variables include (1) state of residence, (2) population density for the total population in PUMAs based on eight categories (less than 100 persons per square mile, 100 to 249, 500 to 999, 1,000 to 2,499, 2,500 to 4,999, 5,000 to 9,999, and 10,000 or more), (3) metropolitan-nonmetropolitan status of PUMAs based on five categories (metropolitan area containing central/principal city; metropolitan area not containing central/principal city; metropolitan area mixed within and outside of central/principal city; non-metropolitan area; and mixed metropolitan and non-metropolitan areas), and (4) relative size of the Latino population in PUMAS based on seven categories (below 5% of PUMA population Latino; 5.0% to 9.9%; 10.0% to 14.9%; 15.0% to 24.9%; 25.0% to 49.9%; 50.0% to 74.9%; 75.0% and above of PUMA population Latino), and 5% of the Latino population in PUMAs who are immigrants based on ten categories (below 10% of Latinos in PUMA are immigrants; 10.0% to 14.9%; 15.0% to 19.9%; 20.0% to 24.9%; 25.0% to 29.9%; 30.0% to 34.9%; 35.0% to 39.9%; 40.0% to 44.9%; 45.0% to 49.9%; and 50.0% or above of Latinos in PUMA are immigrants). While we expect that Spanish-language retention rates vary across states, we expect that the Spanish retention rates will be highest in PUMAs with greater population density, metropolitan areas containing a central/principal city, higher percentages of the population being Latino, and those with higher percentages of Latinos being immigrants.

We also use three individual-level characteristics to examine the relationship between the Spanish-language retention rate and national origin group, age, and educational attainment. First, national origin is based on the country of origin of Latinos for the 12 largest specific Latino groups and a residual category (Colombian, Cuban, Dominican, Ecuadorian, Guatemalan, Honduran, Mexican, Peruvian, Puerto Rican, Salvadoran, Spaniard, Venezuelan, and all other groups). Second, we construct a nine-category age measure (5 to 9, 10 to 14, 15 to 19, 20 to 24, 25 to 34, 35 to 44, 45 to 54, 55 to 64, and 65-and-older). Third, we categorize Latinos 25 and older into one of five educational-attainment categories based on their highest educational attainment level (not a high school graduate, high school graduate, some college but no degree, associate degree, and bachelor's degree or higher). These three attributes will be useful in providing a profile of the Spanish-language retention rates.

The third part of the analysis will examine the language use of Latinos who speak either Spanish or English at home. In this section, we will assess changes in the distribution of Latinos five and older based on the three language-use categories (English-dominant speaker, Spanish-dominant speakers, and bilingual) across five time periods (1980, 1990, 2000, 2010, and 2019).

The final part of the analysis will use multivariate statistics to assess how bilingual and Spanish-dominant Latinos fare relative to Latino English-dominant speakers on job earnings and relative to their respective white counterparts in 2019. This part of the analysis will be based on Latinos and whites 25 to 64 years of age who were employed and had earnings in the previous year. Job earnings are based on workers' wages and salary income earned in the previous year. We use ordinary least squares multiple regression to examine the relationship between language use and earnings given that the latter two variables are continuous variables. We use the logged earnings to minimize outliers and to treat the regression coefficients as percentages. We will include in the regression models variables that are typically used as control variables in the analysis of employment, occupational attainment, and earnings (see Sáenz and Morales, 2019; see also Appendix). The first part of this section of the analysis examines earning inequalities within the Latino population based on their language use (bilingual and Spanish-dominant speakers versus English-dominant speakers) with the analysis conducted separately for subgroups on the basis of nativity and sex. Subsequently, the examines earning inequalities between Latinos and whites for each of the three language-use categories with the analysis conducted separately for subgroups on the basis of nativity and sex. Whites are individuals who identify themselves as non-Hispanic white and for those who are bilingual or non-English-dominant speakers who speak one of 33 non-English Indo-European languages. This part of the analysis will assess whether Latinos pay a cost for being Latino (versus white) for each of the three language-use categories (English-dominant, bilingual, and non-English-dominant) across nativity and sex groups.

Findings

Trends in Spanish-Language Retention

We examine the percentage share of Latinos who speak Spanish at home, a measure that we refer to as the Spanish-language retention rate, from 1980 to 2019. Overall, over the time period from 1980 to 2010, approximately three-fourths of Latinos five and older spoke Spanish at home with a drop of nearly 5 percentage points in 2019 when 70% did so. However, the use of Spanish varies greatly by nativity status. Latino immigrants have retained Spanish at levels at or above 93% throughout the period between 1980 and 2019. In contrast, while a significant majority of U.S.-born Latinos speak Spanish at home, they are less likely to do so compared to those born outside of the country. There

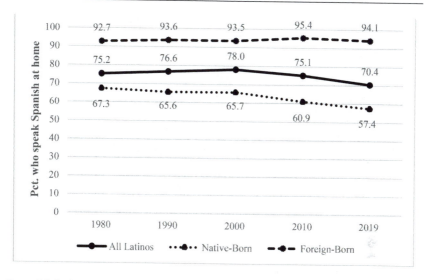

Figure 3.1 Percentage of Latinos five years of age and older who speak Spanish at home by nativity status and year, 1980–2019

Source: 1980, 1990, and 2000 Public Use Microdata Sample and 2010 and 2019 American Community Survey 1-Year Estimates (Ruggles et al., 2021).

has been a noticeable drop in the Spanish-language retention rate of U.S.-born Latinos between 2009 and 2019 with a decline of more than 8 percentage points during this period (Figure 3.1).

Factors Related to Spanish-Language Retention

We now develop a profile of the geographic settings and people who currently have the highest rates of Spanish-language retention using the latest data for 2019. We begin with an examination of the percentage of Latinos who speak Spanish at home across the 50 states and the District of Columbia. There is much variation in the retention of Spanish among Latinos across the nation, ranging from a low of 14.7% in Montana to 81.1% in Florida. Over three-fourths of Latinos speak Spanish at home in eight states (Florida, 81.1%; New Jersey, 77.8%; Rhode Island, 77.5%; Maryland, 77.2%; North Carolina, 76.2%; Georgia, 76.0%; Illinois, 75.2%; and Massachusetts, 75.0%), areas principally located in the northeastern and southeastern parts of the country (Figure 3.2). These eight states feature a critical mass of Latinos with a significant portion being immigrants: Florida (Latinos account for 26.4% of Florida's population and 46.7% of Latinos are immigrants), New Jersey (20.9% and 42.6%), Rhode Island (16.4% and 34.1%), Maryland (10.6% and 46.1%), North Carolina (9.8% and 39.4%), Georgia (9.8% and 39.8%), Illinois (17.5% and 32.7%), and Massachusetts (12.4% and 32.3%).

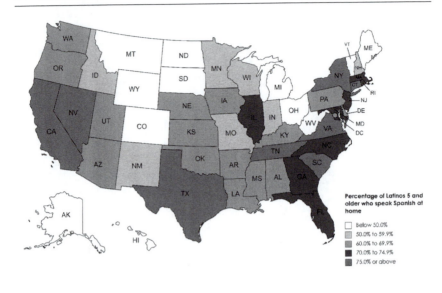

Figure 3.2 States by the percentage of Latinos five years of age or older who speak Spanish at home, 2019

Source: American Community Survey 1-Year Estimates (Ruggles et al., 2021).

Latinos also have relatively high Spanish retention rates—between 70.0% and 74.9%—in eight other states (in the Southwest: Texas, California, and Nevada; in the South: Tennessee, South Carolina, and Virginia; and in the Northeast: Connecticut and New York. This octet also generally has a critical mass of Latinos and a high percentage share of immigrants among Latinos.

Three southwestern states with a large historical presence of Latinos stand out for their fairly low levels of use of Spanish at home. New Mexico (the state where Latinos comprise the largest share of the overall state population at 49.3%), Arizona (31.8%), and Colorado (21.8%) have Latino populations with relatively low percentages being foreign-born (New Mexico, 14.0%; Arizona, 25.0%; and Colorado, 20.9%). As such, a significant portion of Latinos in these states can trace their presence to the United States for multiple generations with the loss of Spanish language being part of this long tenure in the country. Approximately half of Latinos in Colorado and New Mexico and 62% of those in Arizona continue to speak Spanish at home.

States with relatively small Latino populations have the lowest levels of Latino Spanish retention including Montana, Hawaii, North Dakota, Maine, South Dakota, West Virginia, Wyoming, Alaska, and Vermont.

We next assess further geographic factors that are related to the Latino Spanish-language retention rates across PUMAs within states (as noted above,

Table 3.1 Percent of Latinos five years of age and older who speak Spanish at home in PUMAs by the level of selected geographic characteristics by nativity, 2019

Geographic characteristics	Total	Native-born	Foreign-born
PUMA population per square mile			
Less than 250	61.6	50.2	92.4
250 to 999	63.1	50.8	93.0
1,000 to 4,999	67.8	55.0	93.6
5,000 to 9,999	74.5	61.2	94.6
10,000 or more	83.2	72.6	95.9
Pct. of PUMA population Latino			
Less than 5.0%	48.8	34.4	85.7
5.0% to 9.9%	58.0	43.3	89.8
10.0% to 24.9%	65.2	50.8	93.0
25.0% to 49.9%	71.4	58.6	95.0
50.0% to 74.9%	77.6	66.3	95.9
75.0% or more	82.5	73.8	95.9
Pct. of Latinos in PUMA foreign-born			
Less than 10.0%	41.3	37.7	86.7
10.0% to 19.9%	52.0	44.3	90.0
20.0% to 20.9%	65.7	55.3	92.8
30.0% to 39.9%	74.3	62.3	94.2
40.0% to 49.9%	82.1	69.8	95.4
50.0% or more	88.1	74.7	95.7

Source: 2019 American Community Survey 1-Year Estimates (Ruggles et al., 2021).

PUMAs in 2019 had an average total population of 139,617 with a range of 88,540 to 293,328). Table 3.1 contains information on the percentage of Latinos five and older who speak Spanish at home for different categories of three geographic characteristics (PUMA population per square mile, percent of PUMA population that is Latino, and percent of Latinos in PUMA who are foreign-born). There is a clear relationship between each of the three geographic attributes and the level of Spanish retention. PUMAs with greater levels of population density, those where Latinos account for a larger share of the overall population, and those where immigrants comprise a larger percentage of the Latino population are more likely to speak Spanish at home compared to those PUMAs with less concentration of people, representation of Latinos, and lower presence of immigrants. These relationships are quite evident in the level of Spanish retention among U.S.-born Latinos, suggesting that second- and higher-generation Latinos are more likely to maintain the Spanish language in more dense settings with a critical mass of Latinos and immigrants. The relationships between the three geographic factors and Spanish retention are not as strong among the foreign-born due to high levels of Spanish use among Latino immigrants regardless of the geographic context.

Certain individual characteristics are also associated with the Spanish-language retention rate. Table 3.2 presents information on the percentage of

Table 3.2 Percent of Latinos who speak Spanish at home by the level of selected individual characteristics by nativity, 2019

Individual characteristics	Total	Native-born	Foreign-born
National origin of Latinos 18 and older			
Colombian	84.5	62.8	91.9
Cuban	80.7	54.0	93.8
Dominican	90.5	78.6	96.0
Ecuadorian	86.9	66.9	94.0
Guatemalan	89.8	73.4	93.9
Honduran	90.5	67.8	96.0
Mexican	73.3	57.5	95.2
Peruvian	85.1	59.1	92.7
Puerto Rican	64.8	64.4	80.0
Salvadoran	91.2	77.4	95.9
Spaniard	32.0	22.6	75.3
Venezuelan	88.6	64.1	92.3
All others	60.4	41.7	87.1
Age			
5 to 9	56.6	54.5	96.0
10 to 14	59.8	57.7	91.4
15 to 19	62.7	58.5	93.3
20 to 24	66.4	59.2	94.5
25 to 34	69.9	56.9	94.4
35 to 44	76.4	56.0	95.0
45 to 54	79.2	56.4	94.6
55 to 64	77.3	56.0	93.4
65 and older	80.0	64.9	92.7
Educational attainment among persons 25 and older			
Not a high school grad.	88.5	69.2	95.7
High school grad.	76.0	59.1	94.9
Some college, no degree	67.4	54.6	92.6
Associate degree	67.0	54.4	91.1
Bachelor's degree or higher	66.3	50.9	90.6

Source: 2019 American Community Survey 1-Year Estimates (Ruggles et al., 2021).

Latinos who speak Spanish at home by categories associated with the specific national origin of Latinos, age, and educational attainment. Latinos vary tremendously in their length of residence in the United States and in their nativity status. Compared to other Latino groups, the ancestors of Mexicans, Spaniards, and Puerto Ricans, for example, have been in the United States for long periods of time with foreign-born persons accounting for 31.8%, 15.5%, and 2.0% of these groups, respectively. On the other hand, immigrants comprise 58% or more of the overall populations of the other nine specific national origin groups. These nine groups contain the highest Spanish-language retention rates above 80% with more than 90% of Salvadorans (91.2%), Dominicans (90.5%), and Hondurans (90.5%) speaking Spanish among persons 18 and older. The retention rates of Mexicans (73.3%) and Puerto Ricans (64.8%)

are moderate with that of Spaniards (32.0%) being particularly low. Among the native-born, the highest percentages who speak Spanish at home include Dominicans (78.6%), Salvadorans (77.4%), Guatemalans (73.4%), Hondurans (67.8%), and Ecuadorians (66.9%). In contrast, less than one-fourth of Spaniards speak Spanish at home. Among the foreign-born, 10 of the 12 specific national groups have Spanish retention rates above 90% with Spaniards (75.3%) and Puerto Ricans (80.0%) having the lowest levels of Spanish use at home.

Age also appears to be somewhat related to the percentage share of Latinos who speak Spanish at home, though this is the case only for the overall population. Among all Latinos, more than three-fourths of persons above 35 years of age speak Spanish at home, as is the case with approximately two-thirds of those 15 to 34 years of age, and less than three-fifths of persons less than 15 years of age. However, these figures reflect higher percentages of immigrants among populations 35 and older. Indeed, there is not much variation in the Spanish retention rates among native-born Latinos with persons 65 and older (64.9%) more likely to speak Spanish at home compared to persons less than 65. As we have observed above, there is little variation among immigrants with upward of 90% across the age categories speaking Spanish at home. Nonetheless, we observe gender differences in Spanish language retention among U.S.-born Latinos. In particular, across all age groups, Latinas are more likely than Latino males to speak Spanish at home with the greatest difference in the 20–24 age category with 61.2% of Latinas speaking Spanish compared to 57.3% of Latino men. There is less consistency in gender differences in Spanish use among the foreign-born.

Finally, there is a relationship between the educational attainment levels of persons 25 and older and their level of Spanish retention, but these are at the extremes. For the total population and across the two nativity groups, persons who are not high school graduates have the highest levels of speaking Spanish at home and those with a bachelor's degree or higher have the lowest levels. Yet, once again, we see important gender variations in the retention of Spanish. Across all educational categories for all persons, native-born persons, and four of the five educational categories among foreign-born persons, females are more likely to speak Spanish at home compared to their male counterparts. The largest gender difference occurs among native-born individuals with 53.1% of Latinos speaking Spanish at home compared to 48.0% of Latino men (data not shown here).

In this section, we have focused on the extent to which Latinos speak Spanish at home without reference to their fluency in English. We now turn the analysis to an expansive view of language use among Latinos.

Trends in Language Use

In this part of the analysis, we focus exclusively on Latinos five and older who speak Spanish or English at home with those speaking another language in the home front excluded from the analysis. We place Latinos into three language use categories based on the language that they speak at home and, for those

Table 3.3 Percentage distribution of Latinos by language use by nativity and year, 1980–2019

Language use by total and nativity status	1980	1990	2000	2010	2019
Total					
English dominant	23.6	22.6	21.6	24.7	29.2
Bilingual	56.3	55.8	54.7	54.1	54.7
Spanish dominant	20.1	21.6	23.7	21.3	16.1
Native-born					
English dominant	32.2	34.0	34.0	38.9	42.3
Bilingual	58.7	58.5	59.6	57.1	54.7
Spanish dominant	9.1	7.5	6.4	4.0	3.0
Foreign-born					
English dominant	4.3	4.7	5.8	4.1	5.3
Bilingual	50.9	51.6	48.4	49.8	54.7
Spanish dominant	44.8	43.7	45.8	46.1	40.0

Source: 1980, 1990, and 2000 public use microdata sample and 2010 and 2019 American Community Survey 1-Year Estimates (Ruggles et al., 2021).

who speak Spanish at home, their fluency in English: predominant English speaker, predominant Spanish speaker, and bilingual.

Over the last four decades, there have been shifts in the linguistic patterns of Latinos. Nonetheless, one pattern has been consistent from 1980 to the present (Table 3.3). The majority of Latinos overall as well as among the native- and foreign-born have consistently been bilingual, i.e., they speak Spanish at home and speak English "well" or "very well." For the overall Latino population, while approximately 55% have been bilingual across the five time periods, there has been a trend associated with a reduction of Spanish-dominant speakers (falling from 20.1% in 1980 to 16.1% in 2019) and an increase of English-dominant speakers (rising from 23.6% to 29.2%).

Among native-born persons, over time there has been a decline of bilingual (from 58.7% in 1980 to 54.7% in 2019) and Spanish-dominant speakers (from 9.1% to 3.0%) and a rise of English-dominant speakers (from 32.2% to 42.3%). These shifts among the native-born have been most prominent between 2000 and 2019. Among foreign-born individuals, while the percentage of English-dominant speakers has remained consistently low, the trend has been a decline in Spanish-dominant speakers dropping to a low of 40.0% in 2019 and an increase in bilingual speakers rising to a high of 54.7% in 2019. These are interesting trends that portend further diversity in the linguistic patterns of Latinos in the coming decades.

Earnings Differentials on the Basis of Language Use

Research has consistently shown that there are earnings premiums for speaking English and penalties for speaking Spanish in the workforce. In this section of the analysis, we examine these rewards and penalties within the

Table 3.4 Regression coefficients associated with the logged earnings of Latino workers 25 to 64 years of age who are bilingual or Spanish-dominant speakers relative to Latino English-dominant workers by nativity and sex, 2019

Language use	Native-born male	Native-born female	Foreign-born male	Foreign-born female
Bilingual	−0.031**	−0.023**	0.001	−0.050**
Spanish dominant	−0.182**	−0.208**	−0.133**	−0.177**

Source: 2019 American Community Survey 1-Year Estimates (Ruggles et al., 2021).
**Significant at the 0.01 level.

Latino population and in comparison to whites. We use ordinary least squares regressions controlling for variables that are typically held constant in earnings equations (see Appendix for the list of control variables). The focus is on the experienced labor force—ages 25 to 64—who had earnings in the previous year.

We first assess how Latino bilingual and Spanish-dominant speakers fare in comparison to their counterparts who speak English at home with respect to their wage and salary incomes. The results show that workers who have retained their Spanish language pay a cost for having done so, with the exception of Latino foreign-born males (Table 3.4). It is clear, however, that the cost is smaller in the case of bilingual speakers who speak Spanish at home and speak English "well" or "very well." After taking demographic and socioeconomic compositional differences into account, Latino workers who are bilingual, relative to their peers who speak English at home, earn 5.0% lower earnings among foreign-born females, 3.1% lower earnings among native-born males, and 2.3% lower earnings among native-born females. The costs of not being fluent in English, however, are uniformly much greater for Latinos who speak English "not well" or "not at all" with people lacking English fluency earning 13.3% lower wages and salaries (foreign-born males); 17.7% less (foreign-born females), 18.2% less (native-born males), and 20.8% less (native-born females).

Yet, when we shift the focus to examine rewards and penalties associated with all three linguistic categories relative to whites, the findings show that Latinos fare worse, respectively, than their white counterparts who are English-dominant speakers (speak English at home), bilingual (speak a language other than English at home and who speak English "well" or "very well"), and non-English-dominant speakers (those who speak either Spanish or one of 33 Indo-European languages and who speak English "not well" or "not at all"). Table 3.5 shows the regression coefficients associated with being a Latino (relative to a white) worker across nativity, language use, and sex categories. It is clear that, after taking demographic and socioeconomic composition attributes into account, Latinos and Latinas earn lower wages than whites across the board, the only exception being among native-born males who are Spanish-dominant speakers. Furthermore, overall, with only one exception (native-born

Table 3.5 Regression coefficients associated with the logged earnings of Latino workers 25 to 64 years of age who are Spanish-dominant speakers, bilingual or Spanish-dominant speakers relative to white workers by nativity and sex, 2019

Nativity and language use	Male	Female
Native-born		
English dominant	−0.061**	−0.015**
Bilingual	−0.100**	−0.030*
Spanish dominant	−0.034	−0.197*
Foreign-born		
English dominant	−0.269**	−0.152**
Bilingual	−0.240**	−0.175**
Spanish dominant	−0.168**	−0.149**

Source: 2019 American Community Survey 1-Year Estimates (Ruggles et al., 2021).
*Significant at the 0.05 level. **Significant at the 0.01 level.

females with dominance in Spanish), foreign-born Latinos and Latinas pay a greater cost for being Latina or Latino regardless of the language configuration. The greatest cost for being Latino exist among foreign-born male English-dominant speakers (26.9% lower earnings than whites), foreign-born male bilingual speakers (24.0% lower earnings than whites), native-born females who are Spanish-dominant speakers (19.7% lower earnings than whites), foreign-born females who are bilingual (17.5% lower earnings than whites), and foreign-born females who are English-dominant speakers (15.2% lower earnings than whites). Thus, even Latinos and Latinas who speak English at home do not reap economic benefits for doing so compared to whites.

These findings amply show that there are workforce penalties associated with being bilingual and Spanish-dominant speakers within the Latino population and for being Latino across linguistic categories relative to whites.

Conclusion

The Spanish language and Latinos who speak Spanish have a very long history in the United States, particularly in the southwestern part of the United States, lands that once belonged to Mexico. Spanish continues to be the most spoken language, aside from English, in the United States and it has grown tremendously alongside the major expansion of the Latino population between 1980 and today. Our results show that Latinos continue to retain their use of Spanish with the most prominent form of language continuing to be bilingual speakers in which they speak Spanish at home and speak English "well" or "very well." Nonetheless, there have been significant shifts in language use since 2000 among Latinos with U.S.-born Latinos increasingly speaking English at home and foreign-born Latinos becoming more bilingual. Our results also point to the importance of the presence of a critical mass of Latinos and a substantial portion of Latino immigrants as ingredients to support and sustain the retention of Spanish among the native-born. Our findings also show that women are more likely than men to maintain the Spanish language which shows the importance of women in maintaining not only the Spanish language but also the Latino cultures as well.

The results also demonstrate that Latinos experience a long-term economic penalty for speaking Spanish. Latino bilingual speakers earn lower wages and salaries compared to Latino workers who speak English at home. However, the penalties are particularly severe among Latinos with limited or no fluency in English. Furthermore, across the board, Latino workers pay a cost for being a Latino worker compared to being a white worker among those who speak English at home, those who are bilingual, and those with limited or no fluency in English. Thus, even though Latinos who speak English at home enjoy a premium in the workplace over Latinos who speak Spanish at home, they pay the price in their work remuneration compared to whites who speak English at home.

Our results have implications for public policy. As we live in an increasingly global society and economy, the dominance of non-English languages represents a major asset. Indeed, white parents tend to encourage their children to learn foreign languages as a way to increase their academic and economic stock. The mainstream society views Spanish language ability as an asset among whites but as a liability for Latinos. Educational policies and programs need to recognize the asset that the Spanish language represents for Latinos and to encourage its maintenance. Workforce policies and practices also need to protect the rights of Latino workers who speak Spanish to ensure that they are not discriminated against with respect to restrictions against speaking Spanish in the workplace and receive fair compensation for the work that they perform.

References

Acuña, Rodolfo F. 2019. *Occupied America: A History of Chicanos*. London: Pearson Publishing.

Alvarez, Rodolfo. 1973. "The Psychohistorical and Socioeconomic Development of the Chicano Community in the United States." *Social Science Quarterly* 53 (4):920–942.

Benner, Aprile D. and Sandra Graham. 2011. "Latino Adolescents' Experiences of Discrimination Across the First 2 Years of High School: Correlates and Influences on Educational Outcomes." *Child Development* 82 (2):508–519.

Bloom, David E. and Gilles Grenier. 1993. "Language, Employment and Earnings in the United States: Spanish-English Differentials from 1970 to 1990." NBER Working Paper 4584. Retrieved on March 10, 2021 (https://www.nber.org/papers/w4584).

Cobas, José A., Jorge Duany, and Joe R. Feagin. 2016. *How the United States Racializes Latinos: White Hegemony and Its Consequences*. New York: Routledge.

Davila, Alberto, Alok K. Bohara, and Rogelio Sáenz. 1993. "Accent Penalties and the Earnings of Mexican American Men: Implications for Labor-Market Discrimination and Immigration Policy." *Social Science Quarterly* 74 (Dec.):902–916.

Dávila, Alberto and Marie T. Mora. 2000. "English Skills, Earnings, and the Occupational Sorting of Mexican Americans Along the U.S.-Mexico Border." *International Migration Review* 34 (1):133–157.

Davis, Tiffany Y. and Wendy Leo Moore. 2014. "Spanish Not Spoken Here: Accounting for the Racialization of the Spanish Language in the Experiences of Mexican Migrants in the United States." *Ethnicities* 14 (5):676–697.

Feagin, Joe R. and José A. Cobas. 2014. *Latinos Facing Racism: Discrimination, Resistance, and Endurance.* New York: Routledge.

Grenier, Gilles. 1984. "The Effects of Language Characteristics on the Wages of Hispanic-American males." *Journal of Human Resources* 19 (1):35–52.

Guglani, Laura. 2016. "American, Hispanic, Spanish-Speaking? Hispanic Immigrants and the Question of Identity." *Journal of Language, Identity & Education* 15 (6):344–360.

Krogstad, Jens Manuel, Renee Stepler, and Mark Hugo Lopez. 2015. "English Proficiency on the Rise among Latinos." Pew Research Center Hispanic Trends (May 12). Retrieved March 10, 2001 (https://www.pewresearch.org/hispanic/2015/05/12/english-proficiency-on-the-rise-among-latinos/).

Mora, Marie T., Daniel J. Villa, and Alberto Dávila. 2006. "Language Shift and Maintenance among the Children of Immigrants in the U.S.: Evidence in the Census for Spanish Speakers and Other Language Minorities." *Spanish in Context* 3 (2):239–254.

Pease-Alvarez, Lucinda. 1993. "Moving In and Out of Bilingualism: Investigating Native Language Maintenance and Shift in Mexican-Descent Children." National Center for Research on Cultural Diversity and Second Language Learning Research Report: 6. Retrieved March 10, 2021 (https://escholarship.org/uc/item/78p4t7hk).

Portes, Pedro R. and Spencer Salas. 2010. "In the Shadow of Stone Mountain: Identity Development, Structured Inequality, and the Education of Spanish-Speaking Children." *Bilingual Research Journal* 33 (2):241–248.

Ruggles, Steven, Sarah Flood, Sophia Foster, Ronald Goeken, Jose Pacas, Megan Schouweiler, and Matthew Sobek. 2021. *IPUMS USA: Version 11.0 {dataset}.* Minneapolis, MN: IPUMS, 2021. https://doi.org/10.18128/D010.V11.0

Sáenz, Rogelio and Karen Manges Douglas. 2015. "A Call for the Racialization of Immigration Studies: On the Transition of Ethnic Immigrants to Racialized Immigrants." *Sociology of Race and Ethnicity* 1 (1):166–180.

Sáenz, Rogelio and Maria Cristina Morales. 2015. *Latinos in the United States: Diversity and Change.* Cambridge, UK: Polity Press.

Sáenz, Rogelio and M. Cristina Morales. 2019. "Demography of Race and Ethnicity." Pp. 163–207 in Dudley L. Poston, Jr. (ed.), *Handbook of Population.* 2nd ed. Cham, Switzerland: Springer Nature.

Veltman, Calvin J. 1988. *The Future of the Spanish Language in the United States.* New York: Hispanic Policy Development Project.

Section III

Racialization

Chapter 4

What Anti-Spanish Prejudice Tells Us about Whiteness

Bonnie Urciuoli

Introduction: Race Is about Those Who Do the Racializing

The most problematic misunderstanding about race is that the elements that supposedly mark race belong to the people who are racialized. The opposite is true: those elements point, first and foremost, to those who do the racializing. White/black as racial opposites pointed first to those benefiting from the enslavement of black people and later to those benefiting from subsequent economic and political repression of black people. Skin color and other features seem to point to ancestry and place of origin, but they really point to the social locations to which people have been limited, legally, economically, and otherwise. In the same way, the racialization of those with ancestry from Spanish-colonized places points to the limits put on their lives by people classifying themselves as white and American. The Spanish language is a primary marker of that racial construction.

Language as a marker of race is routine and egregious. Rosa and Flores (2017) analyze it in terms of raciolinguistics, the co-naturalization of race and language. Hill (2008) shows how Spanish is made fun of (as "Mock Spanish") in white public space. Zentella (1996) uses the idea of Chiquitafication to show how Spanish speakers are feminized and diminished as an undifferentiated mass speaking a non-language. Silverstein (1996) argues that Americans routinely imagine language as "naturally" a system that must be kept logical, correct, and "unmixed." In short, race gets routinely remapped from biology onto language (Urciuoli 2001), with only a certain kind of English allowable in white public space. In this way, what U.S. Spanish speakers (specifically, those inheriting Spanish from their families) do with language is considered unworthy of a place in U.S. society. This denigration of Spanish is of a piece with the denigration of other "unAmerican" ways of talking, looking, and acting.

DOI: 10.4324/9781003257509-8

Racialization and Language: A Raciolinguistic Perspective

There are two elements to consider here: the general issue of racialization, and the specifics of racialization intertwined with language, which is the jumping-off point for Flores and Rosa. I start with arguments that build on the work of many scholars of race and racialization (summarized in Urciuoli, 1996:15ff and Urciuoli, 2020): the emergence of race from a system of contrasts and its operation as a form of markedness.

As a system of classification, race consists of categories that operate in contrast with each other, one normative and valued, the other or others not. In semiotic terms, the normative categories are unmarked, and the non-normative are marked.[1] Simply being marked or unmarked does not itself create a social hierarchy. What does create social hierarchy is when unmarkedness is read as a sign of inherent superiority and markedness as a sign of inherent inferiority, such that the top of a hierarchy is also taken for granted as not only normative but also as having the natural right to set the rules. What makes this arrangement racial is when superiority or inferiority is signified by "natural" qualities, especially physical markers, supposedly inherited. Thus, what is classified is not just what is there physically but how it is believed to have gotten there; hence the notion of "blood" (pure blood, mixed blood, etc.). This is what makes race particularly intransigent: race at its most marked is embedded in colonization and the slave trade. The most racialized people in the United States are the descendants of the people brought over to be embodied labor: African slaves. Racial markedness is ultimately a classification of descent from those who owned (or could have owned) and those who were owned. This dichotomy, read as "white-black," is complicated by other color-coded markedness contrasts, two in particular anchored in the expansionist visions of Anglo-Saxon manifest destiny: "white-red," "red" marking the people indigenous to the territory; and "white-brown," "brown" marking the residents of former Spanish colonies. In this way, current racializations are historically continuous with the originating conditions of the United States as a slave and a settler society. Nor are these racializations peculiar to the United States, although here I only address the United States. Comparable dichotomies appear in other societies in which enslaved and/or indigenous people have been classified in terms of "naturally" inferior qualities linked to ideas about the descent. Generally, such racializations are a reflex of globally expanding, colonialism-based, early (to later) modern (especially settler) societies.

I have obviously simplified the picture, but I want to clarify the key dynamic here. "Race" as we know it did not come into being independent of these historical dynamics.[2] Racial classifications exist as folk theories about belonging, natural qualities, and descent framed by economically exploitative and politically expansionist privilege. That is the theoretical frame within which we can understand what the demonization of Spanish in the United States is really about.

Part of what brings race as a classification system into being is the dynamic that Rosa and Flores (2017; and see Rosa, 2019 for extended ethnographic analysis) analyze as raciolinguistic, a concept that addresses the co-naturalization of language stigmatization and racial marking of social actors. From a raciolinguistic perspective, the stigmatization of communicative practices is inextricable from other aspects of the construction of race. This is readily seen, for example, in the ongoing delegitimation of the discursive practices of working-class African Americans and of U.S. Spanish speakers, including bilinguals, as linguistic deficiencies or lack of language altogether. A raciolinguistic approach thus connects contemporary manifestations of race and language stigmatization to the "historical and structural processes that organize the modes of stigmatization in which deficit perspectives are rooted" (Rosa and Flores, 2017:622). As this perspective suggests, the widespread assumption that language comes naturally packaged as a standard (made of authorized, correct, unchanging forms and rules) itself emerges from the same conditions of globalized modernity (Bauman and Briggs, 2003) as does (straight, male, non-ethnic) whiteness as an ideally ordered and rational way of being. Language-as-standard and whiteness thus emerge in relation to each other. To again cite Rosa and Flores (2017:623), "A raciolinguistic perspective seeks to understand the interplay of language and race within the historical production of nation-state/colonial governmentality, and the ways that colonial distinctions within and between nation-state borders continue to shape contemporary linguistic and racial formations."

This brings us to U.S. raciolinguistic constructions of Spanish and Spanish speakers rooted in the Anglo-Saxonist expansion of the United States. I should preface this by noting that the Spanish discussed here has been dissociated by elites on both sides of the Atlantic from what is perceived as the educated Spanish of Spain and upper-class Latin Americans. This is the perspective of the Spanish Royal Academy, the national language academy whose mission is to provide the common standard and whose stance on non-standard bilingual practices has been historically purist.

Horsman (1981) points out that the nineteenth-century U.S. construction of Anglo-Saxonism is rooted in beliefs brought by Puritan settlers from six-teenth-century England. As the United States took political shape, beliefs about ideal forms of localized self-government fused with beliefs taking shape in the late 1700s about five human races. In the nascent United States, *Caucasian* became both "scientifically" and popularly understood as denoting the superior race, with that superiority expressed in ever more selective and superior sub-categories of *Germanic*, *Anglo-Saxon*, and *American*, racial visions that mapped onto that of a unified continental United States. The contrast of Anglo-Saxon virtue with non-white (African slave, indigenous American) non-virtue readily set up terms of comparison with inhabitants of the Mexican territory coveted for expanding U.S. settlement. So those inhabitants were cast as "naturally" lazy, stupid, mongrel, degenerate, and so on, with their language cast as similarly problematic. U.S. stigmatization of Mexico became the template for caricaturing the characteristics and linguistic habits of the inhabitants of Cuba, Puerto Rico, and the Philippines, territories formerly controlled by Spain and acquired by the United States in 1898 at the end of the Spanish-American war. The fantasy of U.S. Anglo-Saxonism became the basis for U.S. racialization generally and applied in various ways to the immigrant labor that came from China, Japan, and southern and eastern Europe.

Rosa and Flores note that the perception (and I might add, construction and classification) of racial and linguistic difference is a central element in a raciolinguistic perspective. We see this systematically throughout the history of United States dealings with former Spanish colonies. Let me give, as a detailed example, U.S. dealings with Puerto Rico (drawing from Urciuoli 1996:41ff). (In their chapter for this volume, Alejandrez and Liberato lay out some of the same history that I am about to.) From day one (in 1898) of U.S. occupation, U.S. policy was oriented toward "reforming" what the Spanish had left behind. U.S. policy for about the first half of the twentieth century operated with something like double vision, seeing Puerto Rico as disordered and directionless while at the same time a potential model society and showcase of democracy, assuming they did what the United States told them to do. To that end, U.S. administrators laid out a set of educational, linguistic, and economic directions by which Puerto Rico would be modernized. Policy particularly targeted the working class and rural populations that appeared most disordered and in need of direction.

The new colonial administration sought to establish a public school system that would effectively teach English both to rescue students from illiteracy[3] and to instill English as the medium through which U.S. democratic ideals could be understood (Osuna, 1949:363). English would be the instrument of Americanization (Cabán, 1999:131ff). A three-member Insular Commission, established in 1899, called for a new system of mass education, patterned after U.S. schools, with instruction in English by American teachers. While these recommendations were not altogether practicable, they set the direction for education policy going forward, with school boards patterned after U.S. models established throughout Puerto Rico and English-language fluency becoming a condition for teacher employment (Cabán, 1999:54–55). English was taught in grades 1–8 as a school subject, with grades 9–12 taught in English until 1903, when the U.S. education commissioner decided children were getting insufficient practice at which point English became the medium of instruction at all levels (Osuna, 1949:341–343). This resulted, predictably, in a pedagogical mess, with frustrated teachers and very unhappy students. Despite accusations that they were being un-American, Puerto Rican lawmakers pushed back against this policy and in 1930, José Padín, the first Puerto Rican education commissioner, managed to return primary grades to Spanish instruction until he was forced to resign in 1937. Finally, Mariano Villaronga, education commissioner under Muñoz Marín, the first Puerto Rican elected governor, was able to institute Spanish as the language of instruction for all grades,[4] a policy put into practice in 1949 and made law in 1952 (Zentella, 1981:220–221), with English as a special subject in all grades. But public education, like all sectors of public life in Puerto Rico, has always been badly resourced, which means public school students have never been given a broad basis for English fluency and literacy. This is ironic since public schooling is also the educational background for the working-class people who have been pulled into migration to the continental United States. (By contrast, private schools provide students from middle-class families with excellent English literacy and spoken fluency, giving them educational and economic advantage in Puerto Rico and in the continental United States.) What public education language policies have done is reinforce resentment and insecurity in the presence of unsolicited English use, as I found in fieldwork in Puerto Rico (Urciuoli, 1996:50).

U.S. economic policies extensively shaped migration dynamics. In 1898, when the United States took over Puerto Rico, its agricultural economy included subsistence farming, cattle ranching, small hacienda production of sugar, tobacco, and coffee, and day labor. Puerto Rican farm laborers migrated seasonally around the island, as well as elsewhere in the Caribbean and South and Central America. The shift to U.S. sovereignty meant Puerto Rico became part of the U.S. tariff system, which combined with a devastating hurricane, destroyed the coffee industry.

After 1900, U.S. investment in Puerto Rico's sugar economy shifted its relatively diversified agricultural production toward sugar. This investment was facilitated by the 1900 passage of the Foraker Act, which established civilian government (following the military rule of 1898–1900) and gave Congress direct control over trade and tariffs, in turn benefiting U.S. investors. The tax and trade provisions of the Foraker Act were left intact by the 1917 Jones Act through which Puerto Ricans became U.S. citizens, though under conditions that left them with little practical political representation and minimal control over local economics or external trade (History Task Force, 1979:69–86; Dietz, 1986:89ff; Cabán, 1999:67–80). The increasing monoculture and centralization of agricultural production meant far less agricultural work for day laborers within Puerto Rico, and they accordingly sought work outside Puerto Rico, expanding a pattern already established before U.S. sovereignty. García-Colón (2020) lays out in detail the political, economic, and policy conditions that led to a history of Puerto Rican contract labor in the United States and, despite its hazards, the appeal of non-contract migrant labor to Puerto Rican farmworkers. The outcome was a workforce perceived by their U.S. employers and residents of the areas where they worked as dangerous and disordered – and Spanish speaking.

I have described one piece of the history of U.S. political and economic relations with formerly Spanish colonies. Other distinct and relevant pieces include the United States' history with Mexico, with Central American nations, with Cuba, with the Dominican Republic, with the Philippines – well, the reader gets the picture. All these pieces are embedded in U.S. assumptions about its right to expand, all are informed by U.S. visions of itself. In these visions, assumptions about a "natural" right to call the shots in the Western Hemisphere (reinforced by Protestant Anglo-Saxonist views of Catholic Spain and its legacy) are linked to belief in modernization linked to quasi-religious faith in capitalism and the conviction that natural resources are meant for private development linked to a highly permissive attitude toward U.S. corporate growth and development in the Caribbean and Central America. The raciolinguistic construction of an anti-modern, brown-skinned, directionless, Spanish-speaking figure that emerges from these visions is the antithesis of the Anglo-Saxon American. It matters little where people classified as that Spanish-speaking figure actually came from since, semiotically, the figure itself primarily derives from U.S. expansionist relations with Mexico and Puerto Rico. From an Anglo-Saxonist perspective, all traits marking that Spanish-speaking figure belongs "naturally" to everyone seen to fit that "type." The fallacy of that belief – which is very difficult to point out to those who believe it – is that everyone so categorized is in that position because, historically, the United States has acted in ways that put them there. Attention to historical detail makes clear the ways in which a raciolinguistic take is perpetrated by those in positions of power.

From the perspective of raciolinguistically marked social actors, historical specifics matter a great deal. Labor migrations do not appear out of nowhere. They follow paths established historically, very often retracing specifically colonial or more generally global expansion. This is certainly true of the United States' relation with most of Spain's former colonies, whether or not they became U.S. colonies. The specifics vary. Take, for example, the situation of migrant labor in the United States from Mexico and Puerto Rico. Since Puerto Rican farmworkers are U.S. citizens, their structural place as migrant labor differs substantially from that of Mexican workers. As García Colón (2020) shows, this distinction is invisible to many employers for whom the only real difference is that Mexicans can be sent home when their labor contracts end, and Puerto Ricans cannot. Since from a raciolinguistic perspective, both sets of laborers are brown, foreign, and Spanish speaking, many farm employers prefer to hire Mexicans who can be sent away and not Puerto Ricans who might stick around where they "don't belong."

The Social Experience of English

These processes of raciolinguistic construction set the terms for how English is experienced, as I show using research done with Puerto Rican families in Manhattan and the Bronx in 1978 and 1988 (Urciuoli, 1996). While the work is some decades old, the current xenophobic social and linguistic climate indicates that it remains all too valid. Most working class and rural Puerto Rican families who have moved to continental U.S. cities have done so as part of a labor migration, with family members pursuing better paying or steadier work than they could find at home. Most such families come, as mentioned earlier, from educational backgrounds with few resources to learn English beyond the basics, so they end up learning English after having moved. The people I worked in New York learned an English sociolinguistically continuous, though not identical, with African American varieties spoken by their neighbors. Children overwhelmingly grew up bilingual with everyone code-switching English and Spanish in patterns varying by age, generation, gender, and other social markers less easy to plot. The resulting speech community is formally complex (see Zentella, 1997 for details of language varieties) but united through the coordinated (though not uniform) ways in which people play out the social functions – the pragmatics – of everyday uses of language: gossiping, joking, scolding kids, doing household tasks, flirting, planning, and so on.[5] To understand all this, one must understand that however people talk about codes (e.g., English or Spanish), what they actually do is use available language resources according to local norms (register). People talk about how to use language (i.e., they talk metapragmatically, after Silverstein, 1976) around the neighborhood in terms of "maybe you shouldn't mix but it's OK around here" so long as people respect each other's language preferences, especially younger for older.

The real picture is not people speaking two codes but people speaking registers structured by spheres of interaction: inner sphere and outer sphere (Urciuoli, 1996:77). These are socially distinguishable in terms of equality and familiarity of social relations. All social life involves this distinction to some degree, and while the dividing line between the inner and outer sphere is not always a bright one, the key distinction is how routinely familiar and relatively equal everyone is with each other. Inner sphere relations are with those most familiar and equal: family, relatives, friends, neighbors. Outer sphere relations are with those least equal and least familiar. For people in positions of race and class advantage, inner sphere relations are with others also comfortable and outer sphere relations carry relatively few consequences: dealings with unfamiliar legal or other authorities are not routinely problematic or financially draining. For people in positions of disadvantage, the picture changes. For working-class people of color in a U.S. city, the inner sphere is "poor people together" and the outer sphere is that of relations that put one at a structural (class, race, authority) disadvantage.

It is important to start not by looking at who speaks English and Spanish but at the sociopolitical topography, so to speak, of relations with interlocutors because people's sense of linguistic difference gets mapped onto these inequalities. English is widely spoken in inner sphere relations with family, friends, and neighbors and it is not generally an issue (unless of course in doing so, one shows *una falta de respeto* – disrespect – in which case one will hear about it). People may not be paying attention to whether they are speaking English or Spanish at any given moment. Any English spoken among inner-sphere relations can be code-switched with Spanish. Doing so might sometimes draw such metapragmatic commentary as "you aren't supposed to mix," which might be followed by "but everyone does it anyway." This English is marked by formal features – ways of pronouncing consonants and vowels, intonation patterns, ways of forming sentences and phrase structures – that vary regularly across speakers and that are recognized by speakers as belonging to this sphere. English and Spanish are readily codeswitched in ways that fit the syntactic patterns of either language at the switch junctures (Poplack, 1980). The very existence of such situations – and this one is by no means unique – raises questions about the very idea that codes as such come separately packaged in some essential way.[6] The inner sphere of family threads its way without fixed boundaries into the inner sphere of the neighborhood shared with African American neighbors whose English may not be identical to bilingual inner sphere English but is certainly coherent and continuous in form and pragmatics, a shared, though not identical, register.

The English that fits into the inner sphere is marked in outer-sphere relations, subject to judgment by bosses, teachers, doctors, social workers, landlords, and others in authority, with class and likely to be white. Here, one needs an outer sphere register to use with English speakers who can hire or fire, rent or evict, give grades, and promote or fail: a set of pragmatic functions not found in inner sphere uses. Outer sphere correctness norms have consequences. People focus metapragmatically on accent (comparing an accent to water leaking under a door) or grammar and vocabulary (worrying about endings on words or choosing the wrong word). By contrast, English used at home or around the neighborhood is an English in which one can make mistakes without consequences.

English and Spanish in White Public Space

It is in this contrast of spheres that we see the operation of English and Spanish in a political economy of language (Gal, 1989), in terms of the consequences carried by "correct" or "incorrect" use of a language. Correct English is assumed to open social and economic access. Incorrect English is assumed to trap, undercut, block access to resources, even have legal consequences. This sphere of awareness of English correctness is the sphere of white public space. Hill (2008) characterizes white public space as that in which whiteness is privileged, calling the shots, so to speak, of social and linguistic order. That linguistic order involves constant monitoring, through legislation (English-only laws), education (standard language inculcation), print capitalism (publication and dissemination of prescriptivist texts), media (commentary on correctness norms), and so on. Such public monitoring is routinely reinforced by people who, overhearing even a private conversation in Spanish, feel justified in publicly targeting speakers with metapragmatic statements that boil down to "This is America, speak English." What are these self-appointed patrollers of white public space actually doing?

Zentella (1996:13) describes the 1994 suspension of a clerk in a Jersey City Rite-Aid pharmacy for speaking Spanish to a customer. The clerk had in fact been hired for her ability to use Spanish with a substantial proportion of the pharmacy's customers. An Anglo customer complained, saying in her written complaint, "Isn't this an American store? You are taking an American job and you are working for an American company, so you should speak English." Rite-Aid responded by "indefinitely suspending" the clerk and the New Jersey Labor Department upheld the denial of the clerk's unemployment benefits. I describe this in detail because it keeps happening. For example (and there are many examples), the Associated Press reported in August 2019 that seven bilingual Puerto Rican nurses at a government-run clinic in Haines City, Florida – nurses who had been hired specifically to communicate with Spanish-speaking patients – were told by their supervisors that they could be fired for speaking Spanish among themselves. They submitted complaints to human resources and wrote to the Florida Department of Health. The Equal Employment Opportunity Commission said that English-only rules might violate federal laws unless they are "justified by business necessity."[7] I include some detail here so that readers can see how structurally similar these two incidents are: people are hired because they are bilingual, but they are only supposed to deploy their language skills under the circumstances set by their employers. If they do so at their own discretion, they are subject to discipline. I suspect this is also gendered, that women in particular are likely to be hired for their bilingualism and to be disciplined for speaking Spanish among themselves.

To understand how Spanish is imagined from the perspective of whiteness, let us consider how language generally is imagined from the perspective of U.S. modernity. Silverstein (1996), explicating the social construction that he terms "American monoglot standard English," outlines the modernist language ideology by which Americans routinely imagine language as "naturally" a system that must be kept logical, correct, and "unmixed" for accurate reference. In this "folk-metapragmatics" (cultural expression of how language "should" be used), the key to the expression of "clear meaning" is "just right" pronunciation and word selection (1996:294), a way of imagining language echoed in bilinguals' outer-sphere constructions of English. There is no formal body defining "standard" English which consists largely of "dos and don'ts," but any formal element that can be pointed to as "non-standard" is seen as "interfering" with meaning or "communication." It is the responsibility of English users to patrol their language for such problems, the more so given the modernist assumption that the United States as a nation is made up of individuals in control of their actions and capable of acquiring the means to fix what is wrong with themselves, language included.

It is a short step from imagining language as a manifestation of the modern to imagining that modern as white. A whitened modernist way of imagining English explains the legal decisions accounted for by Matsuda (1991), in which judges routinely rule against cases of accent discrimination (people losing or not getting a job because of their English pronunciation) based on judges' beliefs about "clear communication." In effect, their rulings say, if that person wanted the job, they would get rid of their accent and perform monoglot English. Note the same rationale mentioned by the EEOC in one of the above cases: that prohibiting employees hired for their bilingual abilities from speaking Spanish among each other might not violate federals laws if "justified by business necessity." The idea that individuals "should" thus "take control" of their language habits provides a rationale for mapping race from biology onto language: they may be and look X, but they don't have to sound X or speak X publicly.

But public attacks on languages other than English – most often but not only Spanish; Arabic is a common target[8] – go beyond this modernist ideology. I suggest that what attackers imagine is not the language in any analytic sense. As Zentella (1996) puts it, racialized Hispanophone people are routinely imagined to speak a deformed non-language, feminized and diminished, or as Zentella put it, "chiquitified." The speakers themselves are imagined as a dangerous horde; a point also made by Santa Ana (2002). Incidents like those described by Zentella or in the articles cited here may target discursive activity referred to as "Spanish," but there are also reports of attacks in which attackers make it clear that they do not recognize the language. What attackers recognize is an activity that they assume they have the right to attack because the person engaged in the activity is, in their perception, deliberately acting non-white and un-American in U.S. white public space. In this way, it is like public attacks on women wearing hijabs or on men wearing beards and/or turbans. This hyper-nationalized, hyper-racialized stance is one that a growing number of Americans have felt justified in taking, certainly starting with Obama's election and even more since Trump's. It is the equivalent of attacking people for what they look like physically but justified as an attack on something seen by the attacker as a deliberate action: the attacker justifies the attack because the target "chose" to do it. Similarly targeted are black people reported to the police or even attacked for being somewhere or doing something that the reporter or attacker considers invasive, as has become frighteningly common, as has the justification that the reporter or attacker somehow felt "threatened."

I return for a moment to Hill's (2008) analysis of white public space, which is, ironically, the same space in which non-speakers of Spanish feel free to play with Spanish as a joke (and I might note, in which whites mock racial others in race/ethnic "theme" parties or black/brownface performance). Hill analyzes such linguistic "play" as "mock Spanish," a covert racist discourse whose implications are unacknowledged by those doing it, creating ungrammatical words or phrases that no fluent Spanish speaker would create and that play on stereotypes. Examples include the use of modifiers (*el, mucho*) or endings (*-o*) to construct words or phrases such as the Corona beer advertisement "The drinko for Cinco," the media favorite "mucho macho" (in Spanish, *muy macho*), or puns such as "grassy-ass" (*gracias*, "thanks") or the greeting card perennial "fleas navidad" (*Feliz Navidad*, "Happy Christmas"). An especially well-known example is Arnold Schwarzenegger's "hasta la vista, baby" from *Terminator 2: Judgement Day*. In doing so, people create the kind of language mess that, from their own white public space perspective, Spanish is imagined to be.

White public space is thus best understood as a space of entitlement in which forms of hierarchy and control can be performed in multiple ways without accountability. The very nature of unmarkedness in a hierarchic system is that it need not be accounted for. Within that space, there is a sliding scale of raciolinguistic domination: at one end, carefully positioned and apparently reasoned argument about why people should use "good" English; somewhere in the middle, the kind of "play" that Hill critiques; and at the other end, flat out attacks. But it is a continuum with no bright line. It is important to recognize this continuum for what it is. Hartigan (1997) argues that "white trash" provides cover for more respectable enactments of whiteness, so that "racist behavior" can be blamed on "bad individuals," masking the recognition that all assumptions about whiteness are linked. So too, people may defend seemingly rational notions of English, or "correct" English, as universally appropriate for public space without acknowledging the continuum linking that assumption to "bad individuals" who attack speakers of other languages. But the continuum is there, with multiple whiteness constructions layered onto each other: "English" laminated onto "patriotism" (emblematized as the flag and the military), "law and order" (emblematized as the police), "Christianity," and so on. The more layers of lamination there are, the more these position markers line up with an authoritarian stance. It is very likely that those who see themselves entitled to publicly attack speakers of other languages also see themselves entitled to enact, in equally violent ways, what they see as violations of layers of white public order.

So, What Next?

I started this chapter with the observation that racialization says more about those who do it than those to whom it is done. Does that mean people can be educated out of racializing? Possibly but not probably. The kind of thinking that drives racialization is widely embedded in other (often, not always, related) modes of thinking. These can include other privileged perspectives (gender, class, nation) or they may not be about privilege in any obvious way. But they are all resistant, even impermeable, to social and historical facts on the ground, and they are all about the world as people want to think it exists or should exist for their benefit.

Such perspectives privilege social identification, affective or emotional connection, and a strong sense of *us* versus *them*. They all start from the position of *us* as morally unmarked: right, true, valued. We see this as well in other ways of seeing the world anchored in that binary polarity. To put it in terms of function (Jakobson [1956] 1980), the speech acts making up such discourse are far less about information than they are expressions of emotion and alliance built on rhetoric, persuasion, and confirming feedback. They stress association and familiarity. They connect dots that make sense to an *us*, reinforce *our* sense of who *we* are and how *we* fit into the world. They depend on loose associations of invested concepts and a filter blocking perception of any counter-indicating detail.

Discourses need not be explicitly about race to be racializing; as Dick and Wirtz (2011) argue, racialization is routinely covert. What is critical is that social actors operate together in ways that reinforce their sense of shared reality based on familiarity, feeling, and imagery – dynamics that, as Urban (1991:10–18) points out, are fundamentally mythic. We might also add folkloric, as we see in Mould's (2020) analysis of welfare stories combining elements of racialization and class. Mould points out the importance of a master narrative into which local and personal narratives fit, and the importance of binary distinctions that give racializing elements (implicitly black welfare recipients buying steaks on food stamps while driving Cadillacs) their peculiar charge in distinguishing *them* from *us*. Some points are connected as evidence of causality; others are ignored. Stock characters and moral themes appear regularly, and repetition and parallelism figure heavily. Reported scenes and images are assigned the most damning interpretations and moralized judgment, making any explanatory back story irrelevant. Opposing evidence is not even recognized as such, since beliefs are not about facts but about identities bound up with a position. Nor are such ways of understanding restricted to folklore about race. In her analysis of alien abduction narratives, Lepselter (2016) similarly finds the production of us/them polarities, repetition of key elements and stock characters, meaningful connections among elements unlikely to be related, resonances and parallelism among personal stories that suggest a master narrative, and a resistance to information challenging any of the above; it is safe to say that all these points also apply to conspiracy theories. Many of them also apply to political messaging and its mediation in the press which, as Lempert and Silverstein (2012) point out, is all about us/them polarities, moral certainty, poetics, parallelism, persuasion, connecting unrelated points, attributed causality despite counterevidence, and generally the association of feeling and imagery.

All this thinking is evident in the racializing of language. Evidence is cherry-picked, parallelisms abound, stock themes recur, historical and social realities are ignored, moral judgments are absolute, and it is all about *us* versus *them*. Such thinking is so deeply entrenched in public culture and private life that, much as I wish it were possible to educate people out of it, I cannot see how. However, racialized action in white public space *can* be effectively addressed by legislation and policy change. Company policies that prohibit the use of languages other than English by employees – especially when those employees were hired specifically to use those languages – are particularly hypocritical. There are challenges to white public space by innovative performers, and there are major demographic shifts in the process. But what most needs to happen is serious legal action and some serious counter-messaging from political leaders. Racist executive and legislative political leadership at federal and state levels has made it all to abundantly clear easy it is to generate and validate an atmosphere of entitlement for attacks on not only language but also dress and hair. These are all forms of hate crime and it is not a long leap from those to the murderous targeting of synagogues and mosques, black churchgoers, Latino shoppers, and Asian spa workers. Growing demographics and resistance through performance can only go so far. In the end, it is the responsibility of law and leadership to address such aggression.

Acknowledgments

Particular thanks to Ana Celia Zentella for being an inspiring interlocutor and for keeping the community informed about language discrimination incidents.

Notes

1. The notion of markedness is adapted from linguistics: Unmarked members of a set relate to marked members as typical to atypical or basic to specialized, a concept explored by Jakobson ([1957] 1971). A phonological example would be a language in which most consonants were pronounced as stops but one was pronounced as a fricative, so stops would be unmarked and that one fricative would be marked.
2. Which is not to say there would not have been prejudice. But racism and prejudice operate differently. Racism as a residue of history is structured into the system; not all prejudices are. Racist attitudes are expressed as prejudices, but racism may also operate efficiently without being expressed as overt prejudice.
3. 77.3% of the population was illiterate and 92% of children aged 5–17 did not attend school (Osuna, 1949:341–343).
4. Despite opposition from U.S. presidents Roosevelt (Osuna, 1949:377) and Truman (Zentella, 1981:221).
5. Function as in the social ends accomplished through discourse; see Jakobson ([1956] 1980).
6. Haugen (1972:329) stresses the importance of not assuming that codes naturally exist; Romaine (1989:281ff) questions the assumption that codes themselves are stored in separate cognitive compartments.
7. https://www.latinorebels.com/2019/08/20/floridanurses/ accessed 5-23-2021. Also in 2019, a member of the U.S. Air Force made a phone call in Spanish in a Hawaii Starbucks and was targeted by a stranger for "disrespecting" the uniform by speaking Spanish in public (https://www.nbcnews.com/news/latino/air-force-member-called-distasteful-speaking-spanish-uniform-n1042921 accessed 5-23-2021; the story includes other similar accounts).
8. https://www.sandiegouniontribune.com/news/courts/story/2019-12-05/xx-for-man-in-hate-crime-attack-on-teen-syrian-refugee (accessed 5-23-2021) describes an attack on someone speaking Arabic on public transportation.

References

Bauman, Richard and Charles Briggs. 2003. *Voices of Modernity*. Cambridge and New York: Cambridge University Press.

Cabán, Pedro A. 1999. *Constructing a Colonial People: Puerto Rico and the United States, 1898–1932*. Boulder, CO: Westview.

Dick, Hilary Parsons and Kristina Wirtz. 2011. "Introduction: Racializing Discourses." *Journal of Linguistic Anthropology* 21(S1):E2–E10.

Dietz, James L. 1986. *Economic History of Puerto Rico: Institutional Change and Capitalist Development*. Princeton, NJ: Princeton University Press.

Gal, Susan. 1989. "Language and Political Economy." *Annual Review of Anthropology* 18:345–367.

García-Colón, Ismael. 2020. *Colonial Migrants at the Heart of Empire: Puerto Rican Workers on U.S. Farms*. Oakland: University of California Press.

Haugen, Einar. 1972. "The Ecology of Language." Pp. 325–339 in Anwar Dil (ed.), *The Ecology of Language: Essays by Einar Haugen*. Stanford, CA: Stanford University Press.

Hartigan, John. 1997. "Unpopular Culture: The Case of 'White Trash.'" *Cultural Studies* 11(2):316–343.

Hill, Jane. 2008. *The Everyday Language of White Racism*. Oxford, UK: Wiley-Blackwell.

History Task Force, Centro de Estudios Puertorriqueños, ed. 1979. *Labor Migration under Capitalism: The Puerto Rican Experience*. New York: Monthly Review.

Horsman, Reginald. 1981. *Race and Manifest Destiny*. Cambridge, MA: Harvard University Press.

Jakobson, Roman. [1957] 1971. "Shifters, Verbal Categories and the Russian Verb." Pp. 130–147 in *Selected Writings of Roman Jakobson, Volume II: Word and Language*. The Hague: Mouton.

Jakobson, Roman [1956] 1980. "Metalanguage as a Linguistic Problem." Pp. 81–92 in *The Framework of Language*. Ann Arbor: University of Michigan.

Lempert, Michael and Michael Silverstein. 2012. *Creatures of Politics*. Bloomington: Indiana University Press.

Lepselter, Susan. 2016. *The Resonance of Unseen Things*. Ann Arbor: University of Michigan.

Matsuda, Mari. 1991. "Voices of America: Accent, Antidiscrimination Law and a Jurisprudence for the Last Reconstruction." *Yale Law Journal* 100:1329–1407.

Mould, Tom. 2020. *Overthrowing the Queen: Telling Stories of Welfare in America*. Bloomington: Indiana University Press.

Osuna, Juan José. 1949. *A History of Education in Puerto Rico*. Río Piedras PR: Editorial de la Universidad de Puerto Rico.

Poplack, Shana. 1980. "Sometimes I'll start a Sentence in Spanish *y Termino en Español:* Toward a Typology of Code-switching." *Linguistics* 18(7–8):581–618.

Romaine, Suzanne. 1989. *Bilingualism*. New York: Basil Blackwell.

Rosa, Jonathan. 2019. *Looking like a Language, Sounding like a Race*. New York: Oxford University Press.

Rosa, Jonathan and Nelson Flores. 2017. "Unsettling Race and Language: Toward a Raciolinguistic Perspective." *Language and Society* 46: 621–647.

Santa Ana, Otto. 2002. *Brown Tide Rising: Metaphors of Latinos in Contemporary American Public Discourse*. Austin: University of Texas Press.

Silverstein, Michael. 1976. "Shifters, Linguistic Categories and Cultural Description." Pp. 11–55 in Keith Basso and Henry Selby (eds.), *Meaning in Anthropology*. Albuquerque: University of New Mexico Press.

Silverstein, Michael. 1996. "Monoglot 'Standard' in America: Standardization and Metaphors of Linguistic Hegemony." Pp. 284–305 in Donald Brenneis and Ronald K. S. Macaulay (eds.), *The Matrix of Language: Contemporary Linguistic Anthropology*. Boulder, CO: Westview.

Urban, Greg. 1991. *A Discourse-Centered Approach to Culture: Native South American Myths and Rituals*. Austin: University of Texas Press.

Urciuoli, Bonnie. 1996. *Exposing Prejudice*. Boulder CO: Westview.

Urciuoli, Bonnie. 2001. "The complex Diversity of Language in the United States." Pp. 190–205 in Ida Susser and Thomas Patterson (eds.), *Cultural Diversity in the United States*. Malden, MA: Blackwell.

Urciuoli, Bonnie. 2020. "Racializing, Ethnicizing, and Diversity Discourses: The Forms May Change but the Pragmatics Stay Remarkably the Same." Pp. 108–127 in H. Samy Alim, Angela Reyes, and Paul Kroskrity (eds.), *The Oxford Handbook of Language and Race*. NY and Oxford: Oxford University Press.

Zentella, Ana Celia. 1981. "Language Variety among Puerto Ricans." Pp. 218–238 in Charles Ferguson and Shirley Brice Heath (eds.), *Language in the U.S.A.* New York: Cambridge University Press.

Zentella, Ana Celia. 1996. "The 'Chiquita-fication' of US Latinos and their Languages, or: Why We Need an Anthropolitical Linguistics." Pp. 1–18 in Rebecca Parker and Yukako Sunaoshi (eds.), *Texas Linguistics Forum 36*. Austin: University of Texas Press.

Zentella, Ana Celia. 1997. *Growing Up Bilingual*. New York: Basil Blackwell.

Chapter 5

The Language-Elsewhere
A Friendlier Linguistic Terrorism

Mike Mena

> Las palabras escolarizadas parecían un lenguaje completamente nuevo para mí.
> —Gabriela, UTRGV Student
> (Quoted in Musanti and Cavazos 2018:55)

Introduction

At UTRGV, the Spanish language and English-Spanish bilingualism are often publicly presented as an economic skill, a form of difference that the university markets as its own "competitive edge" over other institutions as well as for its future graduates, who are approximately 90% Latinx and life-long residents to the region (Ostorga and Farruggio, 2018; Ostorga et al., 2020). The economic resource named "Spanish" is marketed as something else and something other than the language spoken in the everyday lives of Rio Grande Valley residents. This "Spanish" is imagined to be located *elsewhere* and is referred to by university actors by a variety of names, such as Mexico Spanish, Spain Spanish, international Spanish, or globalized Spanish. Other times it is called "high-register," "proper," "academic," and "high-level" Spanish or by one of its Spanish language correlates, such as "las palabras escolarizadas" and "español académico" (Musanti and Cavazos, 2018). Each name presupposes and entails a contrastive relation—a blunt dichotomy between a linguistic "standard" and a "substandard"—that is, a rearticulation of a linguistic hierarchy that is the effect of racial and colonial governance meant to separate an allegedly "standard" language, from a perpetually mixed, deficient and racialized linguistic practice (Flores and Rosa, 2015; Rosa and Flores, 2017).

In previous work, I called this standardized linguistic imaginary *the language-elsewhere* (Mena and García, 2020:10), or an imagined set of linguistic features valued in institutional settings that is learned and acquired *anywhere else* but the homes of Latinxs in the United States. The point of this chapter is not to define the parameters of the language-elsewhere, whether it be a so-called "Standard" Spanish or "Standard" English. The goal is the opposite. As we will see, standard language can take a multitude of forms despite it being imagined as a rationally agreed upon universal set of linguistic norms (Silverstein, 1996).

DOI: 10.4324/9781003257509-9

Following Angela Reyes, the idea is not to treat the language-elsewhere (or any of its relational inferiors, such as Spanglish or an imagined "home" language) as definable "real objects," "but as things made to seem real by wider and longer structural processes that regard them as such" (2020:17).

Over 50 years after Anzaldúa attended this university, Mexicans and Mexican Americans are less often explicitly castigated for being "deficient," and are instead told that if their linguistic practice is to be considered legitimate, it must be *disconnected* from familial linguistic practice and *connected* to the university and the global marketplace. What follows is a discourse analysis of ethnographic interviews I conducted with various university actors[1] from UTRGV, including students, faculty, and administration collected during 2019–2021. I illustrate how the language-elsewhere—"standard," "academic," and "pure" language—is being institutionally reconceptualized into an "economic resource," which makes space for a much friendlier form of linguistic terrorism supposedly not based on racial and linguistic deficiency, but on an individual's capacity to remake themselves into economically competitive bilingual workers (Martín Rojo, 2019).

Positioning the Research(er) in Local Histories

For Mexicans and Mexican Americans in Texas, the purpose of primary and secondary education was "Americanization" (Blanton, 2004; Lozano, 2018). Historically, schools used "scientific data" that cast Mexican and Mexican American children as suffering from a diminished mental capacity, often supported by research on language and linguistic practice (Delgado Bernal, 1999; San Miguel, 1987). Indeed, some of this "research" was produced by scholars within the University of Texas System (Montejano, 1987; González, 1990; Haney López, 2003). Over time, Spanish became strongly associated with a "naturally deficient" racialized form of personhood (Valencia, 2010). Flores and Rosa (2015) have asserted that such racialized perceptions are historically produced by "raciolinguistic ideologies," or co-constituting ideologies of race and language that continue to reproduce racial and economic hierarchies in the United States (also see Rosa and Flores, 2017). Such ideological perspectives often gain legitimacy via their institutionalization in, for example, law, scientific discourses, or, for the purposes of this chapter, an institution of higher education.

The university, along with the experience of growing up along the Texas-Mexico border, would come to inform Anzaldúa's (2012 [1987]) "borderlands" theory, where she and thousands of other students would be subjected to the "speech test" and "speech classes" from the 1950s to the mid-1970s (Cole and Johnson, 2013). The speech test was administered by faculty members on registration day and was designed to force Mexican and Mexican American students into remedial speech classes to "fix" their accents. Yet, White students with what were described as "Texas drawls" were not tested, no matter how "thick" their perceived accents were (Cole and Johnson, 2013). Indeed, the speech test was less about spoken accent and more about the racialization of students perpetuated by legitimated institutional actors who were deemed qualified to be "listening subjects" (Inoue, 2003; Flores and Rosa; 2015).

I attended the same institution about 40 years after Anzaldúa and completed one undergraduate and two graduate degrees over the span of approximately 10 years. To the best of my memory, I experienced no overt presence of racism. Instead, I experienced an absence of historical knowledge. I did not know that my university had previously administered a "speech test." I did not take a single Mexican American studies course as an undergraduate. I completed two anthropologically grounded Masters' degrees without reading any original texts by Gloria Anzaldúa. The form of linguistic terrorism I experienced was deceptively friendlier. Growing up, I was not physically abused by local White teachers for speaking Spanish in school like my mother or like Gloria Anzaldúa (2012:75). Instead, I was raised speaking English, which made my experience of monolingual English-language schooling unremarkable. I did, however, experience the embarrassment of being "corrected" nearly every time I attempted to speak or write in Spanish.

Stephanie Alvarez (2013), a current UTRGV faculty member, recalls being publicly embarrassed for misplacing written diacritic markings during a time she was asked to write on the board in front of the class. Alvarez named such a practice "accent terrorism." She collected testimonials of students who reported the experience of UTRGV instructors who took points off their Spanish exams when they wrote *their own name* without an accent (e.g., Garcia instead of García). I did not experience this particular form of linguistic terrorism in any of my time in the Rio Grande Valley education system, which included nearly all of my K-12 education and 10 years at UTRGV. Instead, what I experienced was never knowing which names of my students had accents during my three years as a local high school teacher, simply because they were absent from printed attendance rosters. This kind of historical erasure, such as the knowledge of diacritic markings, represents the kind of friendlier institutionalized linguistic terrorism that is at the heart of this chapter. Here, I focus on the "language-elsewhere" as the conceptual colonial descendent of an always present binary relation between "correct/standard" vs. "incorrect/substandard" linguistic practice. As we will see, this dichotomy is taking a new shape in a globally competitive world and being reimagined as an opposition between language that can become an "economic resource" versus the language of the "home."

A Friendlier Linguistic Terrorism: *The Language-Elsewhere*

Less relevant today is the explicit racial and linguistic terrorism perpetuated by "Anglo" ranchers, murderous Texas Rangers, or White teachers ready to swat their Mexican children with the classroom ruler (Anzaldúa, 2012:75). Instead, a friendlier linguistic terrorism occurs at the conceptual level with the direct and indirect glorification and elevation of a supposed "standard" language. Such elevation may come from our friends, our families, our professors, our institutions, and even our school attendance rosters. The language-elsewhere appears to be a "natural" thing, a neutral, raceless, and standardized linguistic object located nowhere in general, but also potentially everywhere—that is, everywhere else but the homes of the local Mexican[2] and Mexican American population.

Reference in everyday talk to a standardized language-elsewhere gives rise to an oppositional idea of an inferior form of local linguistic practice, and by extension, inferior speakers with a deficient knowledge of "standard" languages (English and Spanish). This is a friendlier linguistic terrorism not necessarily characterized by the presence of aggressive violence, but as the constitution of a particular reality based on ideological presuppositions as well as the absence and erasure of knowledge. Yet, attempting to pin down exactly what constitutes an allegedly perfect set of linguistic practice is a tricky but common exercise that surfaces in a variety of contexts. For example, at times the language-elsewhere emerges as an international entity. When news broke on the re-opening of the university as officially bilingual, Faculty member Victor Alvarado expressed excitement to the online newspaper, the *Rio Grande Guardian*, stating,

> The idea is terrific. [….] But, by the same token I think it is going to be extremely difficult to do unless they begin to actively recruit faculty who come, perhaps, *from other countries* to be in charge [of] those programs.
>
> (Taylor, 2014, my emphasis)

This statement presupposes that worthy prospective faculty members are not currently employed by the university and/or do not live in the Rio Grande Valley region—they must be sought out elsewhere, literally "from other countries." As scholars have shown, the linguistic practices of Latinxs in the United States are particularly stigmatized (Otheguy and Stern, 2011).

Professor Alvarado, himself from Chile, has long supported the idea of bilingual coursework and recounted his experience attempting to teach a course in Spanish at the university in 1972:

> After five minutes[,] I had to stop because the students had no idea what I was talking about. They did not have the technical vocabulary, they did not know how to write or take notes, except for the few who were from *other Latin American countries*. They were very happy to see somebody speaking in their own language, *correctly* and they could follow it.
>
> (Taylor, 2014, my emphasis)

The primary obstacle that Alvarado perceives is that local students are not, as he describes in the same interview, "truly bilingual" and "never studied Spanish formally," except those who came from "foreign countries, Mexico, South America or Spain." This is an explicit spatialization of a "correct" register of Spanish from *elsewhere,* which is then also connected to "correct" language users from *elsewhere.* By elevating a superior language user from elsewhere, the standard/substandard dichotomy is presented not in racializing terms, but as a far friendlier re-articulation via a conversation about geographic regions and nations—that is, a deficiency perspective by proxy.

Locating a "correct" Spanish as geographically not of the Rio Grande Valley surfaced in conversations about local linguistic practice with research participants. For example, one research participant often referred to a "correct" Spanish from elsewhere:

> *Faculty 1*: I call it 'Mexico City Spanish,' but, it's like the *correct* Spanish. I don't know what they call it. Castellano? You know? I think that's what it's called. You might want to Google that. I [don't] remember.
>
> (Interview 2020, my emphasis)

In this conversation, a "correct" Spanish is located in a specific city in the interior of Mexico, which they identify as possibly Castellano, one name of a variety of Spanish spoken in, for example, regions of Spain and some Latin American countries. This is consistent with the widespread ideological premise held by many lifetime Rio Grande Valley residents that a "good" Spanish is located elsewhere, such as in countries like Spain or affluent and cosmopolitan cities in Mexico. These kinds of perceived linguistic boundaries, binaries, and differentiations constitute what scholars have called *language ideologies* (Schieffelin, Woolard, and Kroskrity, 1998; Irvine and Gal, 2000).

Faculty 1 reads, writes, speaks, grades papers, and conducts their courses in English and Spanish. Yet, they regularly characterized their own Spanish-language comprehension as deficient, often reporting they "didn't understand" their own students who spoke "perfect" Spanish. Based on my extended relationship with this research participant, and knowing they also were raised in local poverty-stricken areas, it appears they are attempting to highlight the potential of Latinx students from the region. At times, this faculty member chooses to occupy the position of the "deficient" language user to counter the deficiency perspective. To reassure students of their potential, they often open their classes with,

> *Faculty 1*: "One of the things I always tell them [students] at the beginning, 'Hey guys [….] I grew up 10 minutes away [in public housing]. And if I can make it to be a professor, you guys can do it.' [….] We lived in, I guess what you call 'the ghetto,' or 'projects,' but we got out of there [….] All my siblings have college education or college degrees."

This faculty member offers up their own personal life as "proof" structural inequities can be overcome, not only individually but also as families and communities.

While locating the language-elsewhere in terms of nations, regions, and cities is quite ordinary, the language-elsewhere need not explicitly refer to geography. The standard/substandard hierarchical relation emerges at various spatial scales, especially in locating "academic" Spanish as acquired/learned anywhere else but the home of Rio Grande Valley residents. For example, one student in the Bilingual Education Program described her Spanish speaking home as the following:

> *Miranda*: My parents would always be like, "yo no te entiendo, si no te puedo entender, tienes que hablar en español." ["I don't understand you, if I can't understand, you need to speak Spanish."] [....] So, I feel like that kept us [with] the oral language that we had, it stayed. And also the reading one, but it's more social, like our language is a little bit more social, but now that I'm in school, it's when it's a bit more academic.
>
> (Interview, 2020)

Similar to many conversations I had with participants, there is a reference to a "social" or "home" language, that is differentiated from "academic" language, which also produces a spatialized dichotomy, "home" vs. "elsewhere." This particular student was inspired to go into bilingual education because of her upbringing in Rio Grande Valley schools, which she characterized as utilizing violent, transitional English-language immersion programs.

While at times university actors make valiant efforts to frame the Spanish learned at home as a rich, cultural "asset," it nevertheless exists as a separate entity from that which the public discourse involving UTRGV proposes has potential economic value, or the imagined set of linguistic practices one uses as an avenue of upward mobility. Or, as a student named *Ramona* described (who is quoted extensively below), Spanish with her parents does not include "advanced terminology," or "academic" Spanish, for at home, they speak the language of "the Mexican." Although this characterization was followed by a hardy laugh—it nevertheless positions "academic" Spanish as a raceless, separate linguistic object disconnected from the language learned at home and the racialized body of "the Mexican" (Interview, 2020).

The idea of "adding" academic language to the language learned at home that has been historically "subtracted" from generations of Rio Grande Valley residents is a useful, and likely necessary political stance taken by some faculty and administrators. Yet, such a political stance often involves a double-movement of both the affirmation of home linguistic practice coupled with the implication that what is brought into the classroom from home is *not enough* to become competitive in the marketplace.

> *Faculty/Administrator 2*: At the end of the day, you want them to know that they can graduate and that they can find a job and that they'll be more *marketable* than the monolingual person with the same degree that they have.

Later in the same interview, the research participant followed up with,

> *Faculty/Administrator 2:* I see that you come with your own language. And it's fine. There's nothing wrong with it. We just need to work. I'm trying to *add* to it. I'm trying to *expand* it. I'm not trying to correct it. I'm not trying to erase it. Right, I'm trying to say, "[let's] honor the language you have and how you use it." [...] But we're going to *add* to it and we're going to *expand* it and we're going to improve it, because we can always improve whatever language we have, even if it's our mother tongue.
>
> (Interview, 2020, my emphasis)

This participant has dedicated much time to UTRGVs bilingual initiative and continues to push back against the ongoing legacy of "subtractive schooling" (Valenzuela, 1999). Yet, in order for them to give the name to the deficiency perspective as well as subtractive schooling as an ongoing problem in the Rio Grande Valley, the approach requires students' language be "added to" in order to be legitimized as "marketable"—that is, uniquely competitive with "the monolingual person with the same degree." While the home language is generally characterized by many faculty and administrators as deeply valuable, "culturally enriching," and something that must be "honored," I have never heard the "home" language described as *already* economically valuable or viable as a source of upper mobility without some degree of institutional legitimation.

A student named *Ramona* utilized the notion of "adding" in our interview, particularly when sharing stories of moments she experienced as entailing "subtractive" effects. For example, she described one time her Spanish was publicly "corrected" by her teacher in a local high school. She said,

> "I don't remember what phrase it was, I never said it again. But now I'm trying to get it back, so I feel like *they* robbed a part of my language because they have this idea [that] I'm supposed to transition to academic language, but why would *you* sacrifice our home language? [...] That's not necessary.
>
> (Interview, 2020, my emphasis)

Simply put, corrections entail subtractive effects that often have nothing to do with the intentions of the person doing the correcting. By this point in the conversation, Ramona had already spoken of her experience of subtractive schooling in the Rio Grande Valley. In this sense, the dietics "they" and "you" in her story are not solely referring to the individual high school teacher, but to the wider institutional practice of forcing local residents to "sacrifice" their home language. This is an explicit moment of institutionalized linguistic violence illustrated when Ramona said, "I feel like *they* robbed a part of my language." When Ramona asks, "why would *you* sacrifice our home language?," she is offering a critique of the institutionalized oppositional framing of the local language practices wherein the goal is to get people to "sacrifice" the *home language* for the purpose of "transitioning" to *academic language*.

Faculty/Administrator 2 (previously mentioned) speaks of the complexity of framing the benefits of becoming a bilingual university—including the aforementioned additive framings—in a way that will have specific appeal to various stakeholders while simultaneously dealing with the institutional and political realities of the moment in the late-2010s.

> *Faculty/Administrator 2*: We always have to frame it in the right way and sell it in the right way so that, you know, to make it become a reality. [...] We just have to frame it for the audience, we might frame it in a certain way for a student, a different way for a faculty member, [or] for an administrator. All in the end, it's the same. Our goal is the same, to benefit our university, to benefit our region, to benefit our students.

In terms of wide public marketing, the university foregrounds the economic opportunity and global competitiveness that bilingualism is perceived to offer future graduates. When pushed to a logical endpoint, the language-elsewhere is what the UTRGV marketing strategy and various university actors claim will be "added" to a student's linguistic repertoire that will help create an imagined globally competitive bilingual workforce. Accordingly, tracing the historical emergence of the colonial and racializing binaries that give rise to such linguistic imaginaries from elsewhere as well as the associated representations of language users is recognized by some university actors as potentially having liberatory effects.

¿De Dónde Viene Todo Eso?: The Struggle Against Colonial Legacies

According to several faculty and administrators, excavating the colonial history of the Rio Grande Valley can have both liberating effects as well as produce potential pathways for how the university might proceed into the future. This entails an approach that specifically incorporates forging a new narrative that centers racial, colonial, and cultural histories. For example, when I asked a former faculty member and administrator why students generally characterized their linguistic abilities as substandard and deficient, they said,

> *Faculty/Administrator 3*: It's a vestige of the colonization process vis-a-vis language. I mean, to me that's what it's always been. It's that our Spanish is not good enough. [And Spanish] is connected to our lives, our identity, our set of values, you know? [It's] like a whole slew of reasons that define this sort of colonization process: "substandard *this*, second class *that*, no los dejes entradar aqui [keep Mexicans out of here and there], not as smart as

them, and [our] language is not as good." [....] most of us have language shame issues. You've been through it. I've been through it. My wife has been through it. Every one of my kids has been through it. [...] ¿De dónde viene todo eso? ¿De dónde viene? [Where does all of that come from? From where?]

(Interview, 2020, my emphasis)

This former faculty/administrator, also a life-long resident of the region, asks a complex question: ¿De dónde viene todo eso?, or, specifically, why is the racializing deficiency perspective still prevalent in the lives of people from the Rio Grande Valley?

One approach to denaturalizing the deficiency perspective is advocating for the expansion of Mexican American studies coursework and possibly an Ethnic Studies program, generally considered by many as anti-hegemonic knowledge. However, because of its perceived politicized framing, the effort has been less successful than, for example, offering bilingual coursework in business-related disciplines, which is often described by particular university actors as "an easier sell" (Interview with *Faculty 4*). In a conversation with another faculty member, they noted,

> *Faculty 4*: [If] language is political [....] then ethnic studies is like a bomb. [...] Many people there [at UTRGV] are advocating for it, [but] there's always this pushback, you know, and the pushback seems to come from people who have a lot more say in what's happening, you know, I definitely think the burden has fallen on women of color in the university.
>
> (Interview, 2020)

Faculty 4 agrees that Spanish linguistic practices are important and meaningful for the local student population. They are also aware that individuals, communities, and institutions must contend with the Spanish language being highly politicized, and that at times its speakers are positioned as threats to the United States (Santa Ana, 2002). This faculty member also asserts that it is just as important to exhume local subjugated historical knowledge that has been erased over the last two centuries. There is, however, a problem. As they succinctly summarized: "[If] language is political [....] then ethnic studies is like a bomb." The lexical choice is highly illustrative. As counter-hegemonic forms of knowledge are sometimes framed as iconoclastic weapons, it has triggered an institutional defense from university actors at the highest levels of administration—that is, "pushback [....] from people who have a lot more say in what's happening." But what exactly is so destructive and who's characterization of these forms of knowledge is this?

Four weeks after I conducted the interview with *Faculty 4*, President Trump, speaking at the White House Conference on American History (9/17/2020) said, "We must clear away the twisted web of lies in our schools and in the classrooms, and teach our children the magnificent truth about our country." In this line, Trump's "magnificent truth" refers to hegemonic historical knowledge that positions the United States as an unmatched defender of moral democratic principles. Yet, according to Trump, this magnificent truth is under siege by a "twisted web of lies." Trump would specifically name Critical Race Theory as one such "web," as an unpatriotic enemy and ongoing threat to the United States. He characterized such forms of knowledge as,

> "bear[ing] a striking resemblance to the propaganda of our adversaries. [….] Students in our universities are inundated with Critical Race Theory. [….] Critical Race Theory is being forced into our children's schools [….] and its being deployed to rip apart friends, neighbors and families."

In no uncertain terms, counter-hegemonic knowledge is framed as deeply threatening to the institutional status quo and to the very fabric of friendship, families, communities, and the nation. Having one of the most powerful persons in the United States (and the world) publicly recognize the power of counter-hegemonic histories might be considered a testament to its liberatory potential. Importantly, this also insinuates that *not knowing* these histories can be a means of domination, or at minimum, helps sustain and reproduce contemporary social hierarchies. The vitality of *not knowing* was brought up by another faculty member.

Faculty 5 asserted that there are more "subversive way[s] of keeping people in their place." When asked what these subversive techniques are, they identify one avenue of racial violence is the systematic erasure of history by educational institutions.

> *Faculty 5*: In terms of the historical violence in the [Rio Grande] Valley [...] what I do experience [today] is the *lack* of teaching about it. And that's exclusionary if students don't know about it. The violent history of the Valley at the helm of the U.S. federal government, like the army in 1916 and the Texas Rangers' statewide sanctioned violence. [...] *not knowing* about that violence. I think *that is a violence* [...] it's a violence of education, *having not being taught.*
>
> (Interview, 2020, my emphasis)

Indeed, linguistic and racial terrorism takes many forms, including historical erasures and absences that result from "not having been taught." In the 2020s, institutional racism and linguistic terrorism at UTRGV no longer takes the form of a "speech test" or an explicitly monolingual language policy, but more so through the maintenance of historical erasures coupled with a shift in discourse toward marketplace concepts and economic competition. For example, as illustrated earlier, one such discourse revolves around the friendly and often well-intentioned implication that acquiring "standard" and "academic" language, or a language-elsewhere, is the key to economic and social mobility. This line of reasoning appears to be an apolitical individual choice. However, it can only appear apolitical if disconnected—by not teaching about, or by not knowing about—from the history of the deficiency perspective and how "standard" language ideologies have historically been used against Latinxs in the United States, and in the Rio Grande Valley itself. Yet, there are plenty of students, faculty, and administrators (like *Faculty 3, 4,* and *5* above) who assert a critical consciousness of the racial histories of linguistic terrorism as just as important for the self-determination of Latinxs in the United States.

One of the most comprehensive, counterhegemonic paths forward was offered by a soft-spoken, 19-year-old student named Ramona (previously mentioned), who identifies as an "immigrant, English-learner from Mexico." Ramona is double majoring in bilingual education and Mexican American Studies. When asked why she paired these majors, she responded with,

> *Ramona:* I just feel like it goes hand in hand. Like it's connected. You can't really teach bilingual education if you don't know the history of that. So I feel like a lot of the things that I'm learning in my Mexican American studies classes, it's like, furthering my knowledge of whatever I'm learning in my bilingual education courses.
>
> (Interview, 2020)

Ramona, with her personal immigrant history, her negative experience of Spanish-to-English transitional schooling in the Rio Grande Valley, as well as her commitment to critical history makes her an adversary to normative institutionalized perspectives.

> *Ramona*: I'm usually the one that disrupts the comfort zone and it's like really hard. [….] It's like me against twenty people [in the university classroom]. So yeah, I don't know if I'm wrong, but I think there's no better version of Spanish. It's like, if I speak Spanglish or Tex-Mex, like not one is better than the other.
>
> (Interview, 2020)

Ramona reports that she is often positioned as opposing her classmate's normative stances for explicitly rejecting hierarchical values associated with certain linguistic varieties, particularly the stigma associated with "Spanglish" or "Tex-Mex." Indeed, recognizing such linguistic practices as having always been legitimate is a highly politicized stance (Flores, 2014). Ramona plans to incorporate her perspectives into her chosen profession as an elementary school teacher. She is not, however, celebrated for her political positions by her peers. And, once again, as *Faculty 4* said above, "the burden has fallen on women of color in the university" to resist the normative forces of institutionalized traditions that have not been historically kind to women like Gloria Anzaldúa, or Ramona for that matter. While addressing how local gender ideologies work in tandem with various intersectional dimensions is beyond the scope of this paper, I do not believe it is coincidence that a large majority of the participants that have volunteered for this research self-identify as Latina/x, Chicana, or Mexican and Mexican American women.

The erasure of such histories has been perpetuated by this university and the Texas education system in general, including the historical emergence of the deficiency perspective and the entailed "standard/substandard" binary, which in turn erases the colonial process that *sub-standardized* the linguistic practices of Mexican and Mexican Americans in the region. What makes things all the more complex is that "standard" languages are being conflated into objects of economic value, which allegedly makes graduates more competitive in the global marketplace. This rearticulates the standard/substandard dichotomy into a less politically potent and friendlier framing of what Latinxs should aspire for in terms of linguistic practice—that is, Latinxs should transition from the "home" language to an economically viable standardized language(s)-else-where—both English and Spanish—which are imagined to be pre-legitimized in the marketplace. Note the apparent lack of racial connotations in the later framing, which constructs language(s)-elsewhere as politically neutral, raceless, and economically normative linguistic "resources." It then becomes easier to degrade a group of people by insisting one is *only* talking about an individual's failed competitive drive to learn an economically valuable language, as opposed to talking about a group's overall racial and linguistic deficiencies. The language-elsewhere emerges in everyday conversations, often elevated as superior through the gentle implication that local linguistic practices are simply "not enough" for a competitive marketplace.

Concluding Thoughts: The Hegemony of the Language-Elsewhere

The friendlier form of linguistic terrorism presented in this chapter, the language-elsewhere, is not new, but a re-articulation of the racial and linguistic hierarchies produced within the colonial legacy of the Rio Grande Valley. The language-elsewhere gives name to an imagined linguistic variety and emergent contrastive relation found in everyday discourse, and generally can be traceable to specific spatial-temporal contexts and institutionally legitimized forms of personhood, so long as it does not include the homes of the Rio Grande Valley or Latinxs in the United States. The language-elsewhere changes form, changes names, and is an emergent discursive construction treated as "real" by various university actors.

The practical implementation of bilingualism continues to be a difficult journey for this university. Nevertheless, the effort to make UTRGV both bilingual and critically conscious of relevant histories and structural inequities is being spearheaded by many local researchers and scholars, from the application of a post-colonial critique in the university's Translation and Interpreting Office (Dávila-Montes, González-Núñez, and Guajardo, 2019), to reimagining first-year writing classes (Cavazos, 2019), to the collection of testimonials (Alvarez, 2013; Cole and Johnson, 2013), to critiques of state-sanctioned Spanish proficiency tests (Guerrero and Guerrero, 2017), to the promotion of critical stances toward subtractive schooling in the Rio Grande Valley (Saavedra et al., 2020; Ostorga and Farruggio, 2018; Schall, Alvarez McHatton, and Sáenz, 2020), and through translanguaging in the classroom (Musanti and Cavazos, 2018). Through the work of these university actors, Latinxs in the United States continue to question racial and linguistic hierarchies that have been forming and reforming for centuries, passed along from one generation to the next.

In this political moment, framing Spanish and bilingualism as a potential economic resource provides a "shelter from political tension" (Stephens, 2021) in a nation that views Latinxs as a political and racial threat (Santa Ana, 2002). Using this economic framing is not unique to the region but an identified trend in primary/secondary schools all across the United States (Flores, Tseng, and Subtirelu, 2021; Valdez, Freire, and Delavan, 2016; Stephens, 2021). Caution must be exercised not to simply rearticulate the deficiency perspective by equating the idea of an economically valuable Spanish with the idea of a "standard" Spanish from elsewhere disconnected from the homes of Mexicans and Mexican Americans in the region. As this chapter asserts, this disconnected language-elsewhere is at its core a colonial invention (Makoni and Pennycook, 2005) designed to perpetuate the racializing standard/substandard linguistic dichotomy as a "natural" fact of life. If these histories are not addressed, then the violence of these erasures will be allowed to maintain the institutional status quo. Treating a stigmatized language as a raceless, neutral object of economic value will not work to destigmatize the users of that language, nor will it work against racial and linguistic hierarchies or result in a more equitable society. On the contrary, valuing a people's language while simultaneously devaluing the people who use it has the potential to be one of the friendliest forms of linguistic terrorism to date.

Interviews

Faculty 1, conducted with the author on October 29, 2020.
Faculty/Administrator 2, conducted with the author on September 15, 2020.
Faculty/Administrator 3, conducted with the author on September 6, 2020.
Faculty 4, conducted with the author on August 17, 2020.
Faculty 5, conducted with the author on September 19, 2020.
Ramona (student), conducted with the author on October 28, 2020.
Miranda (student), conducted with the author on November 20, 2020.

Notes

1. Because the university name is identified, hypervigilance is taken to anonymize research participants in an effort to protect the institutional reputation and standing of faculty/ administrator research participants. This includes removing language that might reveal any gender category they identify with as well as pseudonyms. This, however, presents its own epistemological violence as some of these research participants are scholars and women of color. It also risks flattening out power dynamics in statements made.
2. This chapter, more often than not, uses the ethno-racial and identity categories (i.e., "Mexican" and "Mexican American") typically heard in everyday conversations is the region—that is, the contemporary, popular identity category "Latinx" is not widely used in the Rio Grande Valley.

References

Alvarez, Stephanie M. 2013. "Evaluating the Role of the Spanish Department in the Education of U.S. Latin@ Students: Un Testimonio." *Journal of Latinos and Education* 12 (2): 131–151.

Anzaldúa, Gloria. 2012 [1987]. "How to Tame a Wild Tongue." In *Borderlands/La Frontera: The New Mestiza*, 4th ed., 75–86. San Francisco: Aunt Lute Books.

Blanton, Carlos Kevin. 2004. *The Strange Career of Bilingual Education in Texas, 1836–1981*. College Station, TX: University of Texas A&M.

Cavazos, Alyssa G. 2019. "Encouraging Languages Other Than English in First-Year Writing Courses: Experiences from Linguistically Diverse Writers." *Composition Studies* 47 (1): 38–56.

Cole, Deborah, and Rob Johnson. 2013. "'How to Tame a Wild Tongue': Gloria Anzaldúa's Borderlands/La Frontera and the 1960s Era Speech Test and Speech Classes at Pan American College." Pp. 120–134 in *National Association for Chicana and Chicano Studies Annual Conference*.

Dávila-Montes, José, Gabriel González-Núñez, and Francisco Guajardo. 2019. "On Not Taming the Wild Tongue : Challenges and Approaches to Institutional Translation in a University Serving a Historically Minoritized Population." *TTR: Traduction, Terminologie, Rédaction* 32 (2): 33–60.

Delgado Bernal, Dolores. 1999. "Chicana/o Education from the Civil Rights Era to the Present." In *The Elusive Quest for Equality: 150 Years of Chicano/Chicana Education*, José F. Moreno (ed.), 71–110. Cambridge, MA: Harvard Educational Review.

Flores, Nelson. 2014. "Let's Not Forget That Translanguaging Is a Political Act." https:// educationallinguist.wordpress.com/2014/07/19/lets-not-forget-that-translanguaging-is-a-political-act/.

Flores, Nelson, Amelia Tseng, and Nicholas Subtirelu. 2021. "Bilingualism for All or Just for the Rich and White? Introducing a Raciolinguistic Perspective to Dual Language Education." In *Bilingualism for All?: Raciolinguistic Perspectives on Dual Language Education in the United States*, Nelson Flores, Amelia Tseng, and Nicholas Subtirelu (eds.). Bristol and Blue Ridge Summit: Multilingual Matters.

Flores, Nelson, and Jonathan Rosa. 2015. "Undoing Appropriateness: Raciolinguistic Ideologies and Language Diversity in Education." *Harvard Educational Review* 85 (2): 149–172.

García, Ofelia. 2009. *Bilingual Education in the 21st Century: A Global Perspective*. Malden, MA: Wiley-Blackwell.

González, Gilbert G. 1990. *Chicano Education in the Era of Segregation*. Denton, TX: University of North Texas.

Guerrero, Michael D., and Maria Consuelo Guerrero. 2017. "Competing Discourses of Academic Spanish in the Texas-Mexico Borderlands." *Bilingual Research Journal* 40 (1): 5–19.

Haney López, Ian. 2003. *Racism on Trial: The Chicano Fight for Justice.* Cambridge, MA and London: The Belknap Press of Harvard University Press.

Heller, Monica. 2003. "Globalization, the New Economy, and the Commodification of Language and Identity." *Journal of Sociolinguistics* 7 (4): 504–25.

Inoue, M. 2003. "The Listening Subject of Japanese Modernity and His Auditory Double: Citing, Sighting, and Siting the Modern Japanese Woman." *Cultural Anthropology* 18 (2): 156–193.

Irvine, Judith T., and Susan Gal. 2000. "Language Ideology and Linguistic Differentiation." In *Regimes of Language: Ideologies, Politics, and Identities,* Paul V. Kroskrity (ed.), 35–84. Santa Fe, NM: School of American Research Press.

Lozano, Rosina. 2018. *An American Language: The History of Spanish in the United States.* Oakland, CA: University of California Press.

Makoni, Sinfree, and Alastair Pennycook. 2005. "Disinventing and (Re)Constituting Languages." *Critical Inquiry in Language Studies* 2 (3): 137–156.

Martín Rojo, Luisa. 2019. "The 'Self-Made Speaker': The Neoliberal Governance of Speakers." In *Language and Neoliberal Governmentality*, Luisa Marin Rojo and Alfonso Del Percio (eds.), 162–189. New York: Routledge.

Mena, Mike, and Ofelia García. 2020. "'Converse Racialization' and 'Un/Marking' Language: The Making of a Bilingual University in a Neoliberal World." *Language in Society*, 1–22. https://doi.org/10.1017/S0047404520000330.

Montejano, David. 1987. *Anglos and Mexicans in the Making of Texas, 1836–1986.* Austin, TX: University of Texas Press.

Musanti, Sandra I., and Alyssa G. Cavazos. 2018. "'Siento Que Siempre Tengo Que Regresar Al Inglés ': Embracing a Translanguaging Stance in a Hispanic-Serving Institution The University of Texas Rio Grande Valley." *EuroAmerican Journal of Applied Linguistics and Languages* 5 (2): 44–61.

Ostorga, Alcione N., and Peter Farruggio. 2018. "Preparing Bilingual Teachers on the U.S./Mexico Border: Including the Voices of Emergent Bilinguals." *International Journal of Bilingual Education and Bilingualism* 23 (10): 1225–1237. https://doi.org/10.1080/13670050.2018.1438348.

Ostorga, Alcione N., Christian E. Zúñiga, and Kip Austin Hinton. 2020. "Bilingual Teacher Educators at an HSI: A Border Pedagogy for Latinx Teacher Development." In *Teacher Education at Hispanic-Serving Institutions: Exploring Identity, Practice, and Culture,* Janine M. Schall, Patricia Alvarez McHatton, and Eugenio Sáenz Longoria (eds.), 137–155. New York and London: Routledge.

Otheguy, Ricardo, and Nancy Stern. 2011. "On So-Called Spanglish." *International Journal of Bilingualism* 15 (1): 85–100.

Reyes, Angela. 2020. "Coloniality of Mixed Race and Mixed Language." In *The Oxford Handbook of Language and Race*, H. Samy Alim, Angela Reyes, and Paul V. Kroskrity (eds.), 185–206. New York: Oxford University Press.

Rosa, Jonathan Daniel. 2016. "Standardization, Racialization, Languagelessness: Raciolinguistic Ideologies across Communicative Contexts." *Journal of Linguistic Anthropology* 26 (2): 162–183.

Rosa, Jonathan, and Nelson Flores. 2017. "Unsettling Race and Language: Toward a Raciolinguistic Perspective." *Language in Society* 46: 621–647.

Saavedra, Cinthya M., Joy Esquierdo, Dagoberto E. Ramirez, and Isela Almaguer. 2020. "Conducting Research through the Eyes of Chican@ Researchers at a Borderlands HSCOE." In *Teacher Education at Hispanic-Serving Institutions: Exploring Identity, Practice, and Culture*, Janine M. Schall, Patricia Alvarez McHatton, and Eugenio Longoria Sáenz (eds.), 53–68. New York and London: Routledge.

San Miguel, Guadalupe. 1987. *"Let All of Them Take Heed": Mexican Americans and the Campaign for Educational Equality in Texas, 1910–1981*. College Station, TX: Texas A&M University Press.

Santa Ana, Otto. 2002. *Brown Tide Rising: Metaphors of Latinos in Contemporary American Public Discourse*. Austin, TX: University of Texas Press.

Schall, Janine M., Patricia Alvarez McHatton, and Eugenio Longoria Sáenz, eds. 2020. *Teacher Education at Hispanic-Serving Institutions: Exploring Identity, Practice, and Culture*. New York and London: Routledge.

Schieffelin, Bambi, Kathryn Woolard, and Paul Kroskrity. 1998. *Language Ideologies: Practice and Theory*. New York: Oxford University Press.

Silverstein, Michael. 1996. "Monoglot 'Standard' in America: Standardization and Metaphors of Linguistic Hegemony." In *The Matrix of Language: Contemporary Linguistic Anthropology*, D. L. Brenneis and R. K. S. Macaulay (eds.), 284–306. Boulder, CO: Westview.

Stephens, Crissa. 2021. "Common Threads: Language Policy, Nation, Whiteness, and Privilege in Iowa's First Dual Language Program." In *Bilingualism for All?: Raciolinguistic Perspectives on Dual Language Education in the United States*, Nelson Flores, Amelia Tseng, and Nicholas Subtirelu (eds.), 40–62. Bristol and Blue Ridge Summit: Multilingual Matters.

Strategic Plan. 2017. The University of Texas Rio Grande Valley. Accessed January 1 2021. https://www.utrgv.edu/strategic-plan/other-areas-of-focus/bilingual-bicultural-and-biliterate/index.htm.

Taylor, Steve. 2014. "Professor: Making UTRGV a truly bilingual university is going to take time." Rio Grande Guardian, May. Online: https://riograndeguardian.com/professor-making-utrgv-a-truly-bilingual-university-is-going-to-take-time/.

Trump, Donald. "White House Conference on American History." Sept. 17 2020.

Urciuoli, Bonnie. 2008. "Skills and Selves in the New Workplace." *American Ethnologist* 35 (2): 211–228.

Valdez, Verónica E., Juan A. Freire, and M. Garrett Delavan. 2016. "The Gentrification of Dual Language Education." *The Urban Review* 48 (4): 601–627.

Valencia, Richard R. 2010. *Dismantling Contemporary Deficit Thinking: Educational Thought and Practice*. New York: Routledge.

Valenzuela, Angela. 1999. *Subtractive Schooling: U.S.-Mexican Youth and the Politics of Caring*. Albany, NY: State University of New York Press.

Chapter 6

"You Are Not Allowed to Speak Spanish! This Is an American Hospital"

Puerto Rican Experiences with Domestic Discrimination[1]

Alessandra Rosa, Elizabeth Aranda, and Hilary Dotson

In recent decades, the Puerto Rican population has grown substantially in the United States (5.5 million), surpassing the population living in the archipelago (3.2 million) (U.S. Census Bureau 2017).[2] Outmigration from Puerto Rico has especially grown since Hurricanes Irma and Maria struck in 2017 on September 7th and 20th, respectively. Since then, an estimated 220,000 to 255,000 Puerto Ricans have moved to the continental United States (Centro 2018) with a majority of these migrants settling in southern and western states.

Currently, Florida's Puerto Rican population is estimated to be 1,128,000 (U.S. Census Bureau 2017). Central Florida has become home to four of the five largest communities in the state (Duany 2015), emerging as a popular gateway for this group (Velez and Burgos 2010). Moreover, the largest numbers of post-hurricane Puerto Rican migrants are coming to Florida becoming "the epicenter of the new wave of migration" and indicating "an above average number of displaced persons arriving after the storm" (Centro 2018:16). Despite the large presence of Puerto Ricans in the continental United States and Florida specifically, researchers know little about the lived experience of adaptation, particularly with regards to a linguistic discrimination that can be based on Spanish accents or speaking Spanish in public. We examine the nature of linguistic discrimination and the forms it takes quantitatively among a national sample of Puerto Ricans (N = 484) and a qualitative sample of 20 Puerto Ricans living in Central Florida.

Background

Since the early 2000s research has examined the integration of Latinos/as into new destinations (Massey and Capoferro 2008), particularly in the "new south" (Kochhar, Suro, and Tafoya 2005; Winders 2005). Although preliminary studies suggest that Florida, and specifically parts of Central Florida, present advantageous contexts of reception (Velez and Burgos 2010), questions remain as to which populations benefit most from this context, given that

DOI: 10.4324/9781003257509-10

Central Florida attracts both Puerto Ricans from the archipelago and U.S.-born Puerto Ricans from the Northeast from various class backgrounds and levels of English language fluency. This is important given the racialization of Puerto Ricans as an ethnoracial group, and the racialization of the Spanish language spoken by many who come from Puerto Rico with limited English-speaking skills.

We treat Puerto Ricans as an ethnoracial group since they are part of a multi-racial ethnic group. Some ethnicities have been racialized (Grosfoguel 2004) as elements of their culture are perceived akin to racialized phenotypic features. Aranda and Rebollo-Gil (2004) argue that given the racialization of certain ethnicities (usually those coming from the Global South), ethnoracial groups experience ethnoracism. We take this approach to study the racialization of language and the ensuing perceived discrimination resulting from this process.

The Racialization of Language

Racialization is the "sociohistorical process by which racial categories are created, inhabited, transformed, and destroyed" (Omi and Winant 1994:55). The racialization of language is intrinsically tied to the process of minoritizing ethnic groups such as Puerto Ricans. Though ethnic groups such as Latinos/as, and more specifically Puerto Ricans, have been studied through the lens of assimilation (Waldinger and Feliciano 2004; South, Crowder, and Chavez 2005), critical race scholars have argued that it is more appropriate to study their integration outcomes through the lens of racialization (Valdez and Golash-Boza 2017; Sáenz and Douglas 2015).

Perceived limited English proficiency or speaking accented-English imply being a minority or foreigner, invoking stereotypes and discrimination (Bleakley and Chin 2004; Bergman et al. 2008; Zhang et al. 2012). In the United States, language can be racialized or ethnicized depending on context (Urciuoli 2013). Speaking *accentless* standard English serves as a racial marker of whiteness—typically associated with citizenship and perceptions of who is American. Similarly, Spanish language, limited English proficiency, Spanglish, or Spanish-accented English serve as racial markers or indicators of Hispanic or Latino immigrant identities (Silverstein 1976; Bailey 2000); its speakers are seen as racially different and unassimilated, and hence non-white (Urciuoli 2013). Anthropolitical linguist, Ana Celia Zentella (2014:631) states that the "remapping of race from biology onto language facilitates a shift from racialization lodged in the body to racialization lodged in language and culture." She continues:

> It may no longer be acceptable to disparage somebody's race, at least not in public, but it is still acceptable to make negative comments about language in ways that trade on the polarized tropes of inherent superiority versus inherent inferiority, purity versus pollution and intelligence versus retardation that characterize discussions of race.

The racialization of language unfolds as there is a negative bias toward people speaking Spanish or Spanish-accented English in the United States; they are seen as a foreign threat to not just the English language, but more broadly, to American core values and culture (Cobas and Feagin 2008; Feagin and Cobas 2015; Markert 2010; Nelson, Signorella, and Botti 2016;). There exists a sense of linguistic nationalism or purity tied to "the production of an [American] monoglot standard" (Silverstein 1996; Urciuoli 2001; Parsons 2011:231) that only recognizes and values one kind of English as correct (Milroy and Milroy 1999). Consequently, migrants who speak Spanish or have a Spanish accent are perceived as non-citizens, inherently illegal, poor, uneducated, criminally inclined, refusing to learn proper English, and hence, outsiders (Parsons 2011). This is in line with the Latino Threat Narrative (Chavez 2013) that Anthropologist Leo Chavez argues permeates American society. More specifically, sociolinguist, Rosina Lippi-Green (1997:238–239) reminds us that: "not all foreign accents, but only accent linked to skin that isn't white, or which signals a third-world homeland, that evokes… negative reactions." We pay attention to whether darker skin Puerto Ricans face more perceived unfair treatment due to their Spanish accents than lighter skin ones within the context of examining linguistic discrimination.

Data and Methods

We use data from two sources: an online national survey (N = 484) and in-depth interviews with 20 Puerto Rican adults living in Central Florida.

Survey

The survey, available in English and Spanish, was conducted online between October 31 and November 6, 2018 among a national sample of Puerto Rican adults. The analyses use data from a Qualtrics sample of the Puerto Rican adult population living in one of the 50 United States. Qualtrics is a company that offers services for completing online surveys as well as providing a software platform for online surveys. The majority of Qualtrics' samples come from traditional, actively managed market research panels. Qualtrics also uses social media to access respondents and employs niche panels through specialized recruitment campaigns (Qualtrics 2014). Qualtrics' panels contain psycho-demographic profiles of each panelist who can update their information as needed. All Qualtrics' panels have a double opt-in requirement. Potential participants are invited through emails informing them that a survey is for research purposes only, the estimated length of time for completion, and the incentive offered. To avoid self-selection bias, the emailed invitation does not contain details about the survey.

Online surveys have been found to yield advantages such as completion rates that have been found to be reasonable compared to other kinds of surveys

(Miller et al. 2020). They also have been found to exceed any disadvantages in terms of external validity (Heen et al. 2014). In all, Qualtrics provides samples with attributes within a 10% range of their demographic profile in the U.S. population (Heen et al. 2014) and this platform's samples more closely approximate national probability samples than other non-probability samples (Boas et al. 2018). In spite of these advantages, the analyses presented here are not intended to be generalized to the Puerto Rican diaspora population as a whole, and as such, have not been weighted to estimate such values. Given the exploratory nature of this study, Qualtrics has been deemed the best platform due to its ability to survey such a specific population in a relatively short period of time.

We analyzed the data using R statistical programming language in the RStudio environment. After list-wise deletion, the final sample included 484 Puerto Ricans. Perceived unfair treatment due to accent is the dependent measure of interest in this study drawn from the question "Do you think you have been treated unfairly in the United States (referring to one of the 50 states) because of your Spanish accent? Please indicate if this has been a major problem, somewhat of a problem, a small problem, or no problem at all?" 39.5% (n = 191) stated it had been "no problem at all," while 16.6% (n = 80) stated it did not apply to them (which could be because they did not have an accent when speaking English). Among those who answered that unfair treatment as a result of having a Spanish accent had been a problem for them at all (n = 212), 50.9% stated it had been "a small problem" (n = 108), 34.0% (n = 72) stated it had been "somewhat of a problem," and 15.1% (n = 32) stated it had been "a major problem." We analyze this measure as a binary variable, comparing those who stated it had been "no problem at all" or that it did not apply to them as one group, and those who experienced any problems as a result of unfair treatment due to accent as another group.

In the predictive model, we employed the following predictors of unfair treatment due to accent: gender, skin tone (see Ethnicity Module Color Palette—often referred to as the PERLA chart—https://perla.soc.ucsb.edu/about-perla), educational attainment, marital status, language proficiency, birthplace, living in a Puerto Rican neighborhood, annual family income prior to Hurricane Maria, and age.[3] In reference to the PERLA chart, it is a chart with nine gradations of skin color that we have labeled as follows: 1–2 refer to light skin, 3 is light-medium, 4–5 is described as medium, and 6–11 refers to having dark skin.

Qualitative Sample

In addition to the quantitative survey, we conducted in-depth, in-person interviews with 20 Puerto Ricans who either migrated to Florida after the hurricanes or were already living in the continental United States prior to the hurricanes. Interviews typically lasted about two hours and were conducted in the language of their choice. We used snowball sampling and a couple of referrals from agencies that had helped Puerto Ricans upon post-disaster relocation. We asked about biographical histories, including questions about major life events and migration histories, experiences adapting to their new homes in Florida, and experiences with discrimination, among other topics. Participants consist of 11 women and 9 men, with ages ranging from 20 to 70 years old. Eleven had been living in Puerto Rico when Hurricanes Irma and Maria struck the archipelago. For these interviewees, questions also focused on the lived experience of going through the disaster and the ensuing problems such as getting supplies in Puerto Rico, and their decisions to leave Puerto Rico. All of those who had migrated after the hurricanes chose to do their interviews in Spanish, with one exception. Of the remaining interviewees, one chose to do his interview in English and the rest in Spanish. All of them were conducted by the first and second authors, both bilingual Puerto Rican natives. The positionality of the researchers allowed them to understand the cultural nuances that arose in the interviews and also helped to foster a social connection, given that the two researchers who did the interviews also had close families that experienced Hurricanes Irma and Maria.

All interviews were transcribed verbatim and the transcripts were coded thematically in the data analysis software package MAXQDA. Thematic codes categorized participants' responses. Data related to perceived unfair treatment due to language or one's Spanish accent were coded as linguistic discrimination. Excerpts of data in Spanish were translated by the authors.

Findings

Quantitative Results: Spanish Accents and Perceived Unfair Treatment

To determine whether there was a relationship between experiencing unfair treatment due to one's accent and the independent variables of interest, we ran a binary logistic regression model, predicting whether individuals experienced problems with unfair treatment due to accent compared to those who did not experience such problems. We hold gender, education, marital status, language proficiency, birthplace, neighborhood composition, annual family income prior to Hurricane Maria, and age constant. Several independent measures were statistically significant in the models. Skin tone, educational attainment, birthplace, marital status, and annual family income prior to Hurricane Maria were all independently associated with perceived unfair treatment due to accent (see Table 6.1).

Dark-skinned participants (based on self-reported Perla chart skin tone ranged from 6 to 11) were about twice as likely as those with a lighter skin tone (3 in Perla chart, light-medium skin color) to indicate experiencing problems with unfair treatment due to accent. Several factors may be at work here. It is

Table 6.1 Binary logistic regression

	Coef.	SE	OR
Woman (ref. man)	−0.16	0.21	0.85
Perla chart skin tone			
Light (1–2)	−0.08	0.28	0.93
Light-medium (3) (ref.)	–		–
Medium (4–5)	−0.03	0.25	0.97
Dark (6–11)	0.81*	0.35	2.24
Educational attainment			
Did not finish high school	−0.65	0.60	0.52
High school diploma or equivalent (ref.)	–		–
Some college	0.25	0.31	1.28
College degree (BA/BS)	0.91**	0.32	2.49
Graduate degree or professional school	0.93**	0.36	2.54
Marital Status			
Married	0.50*	0.24	1.65
Cohabiting	0.80*	0.36	2.22
Not married/cohabiting (ref.)	–		–
Fluent in which language			
English	−0.40	0.29	0.67
Spanish	0.30	0.27	1.35
English and Spanish (ref.)	–		–
Born in Puerto Rico (ref. U.S. state/international)	0.92**	0.30	2.52
Agree that neighborhood mostly Puerto Rican (ref. disagree)	−0.11	0.26	0.89
Annual family income before Maria			
No response	−0.58	0.48	0.56
$0–$19,999 (ref.)	–		–
$20,000–$39,999	−0.33	0.33	0.72
$40,000–$59,999	−0.46	0.35	0.63
$60,000–$79,999	−0.65	0.40	0.52
$80,000–$99,999	−0.40	0.51	0.67
$100,000–$125,000	−1.21*	0.49	0.30
$125,001–$149,999	−1.44*	0.58	0.24
$150,000 or more	−0.54	0.56	0.58
Age	−0.01	0.01	0.99
Constant	−0.74	0.54	0.48

N = 484

Log likelihood = −296.901.

$p < .05$*; $p < .01$**

Source: Qualtrics survey sample.

possible that unfair treatment due to accent may be more commonly experienced among those who are already racialized due to phenotype and who do not pass as white. It is also possible, however, that unfair treatment is more likely to be perceived and interpreted as such by those with darker skin, as they may have been more likely to be socialized into the U.S. system of racial discrimination than their lighter skin counterparts. These findings mirror Waters' (1999) research suggesting that the longer West Indian immigrants were in the

United States (i.e. socialized into the system of U.S. racial discrimination), the more they became attuned to naming unfair treatment as discrimination and to identify racism.

With respect to educational attainment, participants with a college degree and those with a graduate or professional degree were about two times as likely as those with a high school diploma to indicate experiencing problems with unfair treatment due to accent while accounting for all control measures listed above. One explanation for this could be that as Puerto Ricans rise in the occupational ladders due to their returns on human capital, they may be more likely to come into contact with whites and white spaces, and thus, subject to perceived unfair treatment because of their accents. This finding is along the lines of prior research on Latinos/as who achieve occupational mobility (Kasinitz et al. 2008; Aranda et al. 2014s).

Birthplace is also a significant predictor of differences with unfair treatment due to accent. Puerto Rico-born individuals were two and a half times more likely than those who were born in one of the 50 states (and the one person born abroad) to indicate experiencing problems with unfair treatment due to accent.

Having been born in Puerto Rico is tied to one's migratory status and is likely to shape whether one has a Spanish accent when speaking English, thus subjecting the Puerto Rican-born participants to greater scrutiny. As Jorge Duany (2003:426) has argued, when Puerto Ricans migrate to any of the 50 states, they "cross significant geographic, cultural, and linguistic borders between the Island and the mainland." Upon this crossing, as a U.S. ethnoracial group, they are subject to racialization by whites who may perceive them as foreigners despite Puerto Ricans' U.S. citizenship (Aranda 2007). Linguistic factors contribute to the racialization of island Puerto Ricans as the process of ethnoracism reveals (Aranda and Rebollo-Gil 2004).

Last, those who were married and cohabiting have higher odds of facing unfair treatment due to accents. It is unclear from the literature how to explain these patterns; as such, we can only hypothesize what accounts for this. Our qualitative data supports that that having a co-ethnic partner may provide a frame of reference when it comes to interpreting experiences with linguistic and other forms of discrimination when such incidents are discussed within the context of close relationships. Thus, it is not necessarily that experiencing unfair treatment is related itself to marital status, but more so, it may be having a partner with whom to compare experiences and thus interpret these as unfair treatment.

Unlike each of the relationships discussed above, annual family income prior to Hurricane Maria appeared protective against experiencing problems with unfair treatment due to accent. More specifically, higher incomes were related to lower odds of unfair treatment because of one's Spanish accent. Those whose annual family income prior to Hurricane Maria was between $100,000 and $125,000, and $125,001 and $149,999, had significantly lower odds of experiencing problems with unfair treatment due to accent, compared to those whose annual family income was between $0 and $19,999. It is possible that those with the lowest income levels have the most problems with English compared to those who make above $100,000, even if the former group is somewhat fluent, possibly subjecting them to perceived unfair treatment. To note is that among those whose annual family income was above $100,000, 23.5% (n = 19) stated that the unfair treatment due to accent question did not apply to them, compared to only 15.4% (n = 62) of all other respondents, though this difference was not significant.

In short, darker skin tone, higher levels of education, being married or cohabiting, and being born in Puerto Rico all increased odds of experiencing problems with unfair treatment due to one's accent, while higher levels of income helped to protect against experiencing problems from unfair treatment due to accent. These findings confirm the presence of ethnoracism in the form of linguistic discrimination in the lives of Puerto Ricans residing in the continental United States. We now turn to our qualitative data to illustrate how linguistic discrimination works in the lives of Puerto Rican migrants who reside in Central Florida.

Qualitative Results: Linguistic Discrimination

Puerto Ricans feel vulnerable when speaking Spanish or Spanish-accented English in public spaces, job interviews or workplaces, parent-teacher conferences at children's schools, among other situations. Puerto Ricans speaking Spanish or Spanish-accented English can suffer from linguistic profiling or "the auditory equivalent of visual racial profiling" (Baugh 2003:155) since they can be seen less favorably as job applicants as an example (Purkiss et al. 2006; Hosoda, Nguyen, and Stone-Romero 2012). Thus, in spite of being U.S. citizens, Puerto Ricans continue to be *Otherized* as *foreign in a domestic sense*.[4] As Cultural Sociologists Lamont and Molnár (2002) theorize, symbolic boundaries are drawn between American whites and Puerto Ricans based on language and accents in combination with phenotype; all are acting as ethnoracial markers that reinforce social boundaries (Lamont and Molnár 2002). Both our quantitative and qualitative data point in the same direction. For instance, in constructing these boundaries, language and phenotype interact to construct who "looks" and "sounds" more Puerto Rican, which subjects them to more or less instances of ethnoracial discrimination or ethnoracism, depending on how they are perceived by others.

To show how language can be a marker of racialization and construct Puerto Ricans as *other*, Gaby, who is white passing, and who has lived in the United States for close to 10 years, explains:

> Sometimes, I think in Spanish, *so*[5] when I am with persons who speak English sometimes it takes me a second because I have to translate,

because I think in Spanish and then translate to English. *So*, it takes a bit of time. And that's when you notice that people say, "Wait, *you are not from here, so where are you from?*" And that's when it begins... that's when it feels different.

Language or linguistic diversity becomes a signifier of not just an *other* status, but a racialized, unassimilated, and foreign *other*. In other words, even though Puerto Ricans are U.S. citizens, having accented English (and specifically, a Spanish accent) denotes them as members of a group that stands in opposition to white Americans. "So where are you from?" often arises when symbolic boundaries (Lamont and Molnár 2002) are drawn based on cues such as accents. The fact that these are Spanish accents draws the social boundary that denotes the person as foreign. These boundaries call into question Puerto Ricans' sense of belonging to a nation-state of which they are citizens, which runs contrary to assumptions of foreignness. Gaby contrasts her treatment with that received by her husband in the following quote: "[Speaking about racism] Not him, because I look a bit more Puerto Rican. Not him; and his English has much less of an accent. So, he passes and in reality... He has not felt anything." This quote supports our theorizing about the relationship between marital status and perceptions of unfair treatment due to having a Spanish accent discussed earlier, since by comparing their experiences, Gaby notices that she is more likely to be exposed to such treatment.

The racialization of language can work in a number of ways. For some in our sample, the case was that their accents and even speaking Spanish in public were subject to surveillance, a process that had material and psychological consequences for jobs, promotions, and feelings of belonging or feeling marginalized within their social groups and organizations. For example, John, who has black hair, brown skin, and a beard, described his experience when he was in the military, at boot camp:

> But definitely at the beginning. I remember being called—what did they used to call—even in boot camp, because I would help—there were another couple guys that didn't speak a lot of English that I would help sometimes, translate to them, and we would get in trouble for speaking Spanish and things like that. I'm like, "Well, I'm trying to help them out." It's like, "Well if you want to be in Mexico, you should have stayed in Mexico." And in boot camp, a lot of it's to get in your head... or there was a lot of—I think there was a lot of insult meant behind it. They knew they could get away with it, "So let's just do it. It's boot camp. We can say whatever we want, basically."

There are a number of issues to consider in this quote. First, speaking Spanish is tied to being from another country, and by singling out Mexico, it reveals a process of racialization in which Latinos/as are homogenized. Moreover, speaking Spanish is followed by remarks that one should go back home, or in this case, "stayed in Mexico," sending the message that any language other than English is not compatible with living in the United States.

The racialization of language in this form can also lead to escalations that can result in violence in some cases. For instance, José, who can be considered white passing, is a midwife nurse who migrated in 2013. He recounted an incident at the Veteran's hospital where he worked with other Latinos/as who often spoke to one another in Spanish. He told us about an occasion when he was speaking to a co-ethnic in English in the hospital but since they were in the middle of a nursing shift change, there was more noise than usual, and his co-worker could not hear him well. He explained,

> When someone doesn't understand me, I think it is because of my accent, I won't think it's the noise… I'll think, "It's José's poor English." So, I changed to Spanish; I changed to Spanish for only four words. The person who was behind him who is American, light eyes and immediately and rapidly opened his mouth and said, "You are not allowed to speak Spanish" in a nasty way. I was like not believing if I heard him right.

José confirmed with another colleague that he, in fact, had heard correctly and continued, "And well my reaction was… well, if you say I cannot speak Spanish here, now is when I will speak Spanish even more." He stated, "To make a long story short, he came out yelling at me, *'You are not allowed to speak Spanish! This is an American hospital!'* And I said, *'So? I'm allowed.'* [He said] *'No, per VA policy'* of the hospital, *'per VA policy you are not allowed to speak Spanish.'* [I answered] *'That's not true.'*" José does not accept the linguistic discrimination he was experiencing by continuing to correct the man that insists he could not speak Spanish in the hospital. His resistance is also visible in his comment that if someone tells him, he cannot speak Spanish, he's going to speak it even more. However, this encounter did not stop there and could have led to violence if the police had not been called. José explained:

> So, he got ferocious. He started walking to leave, and I asked him his name so that I could file a report. And he told me his name was *asshole* and I walked towards him and I told him, "You don't talk to me like that," and I signaled him with my finger, and he hit my hand. He lowered my hand. So, to summarize, then the police arrived… And the VA policy said that I could speak Spanish…

José explained that he did file a report but that it did not go anywhere, the fact that he attributed to "VA culture" and a few other things he did not want to elaborate. Like this incident shows, language discrimination occurs in the workplace environment, though it is not just there. Even in leisure, Puerto Ricans face the prospects of having their language scrutinized.

Like José and John, other participants felt that their language was policed by ordinary people with whom they came in contact in public. The cumulative effect of these experiences is seen in one of our participant's stories, who recounted policing himself for fear of aggression from people who support the likes of President Trump. Papo, who is a box office manager and came from Puerto Rico in 2017 after the hurricanes, talked to us about his experience of attending baseball games and how it had changed over time. He explained,

> With the Trump effect there are many things that I reserve, I cannot be as expressive like in a moment of… for example, I'll go to a sporting event and if there's a baseball player, I'm a baseball fanatic…. Before, I can tell you…that I felt completely comfortable, I did it at a sporting event, in the past here in Tampa, and I'd yell, "Boricua voy a ti." (Boricua I'm rooting for you) Now, no, I don't dare. But before… The way things are and how I see society, or maybe it's… it's like they [Trump supporters] now feel more liberated and they can express themselves more, and if they don't like something they are going to say something now, without any fear because they have a certain [entitlement]. It's their season. It's like, "Shut up because this now here is mine." I don't know, that's how I feel… So, I reserve those things, in those situations. So basically, before I'd yell, "Voy a ti Boricua!" Now, well I stay there, because I don't know if someone will see it as something bad and will form an issue.

Papo, who has brown skin, brown eyes, and brown hair, explains the process by which he has come to self-regulate his excitement at sporting events because he feels that an expression of solidarity with a Puerto Rican baseball player in Spanish will be perceived as "bad" to the kind of people who have pledged support to President Trump. This is important because it has moved the policing of language from other whites to Puerto Ricans themselves who, in this case, censor themselves to not attract attention and to avoid an "issue."

Ever since Trump became president, there has been an increase in attacks perpetrated by white Americans to Spanish speakers in public spaces, telling them to "Speak American!" or "This is America, speak English!" Since 2016, hate crimes have increased to the point that "four-in-ten Latinos say they have experienced discrimination in the past year, such as being criticized for speaking Spanish or being told to go back to their home country" (Pew Research Center 2018:22). These incidents depict language policing by drawing an explicit link between language and national identity, and at a broader level, racialization (Brown and Dick 2019).

Though Papo internalized this policing, others resisted what they perceived to be unfair treatment. Pancho, who also has brown skin, brown eyes, and brown hair, is a truck driver and has lived in the United States for two years. He talked about being out with some friends, and as they were speaking Spanish to one another, how a group of men began hassling them as they went to exit the bar they were at. He explained, "I looked at him... and I began to analyze... I said, 'This asshole'... And I got angry and I yelled, because when I was leaving, I said I'm leaving because there's no... And I said, '*Hey, we are Puerto Rican, we are United States citizens. We fight in the wars and we have the right to be here.*'" During our interview, Pancho's spouse chimed in, "And we pay taxes, we pay taxes." Pancho echoed what his wife said, "We pay taxes and we are here." He continued, "I was so mad! I said, I was going to go back, but my brother-in-law grabbed me. Because it bothered me. I said, 'We have the right to be here, we are Puerto Ricans.' He was wrong. '*You're wrong. You're wrong.*'"

In this case, Pancho used his U.S. citizenship to claim that they belonged in that space; that Puerto Ricans had put their bodies on the line by fighting in U.S. wars. He made it clear he did not take what the men were doing quietly. He laid his claim to that space by speaking out and denouncing the way the men were acting toward him and his family and friends. But clearly, in this case, Pancho and his group faced backlash because the "soundscape" (Maldonado 2014) at that bar was not exclusively English. Just hearing Spanish invokes a sense of proprietary control over white spaces that in the view of white Americans, should sound white as well. By transgressing that line, Pancho felt the backlash and actively resisted it.

Conclusion

In this book chapter, we have analyzed Puerto Ricans' experiences with unfair treatment due to speaking English with Spanish accents and more broadly, linguistic discrimination in which they have been racialized based on aspects of their culture. Using a unique mixed-methods approach, we find that having dark skin, a college education or higher, having been born in Puerto Rico, and being married or cohabiting increase the odds of reporting that Puerto Ricans faced unfair treatment due to their Spanish accents. Further, higher income was associated with lower odds of reporting such treatment compared to low-income participants. Finally, linguistic discrimination takes many forms that go beyond unfair treatment based on accents, to involve having one's language policed in spaces that are deemed to be white. This latter finding was reported by those with both light and dark skin.

There are limitations to this research. The Qualtrics sample is a non-probability sample and not necessarily generalizable to the Puerto Rican population living in the continental United States. Moreover, there could be a selection bias in those participants in the quantitative sample who had to be literate and have access to a computer. That said, given that this research is exploratory, it yields initial findings that can be further explored in population surveys that use generalizable samples. In addition, given that the qualitative sample is limited to Puerto Ricans, it is unclear if other groups face similar forms of linguistic discrimination. For example, how much more or less likely is a Black, West Indian immigrant with a British accent to face linguistic discrimination compared to a white or Afro-Latino/a immigrant with a Spanish accent? What are the mechanisms behind linguistic discrimination? Last, the qualitative sample involves Puerto Ricans from Central Florida, therefore we must not generalize to the experiences of all Puerto Rican in the diaspora. It is possible that there are regional effects that comparative work is more likely to capture.

This chapter contributes to the field by highlighting the importance of broadening our view of the racialization processes to include factors related to culture and ethnicity, such as language and accents. Future work should examine whether cultural expressions, be it customs or traditions, are racialized in the same form that language is. In short, what does the full scope of ethnoracism look like and for whom?

Notes

1. We would like to acknowledge Juan Arroyo-Flores for his assistance with the survey and Elizabeth Vaquera for her constructive comments on this manuscript.
2. Important to note that ever since the invasion of Puerto Ricans by the United States in 1898, and particularly more so after Congress granted Puerto Ricans U.S. citizenship in 1917, there has been constant migration of Puerto Ricans to the continental United States and back (Duany 2011).
3. Descriptives of the sample are available upon request.
4. "In 1901 the United States Supreme Court stated that Puerto Rico was 'foreign to the United States in a domestic sense' since it was neither a state or a sovereign republic" (Duany 2003:1; Burnett and Marshall 2001).
5. Words in italics within the quotes indicate they were spoken in English during an interview conducted in Spanish.

References

Aranda, Elizabeth M. 2007. *Emotional bridges to Puerto Rico: Migration, return migration, and the struggles of incorporation.* Lanham, MD: Rowman & Littlefield.

Aranda, Elizabeth M. and Guillermo Rebollo-Gil. 2004. "Ethnoracism and the 'sandwiched' minorities." *American Behavioral Scientist*, 47 (7): 910–927.

Aranda, Elizabeth M., Sallie Hughes, and Elena Sabogal. 2014. *Making a life in multiethnic Miami: Immigration and the rise of a global city.* Boulder, CO: Lynne Rienner Publishers.

Bailey, Benjamin. 2000. "The language of multiple identities among Dominican Americans." *Linguistic Anthropology*, 10 (2): 190–223.

Baugh, John. 2003. Linguistic profiling. In S. Makoni, G. Smitherman, A.F. Ball, and A.K. Spears (eds.). *Black linguistics: Language society and politics in Africa and the Americas*, pp. 155–168. London: Routledge Press.

Bergman, Mindy, Kristen M. Watrous-Rodriguez, and Katherine M. Chalkley. 2008. "Identity and language: Contributions to and consequences of speaking Spanish in the workplace." *Hispanic Journal of Behavioral Sciences*, 30 (1): 40–68.

Bleakley, Hoyt and Aimee Chin. 2004. "Language skills and earnings: Evidence from childhood immigrants. *The Review of Economics and Statistics*, 86 (2): 481–496.

Boas, Taylor C., Dino P. Christenson, and David M. Glick. 2018. "Recruiting large online samples in the United States and India: Facebook, Mechanical Turk, and Qualtrics." *Political Science Research and Methods*, doi:10.1017/psrm.2018.28.

Brown, Melanie and Hilary Parsons Dick. 2019. "Speak American." Anthropology News. Retrieved from: https://www.anthropology-news.org/index.php/2019/08/16/speak-american/

Burnett, Christina D. and Burke Marshall. 2001. *Foreign in a domestic sense: Puerto Rico, American expansion and the constitution*. Durham, NC: Duke University Press.

Centro. 2018. "Puerto Rico two years after Hurricane Maria." *Research Briefs*. Hunter College: CUNY. Retrieved from https://centropr.hunter.cuny.edu/research/data-center/research-briefs/puerto-rico-two-years-after-hurricane-maria

Chavez, Leo. 2013. *The Latino threat: Constructing immigrants, citizens, and the nation*. Palo Alto, CA: Stanford University Press.

Cobas, José A. and Joe R. Feagin. 2008. "Language oppression and resistance: The case of middle class Latinos in the United States." *Ethnic and Racial Studies*, 31 (2): 390–410.

Duany, Jorge. 2003. *The Puerto Rican nation on the move: Identities on the island and in the United States*. Chapel Hill, NC: University of North Carolina Press.

_____. 2011. *Blurred borders: Transnational migration between the Hispanic Caribbean and the United States*. Chapel Hill, NC: University of North Carolina Press.

_____. 2015. "Florirricans" en crecimiento. *El Nuevo Dia*. October 14, 2015.

Feagin, Joe R. and José A. Cobas. 2015. *Latinos facing racism: Discrimination, resistance, and endurance*. New York: Routledge.

Grosfoguel, Ramón. 2004. "Race and ethnicity or racialized ethnicities? Identities within global coloniality." *Ethnicities*, 4 (3), 315–336.

Heen, M.S., Joel D. Lieberman, and Terance D. Miethe. 2014. "A comparison of different online sampling approaches for generating national samples." *Center for Crime and Justice Policy*, 1: 1–8.

Hosoda, Megumi, Lam T. Nguyen, and Eugene F. Stone-Romero. 2012. "The effect of Hispanic accents on employment decisions." *Journal of Managerial Psychology*, 27 (4): 347–364.

Kasinitz, Phillip, John Mollenkopf, Mary Waters, and Jennifer Holdaway. 2008. *Inheriting the city: The second generation comes of age*. New York: Russell Sage Foundation.

Kochhar, Rakesh, Roberto Suro, and Sonya Tafoya. 2005. "The New Latino South: The Context and Consequences of Rapid Population Growth." Pew Hispanic Center. Retrieved from http://www.pewhispanic.org/2005/07/26/the-new-latino-south/

Lamont, Michèle and Virág Molnár. 2002. "The study of boundaries in the social sciences." *Annual Review of Sociology*, 28 (1): 167–195.

Lippi-Green, Rosina. 1997. *English with an accent: Language, ideology, and discrimination in the United States*. New York: Routledge.

Markert, John. 2010. The changing face of racial discrimination: Hispanics as the dominant minority in the USA—a new application of power-threat theory. *Critical Sociology*, 36 (2): 307–327.

Massey, Douglas S. and Chiara Capoferro. 2008. "The geographic diversification of American immigration." In Douglas Massey (ed.), *New faces in new places: The changing geography of American immigration,* 25–50. New York: Russell Sage Foundation.

Miller, Carrie A., Jeanine P.D. Guidry, Bassam Dahman, and Maria D. Thomson. 2020. "A tale of two diverse Qualtrics samples: Information for online survey researchers." *Cancer Epidemiology, Biomarkers & Prevention*, doi:10.1158/1055-9965.

Milroy, J. and L. Milroy. 1999. *Authority in language: Investigating standard English*. New York: Routledge.

Nelson, Larry, Margaret L. Signorella, and Karin G. Botti. 2016. "Accent, gender and perceived competence." *Hispanic Journal of Behavioral Sciences*, 38 (2): 166–185.

Omi, Michael and Howard Winant. 1994. *Racial formation in the United States: From the 1960s to the 1990s* (2nd Ed). New York: Routledge.

Parsons, Hilary. 2011. "Language and migration to the United States." *Annual Review of Anthropology*, 40: 227–240.

Pew Research Center. 2018. "More Latinos Have Serious Concerns about Their Place in America under Trump." Retrieved from https://www.pewresearch.org/hispanic/2018/10/25/latinos-and-discrimination/

Purkiss, Sharon L. S., Pamela L. Perrewé, Treena L. Gillespie, Bronston T. Mayes, and Gerald R. Ferris. 2006. "Implicit sources of bias in employment interview judgments and decisions." *Organizational Behavior and Human Decision Processes*, 101 (2): 152–167. https://doi.org/10.1016/j.obhdp.2006.06.005.

Qualtrics. 2014. "ESOMAR 28: 28 Questions to help research buyers of online samples." June 20.

Sáenz, Rogelio and Karen Manges Douglas. 2015. "A call for the racialization of immigration studies: On the transition of ethnic immigrants to racialized immigrants." *Sociology of Race and Ethnicity*, 1 (1): 166–180.

Silverstein, Michael. 1976. "Shifters, linguistic categories, and cultural description." In K. Basso and H. *Shelby* (eds.), *Meaning in anthropology*, 11–55. Albuquerque, NM: University of New Mexico Press.

———. 1996. "Monoglot 'standard' in America: Standardization and metaphors of linguistic hegemony." In D. Brenneis and RKS Macaulay (ed.), *The matrix of language: Contemporary linguistic anthropology,* 284–306. Boulder, CO: Westview.

South, Scott J., Kyle Crowder, and Erick Chavez. 2005. "Migration and spatial assimilation among U.S. Latinos: Classical versus segmented trajectories." *Demography,* 42: 497–521.

The Project of Ethnicity and Race in Latin America. 2019. https://perla.soc.ucsb.edu/about-perla

Urciuoli, Bonnie. 2001. "The complex diversity of language in the United States." In I. Susser and T.C. Patterson (eds.), *Cultural diversity in the United States: A critical reader*. Oxford, UK: Blackwell Publishing.

———. 2013. *Exposing prejudice: Puerto Rican experiences of language, race, and class*. Long Grove, IL: Waveland Press.

U.S. Census Bureau. 2017. "American Community Survey (ACS) 1-Year Estimates." *Selected Population Profiles*. Retrieved from https://centropr.hunter.cuny.edu/research/data-center/selected-population-profiles

Valdez, Zulema and Tanya Golash-Boza. 2017. "US racial and ethnic relations in the twenty-first century." *Ethnic and Racial Studies*, 40 (13): 2181–2209.

Velez, William and Giovani Burgos. 2010. "The impact of housing segregation and structural factors on the socioeconomic performance of Puerto Ricans in the United States." *Centro: Journal of the Center for Puerto Rican Studies*, 22 (1), 174–197.

Waldinger, Roger and Cynthia Feliciano. 2004. "Will the new second generation experience 'downward assimilation'? Segmented assimilation re-assessed." *Ethnic and Racial Studies,* 27 (3): 376–402.

Waters, Mary C. 1999. *Black identities: West Indian immigrant dreams and American realities*. Cambridge, MA: Harvard University Press.

Winders, Jamie. 2005. "Changing politics of race and region: Latino migration to the US south." *Progress in Human Geography*, 29 (6), 683–699.

Zentella, Ana Celia. 2014. "TWB (Talking while Bilingual): Linguistic profiling of Latina/os, and other linguistic *torquemadas*." *Latino Studies*, 12: 620–635.

Zhang, Wei, Seunghye Hong, David T. Takeuchi, and Krysia N. Mossakowski. 2012. "Limited English proficiency and psychological distress among Latinos and Asian Americans." *Social Science Medicine*, 75 (6): 1006–1014. doi:10.1016/j.socscimed.2012.05.012.

Chapter 7

Blanqueamiento Dreams, Trigueño Myths, Refusal of Blackness

Michelle F. Ramos Pellicia and Sharon Elise

> *Forgive my silence but I can't even believe this is still happening...I was always taught that we are all the same...I swear it hurts! It hurts to know that people are still being killed because of the color of their skin. Living in a world like this none of us can breathe! ...Don't stop the fight. Don't lower your fists. I remember the white boy with the "bad hair," that's what they would say...*
>
> (from Bad Bunny, "Perdonen," 2020)

Introduction

Increasing numbers of his compatriots are joining the popular Puerto Rican rapper, singer, and songwriter Bad Bunny in extolling Blackness and criticizing racism, along with misogyny and homophobia. Bad Bunny explicitly takes the position of cultural critic alongside other artists, writers, and performers to contest Puertorriqueño culture where it is silent on racism. When critical artists like Bad Bunny take a stance like this, risking celebrity for principles, they are performing an exorcism of colonialism, white supremacy, and heteropatriarchy. Given his explicit condemnation of racism, Bad Bunny is part of the growing tide of radical artists who break from the blanqueamiento vision idealizing whiteness and from a false claim of racial harmony.

Why does this matter? If we are at all concerned with the outcome of the white supremacist project of colonialism born 500 years ago in the Caribbean, we must attend to the ways that everyday people dialogue with race and white supremacy, whether to contest it, to hide it, or to deny it. If we long for racial harmony, we must attend to racial justice.

These issues of racial justice are embedded in our everyday speech and social interactions, in everyday references to certain kinds of bodies that are found in everyday cultural representations. Puerto Rico represents an ideal location for exploration of these issues and practices given its long history of colonialism, its self-identification as racially harmonious, and its more recent engagements with Black identity movements. For scholars of linguistics and race, Puertorriqueño culture offers an opportunity to witness the myriad turns and twists of race, culture, and identity that are the legacy of colonialism and

DOI: 10.4324/9781003257509-11

imperialism. We are interested in how everyday people situate themselves in this conundrum and what that means for social justice. When we "read" language and representation, we can discern how people encode their beliefs about race into language and further, even how they create race as they speak. In the process of language, ideals are re/created, recast, and reinforced that tell us what is beautiful and what is ugly, what is acceptable and what is scorned, what is valued, and what shall be cast aside.

In this chapter, we unpack racial meanings in Puertorriqueño discourses from a variety of sources—popular, public, and private—to see what these can tell us about how race is understood and practiced in Puerto Rican culture. We consider the social context of talk in which bodies are referenced as racial to understand what this says about racial hierarchies in Puerto Rico. We consider the cultural and interactional context, as well as whether the subject of race is introduced through a formal interview process or whether racial meanings are produced through everyday talk or public discourses. Our analysis reveals silence on systemic racism—interview subjects did not want to talk about race or racism. As researchers, when we pushed people to talk about race, they were very resistant and even, at times, angry with us forcing them to take a position because they were pushed from their comfort zone. Further, if we said racism exists, they often denied it and issued forth a series of arguments to contest it.

In our ethnographic work, we found a discourse on Puerto Rican society and culture that routinely characterizes Puerto Rico as a racial melting pot of three groups, Taíno (indigenous), African (Black), and Spanish (white). We also witnessed a wide vocabulary of words that reference Black racial identity in derogatory ways while leaving whiteness unmarked. We examine these formal and informal conversations to illustrate their negative valuation of Blacks and Blackness, white supremacist culture, and racial polarity in Puerto Rican society. But Puerto Ricans do not generally acknowledge the poles of race and instead prefer to situate themselves as "trigueño"—a celebrated hybrid identity that signals racial harmony based on equal appreciation of all three parts of the indigenous-white-Black narrative, with the (supposedly extinct) indigenous Taíno (or *indio*) identity recasting many signs of non-whiteness as *indio* rather than Black heritage.

Despite this verbal allegiance to hybridity, there remains a polarity with whiteness and Blackness at the extremes. The designation of Black bodies and various physical features (hair, skin, lips) and social features (laziness, welfare dependency, unwed motherhood, hypersexuality, criminality) named to mark Blackness establish it as deviant from a racial norm that remains unmarked—whiteness. This leaves the preferred identity, the *Trigueño mixture of Spanish, Taino/Indigenous, and African*, to be venerated but marked only when speakers are forced to perform a racial identification. In this scenario, played out repeatedly in our research, Trigueño identity becomes a neutral category whose most important feature is that it is not Black.

Finally, we examine new and growing trends of a racial contest and growing Black consciousness as the Black Lives Matter Movement comes to Puerto Rico bringing new attention to Afropuertorriqueño identities and culture, affirming their existence and struggles. We argue for the need to link cultural representations to the social structure that situates racialized bodies in a hierarchy of wealth, power, and status that is also gendered, sexed, and classed.

Theoretical Framing

Raciolinguistics has strong parallels to and connections with Critical Race Theory and Black feminism. The concept of raciolinguistics developed by Rosa and Flores (see, e.g., Rosa 2019; Rosa and Flores 2017) addresses the co-construction and co-naturalization of race and language in terms of social processes that simultaneously give rise to racial classifications and to the racialized classification of language forms and practices. Like Critical Race Theory and Black Feminism, raciolinguistic analysis *centers race in discursive analyses* even when those discourses deny the significance of race. Raciolinguistic analyses reveal *and contest* racism while also advancing, as Black Feminist theory does, an *intersectional framework* that *recognizes racial oppression as co-constructed with gender/sex and other identities* (Crenshaw 1989; Collins 1990; Alim 2016). Like Critical Race Theory, raciolinguistic analysis suggests that the stories people tell in the course of our everyday social interactions, as well as narratives they offer on identity and culture, can and should be the basis for theorizing racism and discourse (Bell 2003; Alim 2016). But not all linguistic treatments of race do this work, and many are silent on how these discourses are linked to social structure, a connection strongly asserted in the work of the Puerto Rican critical race scholar and sociologist, Eduardo Bonilla-Silva (1997).

Bonilla-Silva advances a *structural theory of racism* that defines racism as the ideological apparatus for "racialized social systems," which are, in part, "structured by the placement of actors in racial categories or races" (1997:468–469). Bonilla-Silva argues that a *racialized social order* is formed "when a racial discourse is accompanied by social relations of subordination and superordination between the races" (1997:473). *Social relations are structured by race and are hierarchical,* so the race on top gets the greatest share of social goodies: wealth and income, prestigious occupations, political power, and social regard, leading to a power struggle between the races (1997:470). In Bonilla-Silva's theory, these group relations and the unequal material and ideational resources that accrue are rationalized by racism, a racial ideology that shifts as those relations shift. Bonilla-Silva (2010) argues that the prevalent racial ideology now is based on *color-blindness.* This ideology centers on the notion that *race no longer matters.*

Raciolinguist analysis can offer a cultural criticism of how discourses create and reproduce race in society in ways explicitly tied to structural racism per Bonilla-Silva (1997). They thus offer an important intervention in earlier linguistic scholarship that often ignored the role of culture and language in racial reproduction. Many works by sociolinguists and linguistic anthropologists on which current raciolinguistic scholarship builds have examined the relationship between race and discourse, and the ways in which languages and language users are racialized, for example with the *racialization of Spanish and Spanish speakers* in U.S. society, where racial meanings have been attached to Spanish speakers (e.g., assumptions of their ethnicity and citizenship status); see for example work by Zentella (1997), Urciuoli (1996), Santa Ana (2002), and Hill (2008). Given the multi-racial and multi-ethnic identities of Spanish speakers, it is important to note their social context in societies that privilege whiteness and derogate Blackness whether in the United States, Mexico, Central and South America, or in the Caribbean. "Hispanic" is a category of identity in the U.S. context, but as U.S. Census questions reveal, it is composed of multiple races. In this work, we go inside the "box" of "Hispanic" identity or, as we prefer, Latinx—in our case, examining Puertorriqueños—to look at racialization in discourse with a focus on whiteness and Blackness.

Hudley et al. (2020) advocate the importance of an interdisciplinary raciolinguistic scholarship to examine race and racism in language by drawing on sociology and critical race studies. They see language as central to theorizing race and argue that more traditionally formal linguistic models are seldom informed by race theories. They propose linguists draw from work that centers race to engage critically with race and challenge racism, particularly work by scholars of color who "have been at the forefront of theorizing race and racism, often in ways of direct relevance to linguistics" (2020:7). They argue further that, "whether acknowledged or not, race is central, not peripheral or irrelevant, to every aspect of academic knowledge" (2020:12). They call for sociologists and linguists to study the role of language in racialization, rhetoric, bias, discrimination, and microaggressions throughout society along with racial discourse and the role of language in activism around racial equity (2020:21). We engage raciolinguistics and critical race studies through an analysis of Puertorriqueño discourses below.

Research Findings

We draw from ethnographic work—participatory observations, formal and informal interviews—to examine, following Hudley et al. (2020), *how race is invoked in everyday discourse* in Puerto Rico and in the processes through which Blackness and Black people are often disparaged. Yet, this hegemonic discourse also regularly invokes a critique of upper-class elites. A rhetoric of race rationalizes and rarely contests social relations and ideals based on white supremacy while contesting class relations. These practices exist within a nationalist discourse, also hegemonic, that celebrates and gives allegiance to Puerto Rican identities while eschewing race and denying racism. Except for those prepared to flee the island for the U.S. mainland, joining the mighty stream of the Caribbean's greatest export—its people—most individuals situate themselves in a discourse of Puerto Rican pride and devotion to the island, its people and culture. Speaking Spanish, not English, is central to Puerto Ricans' allegiance to their culture.

We pursue this analysis along three lines: the "slippery semantics" of supposedly colorblind discourse; the ways in which discourse involving reference to races pose challenges to Grice's principles of cooperation and politeness which, we argue, are premised on idealized speaker groups divorced from real-world structures of inequality; and the large number and a wide variety of terms in everyday discourse that highlight the marked nature of Blackness.

A Colorblind Racism Discourse and "Slippery Semantics"

The most prevalent discourse on race that emerged from our ethnographic work echoes what Bonilla-Silva has theorized as colorblind racism. This form of racism is more covert than overt, where racism is coded/hidden in discourse. *Colorblind racism insists that there is no racism*, that "we are all Americans," or in this case, "we are all Puertorriqueños," and inequalities are solely based on economics. There is a taboo against calling attention to race because "race doesn't matter;" to call attention to it makes it matter. The discourse contains contradictions; it is transgressive in rendering a negative view of elites but complacent in casting the poor through a deficit lens based on a "culture of poverty" mindset that says the culture of the poor, especially the Black poor, is to blame for their poverty. Though the discourse suggests race doesn't matter, it links Blackness to poverty. A central feature is the treatment Blackness receives in this discourse: disparaged, dehumanized, and objectified.

Godreau's (2008) concept of *"slippery semantics"* parallels Bonilla-Silva's discussion of colorblind racism discourse, where people are reluctant to acknowledge a white supremacist racial hierarchy and therefore their *racial designations and realities are not often specified* in accordance with that hierarchy. Instead, their discourses on race are "slippery"—imprecise and scattered, marked by hesitations, stuttering, pregnant pauses, and multiple assignations of racial terminology to describe the same body. Godreau uses the concept of "slippery semantics" to address how *social context alters the ways that people are willing or unwilling to mark someone as Black*: such marking is considered rude as Blackness is undesirable. However, this does not address racial hierarchy or prove racially harmonious. Similarly, colorblind racism as a discourse hides the reality of white supremacy in favor of a seemingly polite discourse. In this polite discourse, it is rude to mark people, systems, or behaviors as racialized or racist, and instead asserts the myth of meritocracy.

There is another practice perhaps related to "slippery semantics" where racism is displaced as something "over there" somewhere, along with Blackness. "Oh, you want to study Blacks," says a person (who looks Black to me), "well you should go to Loiza. You should go to Carolina." This statement denies the Blackness of people who do not reside in Loiza or Carolina, as well as denying the Blackness of the speaker and their racial experiences. It is also funny because people in Carolina would tell us to go to Loiza if we want to study Blackness, as though they didn't realize people outside Carolina locate Blackness there.

Black communities "over there" are described by many as places "you don't want to go" because they are seen as crime ridden and unsafe. In this discourse, the problem of anti-Black racism is unnamed even though it is obvious to those with a critical eye. As Godreau similarly argues in her intersectional analysis, this discourse intersects race with class and social standing. Class is merged with race in the thesis that those who are poorest are so because they are lazy and don't want to work hard for Puerto Rico, or because they have too many babies by different men and just want the government to pay. This racial coding of Blackness is endemic to colorblind racism and apparent in the "slippery semantics" of everyday discourse in Puerto Rico.

Nevertheless, *Puerto Rican society is racially stratified* such that inequality is still largely structured by race. Blacks sit at the bottom of the socioeconomic ladder and are absent, except in token numbers, in seats of power and in the public face presented to tourists save that which is folklorized as a quaint relic of the past. In reality, race is central to Puerto Rican identity and culture and the society is racialized despite the denial of "doing race" and practicing racism. Related to this is the insistence that Puerto Rico is a hybrid society, a success story for assimilation as a *trigueño melting pot*.

Many Puertorriqueños we spoke with are vehement that they do not have races and everyone is equal, and that to talk about race is problematic. This sentiment is shared among low-level workers and shop owners, among gay and straight, among people who are dark skinned and people who are light:

> "*Aquí no hay raza; todos somos iguales. No hay negros, ni blancos. Todos somos Puertorriqueños.*"
>
> "Here there are no races, everyone is equal. Here there are no Blacks, no whites. We are all Puerto Ricans."

Below we see a refinement of this argument, where people insist that each heritage, not just Spanish, has value in Puerto Rico, race—Black or white—doesn't matter here, and there is no racism. As we pushed people to speak on race and racism, they became emotional, either strident, voices raised, or hesitant and stammering, stuttering their replies as described in the works of Bonilla-Silva (2010) and Godreau (2008). Notice how *Indian* mediates *African* and *Spanish*, making each a piece of "heritage," part of the past, so that "Black" and "white" are not faced directly in the present:

> I know someone who looked in his family tree and found out that his grandpa was a Spaniard and I say that's bullshit because you and I are the same...but if I have to remind the person where they come from, you don't know that you're a Spaniard

between all of this until now, there were Africans and Indians on this island so
you don't know if that Spaniard had any relations with Africans or Indians so
you cannot say that because of that, it doesn't mean that because your grandpa is
Spaniard everything else has not value and that is why we are Puerto Ricans, our
history has value…

Related to this is the notion that *class matters, not a race*. From the café owner
to the machinist to hotel and shop workers, it is the work ethic that defines
identity as well as being Puerto Rican for nearly everyone we talked with.
Many said one's treatment is based on whether they "have money" not on race.
Working-class values of humility, honesty, and hard work are praised and contrasted to those who take money from the government, who are looked down
upon. They also contest the elitism of the affluent classes and related snobbery:

Everybody is treated the same, because what I've seen, everybody is treated the same,
who is treated well is the people who have money, the people on the top, us who are
here, who have to work, we are not going to be treated the same, but people who
have money are going to pay for the services and those of us who don't have money,
we have to bust our asses off…
    {T}he people who are lower, lower, lower, {are} the person who is not working,
who lives by the support of the government.

Some render a class/race analysis that says race only matters to the upper classes,
one that further underscores the class antagonism we observed among working-class people that valorizes the collaborative relations they profess among
working-class people.

We have prejudices, prejudices do exist here like in any other place—racism, not
as much. But there is racism in the upper social classes. In the working class there
is prejudice but there is no racism as it exists in the United States but in the upper
and middle classes there is racism.

In addition to situating racism in the affluent classes, in the cases below, we
also see a conflation of white attributes with affluent class standing among
some of the same people who earlier extolled the racelessness of Puerto Rico.
Some even equate class and intermarriage:

For the working class the main goal is to find a job and to achieve that goal you
have to help each other so race is not a priority.…there's not so much prejudice in the
working class—our goal is help other…but up there, when they already achieve,
when they have the money, what matters is to make those family connections, become
related to people who are white with blue eyes.
    If you like a prieto (a colored person) and he has dough you marry him. If not
you don't marry him.

This is a contradictory discourse on race that denies racialization and racism in Puerto Rico while averring that race and class are interrelated and hierarchical with whiteness on top. Pushed to discuss racism, most insisted, again stridently, there is no racism in Puerto Rico, but you can see racism in other places like the United States, Cuba, and the Dominican Republic:

> *I think everybody here, white, black, bad hair, I don't see that racism, that discrimination among Puerto Ricans and I work with many people in different towns and I don't see it that way. And I have met Cubans who are racist, with Puerto Ricans, with blacks with whites!*

The speaker above decries the existence of racism in Puerto Rico but associates "bad hair" with Blackness, displaying anti-Black racism while arguing racism is "over there," not in Puerto Rico. When I ask him who is Black in Puerto Rico, he replies, "everyone." Asked who is white in Puerto Rico, he again replies, "everyone."

So, what is the problem with this discourse? The silencing of racism is a discursive strategy that maintains the status quo of a racialized society that privileges whiteness. This is a preemptive strike against anti-racism and social justice activism, delegitimizing protests and silencing testimonials on experiences of anti-Black racism. Those who self-describe as Afropuertorriqueño are resisting just by proclaiming that identity. The hegemonic denial of race and racism means their lived experiences are hidden just as Afropuertorriqueño perspectives are erased.

This practice is symbolized in a well-known poem *¿Y Tu Agüela, Aonde Ejtá?*—"And Yo Granma, Where She At?"—rendered in a vernacular Black Spanish to reference the commonly shared African heritage that is the "skeleton in the closet" or, in this case, the grandmother in the kitchen (Vizcarrondo, www.elboricua.com/Poem_Y%20tu%20abuela.html).

> *"yesterday you called me black/today I'm answerin' back"...You say my bubba-lips big, that my kinks high yella red, for lord sakes, why 'ont you tell me 'bout yo granma, where she at?" "Yo whiteness ain't but veneer...hopin none knows to invoke who's yo momma's momma dear?*
>
> *Ayé me dijite negro/Y hoy te boy a contejtá...¿Disej que mi*
> *bemba ej grande Y mi pasa colorá? Pero dijme, por la binge,*
> *¿Y tu agüela, aonde ejtá? Erej blanquito enchapao ...*
> *Temiendo que se conojca La mamá de tu mamá.*

The poem references the Black grandmother, who is out of sight and working in the kitchen just as the commonly shared African heritage on the island, is to be kept out of sight, a shameful family secret. The poem's protagonist is basically asking, "who are you to call me Black?" because "there is blackness in you too" and "you" refers to those who call others Black without seeing their own African heritage. They too have a Black grandmother and Black/African roots they are denying. Unlike them, the protagonist keeps their own Black grandmother "in the living room," in a place of pride, suggesting that is how African/Black heritage ought to be treated.

Performing Politeness

Puerto Rican speakers don't just avoid noticing their Black/African heritage; they also avoid issues related to race in conversations and explain this, if asked, as not being rude or as an act of politeness. This attention to politeness is addressed by two principles developed by Grice (1975 and 1989): the Cooperative Principle and the Politeness Principle.

Grice's (1975) Cooperative Principle (CP) is that you say what you mean; the hearer needs to understand two levels of meaning from the speaker, the level of expressed meaning and the level of implied meaning. In other words, there should be no hidden message that needs decoding. Conversations need to be an "effective exchange of information" (Grice, 1989: 28), so there is some level of common agreement between conversationalists to meet this need. Speakers adhere to this principle in conversation, recognize common aims, and ways of achieving them.

The Politeness Principle minimizes the use of impolite beliefs and maximizes the use of polite beliefs (Leech 1983:81). This principle is an extension of Grice's Cooperation Principle. The speaker chooses phrasings to satisfy the politeness principle based on assumptions about the hearer and the social context, to conform to a principle that serves the aim of meeting a standard that defines politeness.

We contest whether these two principles really do operate. There do seem to be hidden messages, and the principle of politeness ignores what happens when the race is part of the conversation/discourse. Proclaiming a principle without attention to how the speaker's standpoint and social context raise consequences for adherence to said principle is problematic. In the context of racial hierarchy, it means that politeness speech acts are defined based on what is considered acceptable to white speakers, and ignoring what may be offensive to Black speakers, and ignoring the whole question/issue of race.

In interrogating these principles, we raise the question of standpoint. We challenge the Politeness Principle since the neutral standpoint of politeness reifies whiteness.

Critical race theorists argue for recognition of the centrality and persistence of racism and white supremacy. It follows then, that there can be no universal principles or laws of human behavior that elide consideration of racial realities. When theorists consider politeness, from whose perspective is this politeness defined? What is the lens used? If it is polite for you to ignore my Blackness, must I join you in my subjugation? And if it is polite to you, when we speak, to avoid any conversation on white supremacy or racism, how does that help me in my project to advance my freedom and self-determination? Politeness rules silence resistance to everyday oppression, providing cover to practices that maintain white privilege. How can we lay rules for discourse that ignore status in social interactions? We need to use a different lens and expand the scope of our analysis to truly include Black speakers' experience when studying language use.

In the ideal world imagined by linguistic theorists who ignore social history and structure, speakers engage in conversation that follows (or doesn't) expectations or maxims. When rules for politeness are not followed, speakers lose face. However, it is important to note that there are reasons to violate these expectations in service of a higher purpose. For instance, speakers may engage in an exchange where direct speech and impoliteness as a speech act are needed to explicitly express views that contest racism and white supremacy. Theorists who ignore the world in which language is embedded do not concern themselves with an evaluation of speech based on its impact on social justice. And they should. At the same time, these conventions, or principles, help us understand people's responses to how we regularly break with them, committing daily acts of rudeness about race and racism.

Lexical Performances of Anti-Blackness in Everyday Language

It is interesting that, even as there is a common avoidance of talk about race to follow politeness conventions among most Puertorriqueños, there are many terms to reference Blackness. The wealth of words about Black bodies suggest Blackness plays a significant role in Puerto Rican culture and identity. Language is weaponized against Black people through linguistic maneuvers that render them negatively, as illustrated in the following tables.

We concentrate on how Blackness is described by decoding lexical items following Wheeler's proposal (2015) that people base their choice of words on a prototype. We argue that the prototype that Puertorriqueños use is a non-marked white model. We base this proposition on the evidence presented in the previous sections. Puertorriqueños base their race ideas on a white supremacist model that does not see race yet promotes *blanqueamiento, a process and an ideal of whitening.* In the construction of race through language, we observe a variety of lexical strategies to designate the salient/marked race that is not white versus the unmarked "standard" or neutral race.

Nouns refer to feelings, people, and objects. In Puerto Rican discourse, several nouns reference Black people and Blackness. *Mono* or "monkey" is used to refer to Blacks. The name also references Mono Yuyo, a famous chimpanzee (https://www.youtube.com/watch?v=3XkZHDT9tUc) in Puerto Rico who died in 2012, whose name is used to refer to Black men in Puerto Rico. This reference ascribes the untamed characteristics of an animal to a Black human being.

Puertorriqueños discourage the use of *Negro* or "Black" to reference people because of its negative, pejorative, and dehumanizing connotation. *Negro* is a bad word, to be avoided, replaced instead with: *una persona de color,* a term which erases Black people, Blackness, and the Black experience. The ideology behind the avoidance through the use of euphemisms and silences needs to be contested. Blackness in and of itself is not demeaning, it is the white supremacist social context that conjures this interpretation. The lexical item *Negro* is allowed, however, in a context where the noun is qualified by an adjective, as we will see in the following paragraphs.

Puertorriqueños also use a *nouns + adjectives construction* which means a description is offered along with the person, object, or feeling. Our data includes expressions where the nouns *negro* and *pelo* (hair) are paired with adjectives that qualify the noun negatively. These include: *negro africano* (African Black), *negra loca* (crazy Black woman), *negra bembona* (big lipped Black woman), *negra pasúa* (Black woman with bad hair), and *negro carbon* (charcoal Black). These constructions adjectivize the word *negro*, which normally describes skin color, but in these cases, a Black person is defined by their skin color. Another adjective used to describe the noun refers to the continent of origin, Africa, which displaces the Black person. If one is Black, one is from somewhere else—*otro planeta* (another planet) or another town like Loíza, Carolina, Santurce, Barrio Antón—not from "here," the place where the speaker is. Still, other descriptive adjectives, as we see above, refer to mental state, behavior, as well as physical traits like skin color, lips, and hair.

Mintz (1956) argues that Black hair has been given "more (mostly demeaning) names than any other racialized body part" and this is apparent in Puerto Rican discourse. The noun *pasas* (raisins), normally referencing a dried fruit, is used to refer to Black hair texture as in *Tienes que peinarte las pasas* (you need to comb your messy hair) and denotes the quality of Black hair negatively vs. white or *lacio* (good) hair. Black hair needs an adjective because it varies from the white standard, so it must be marked as bad, *pelo malo*, as rough, *pelo grifo*, as kinky and wild, *pelo kinky*, and like a broom, *pelo de escoba*. By extension, the Black woman who has Black hair is described by her hair texture: *negra pasúa*, a messy-haired Black woman. *Arreglarte el pelo* (meaning "fix your hair") refers to Black hair that is characterized as unkempt, uncombed, and unprofessional in its natural state.

We also hear Black people described in terms of their lips and how they speak, *bembe trueno*—big lips, loud voice (loud as thunder). Using *bembe* is racially coded to reference Black lips as white lips do not need to be defined, they are the norm. And they are never big.

Bonilla Silva (2010:66) describes how "whites rely on diminutives to soften their racial blow" such as "I am just a little bit against affirmative action," instead of directly stating: "I am against affirmative action." As Hudley et al. (2020:21) suggest, we consider this a microaggression. Reinat-Pumarejo (2013) from Colectivo Ilé activists describes the use of diminutives as *racismo afectivo* where terms of endearment are racially coded and Black bodies are objects of possession. Following this interpretation, the following expressions with the diminutive suffix—*negrito* (Black boy), *el negrito* (the Black boy), *mi negrita linda* (my cute Black girl), *Es negrita pero es buena* (she is a Black girl but nice)—considered expressions of affection, in fact, diminish the personhood of Black people (reinforced by *pero* in the last example). Further, when used in combination with the possessive adjective "mi," they convey possession of a diminished/little Black, and reproduce notions of subjugation through bondage or enslavement. Similar expressions are: *Ay, mi negro lindo* (oh, my cute Black boy) or *mi negra chula* (my cute Black girl), which also minimalize Black people as "cute."

Adjectives are sometimes used as nouns, where the person becomes their race instead of their name. The characteristics of an individual are nominalized, underscoring the marked/salient race, denying personhood: *negro* (Black), *prieto* (dark/Black), *jabao* (yellow), *betún* (Black as shoe polish) and *cafre, cafrerías* (Kafir, a South African slur similar to the n-word) among too many other expressions (see Tables 7.1 and 7.2).

This is a small sample of how Puerto Rican usage of "slippery semantics" following principles of politeness still dehumanizes Black people. It is common for expressions that describe actions and qualities of Black people to use a pejorative lens: *¡qué cafre!*, What a Kafir! (slur comparable to the n-word) *esas cafrerías que dice*, the Kafir things they say! *voluntariosa* She acts like she is free! Similarly, expressions such as *negra acomplejá* (a Black woman with a complex), *parejera* are used to describe the so-called "angry Black Woman," and to decry women who are vocal about defending their rights. More recently, a political analyst even used the "n-word" on the radio to protest the removal of the puppet "La Comay" that many critics promulgated stereotypes, racism, and misogyny. In this case, people broke the taboo against using English to use this racial slur.

Reclaiming Blackness: An Anti-Racism Discourse

Despite the pandemic that brought curfews and quarantine to the island, Borikuas took to the streets in huge numbers to support the Black Lives Matter Movement and protest the police lynching of George Floyd. They echo protests on the mainland in calling attention to structural racism, white supremacy, and police brutality against Black Puertorriqueños. These conversations in Puerto Rico are not new, like the questioning of the racist language. However, the lynchings of George Floyd, Ahmaud Arbery, and Breonna Taylor have brought conversations on anti-Black racism to Puerto Rico. In Loiza, marked in everyday discourse as a Black space, protestors simultaneously called attention to George Floyd and to Adolfina Villanueva, a young mother of six who was shot to death by Puerto Rican police during an eviction in 1980 (Leandra 2020). News stories featured protestors who echoed the criticisms lodged in this paper: the covert racism hidden in a trigueño mythology that decries its African roots, negative judgments of Black hair and skin, positive valuations of white features, and diminutive characterizations of Afropuertorriqueños.

Table 7.1 Words to describe Black people

Nouns	Diminutives/racismo affectivo	Nouns + adjectives	Possessives	Expressions
Negra, -o Black	Negrita, -o Little Black	Negra, -o Africana, -o Black African	Mi negra, -o Mi negrita, -ito My little Black Ay, mi negra, -o linda, -o, o or mi negrita, -o chula, -o Oh, my beautiful little Black; my cute little Black	Es negrita, pero es buena. She is a little Black woman, but she is nice/good
La, el negra,-o, Black woman	La, el negrita, -ito The Black girl	Negro chazuli A dark Black person Negra loca Crazy Black woman Negro carbón Black charcoal		Negro, -a de África Black from Africa negro como la noche Black as the night
Mono Monkey (las) pasas (the) messy hair	Monito Little monkey	Negra pasúa A messy haired Black Woman	Mi monito My little monkey	Mono Yuyo Yuyo, the Monkey Tienes que peinarte las pasas You have to comb your messy hair
Grifa A Black woman with rough hair		Pelo grifo Rough hair pelo de escoba, mapo hair like broom/broom hair hair like mop/mop hair Pelo kinky Kinky hair Pelo malo Bad hair		Arréglate el pelo. Fix your hair Ese pelo no se ve profesional That hair does not look professional

Table 7.2 Characteristics of Black people

Nouns	Diminutives/racismo affectivo	Nouns + adjectives	Possessives	Expressions
Bembes Big lips Bembe also an African ethnic group	Bembe trueno Big lipped and loud	Negra, -o bembona, bembón Black woman/man with big lips		El bembé Big loud party Se formó el bembé The (big loud) party has started
Jabao Yellowish		Negro jabao Yellowish Black		De color Of color Mujer, hombre de color Woman, man of color
Cafre A slur from South Africa analogous to the "n- word"		Negro cafre		¡qué cafre! ¡Esas cafrerías que dice!
Prieta, -o Black	Prietita, -o Black girl, boy		Mi prietita, -o My Black girl, boy	Mi prietita, -o linda, -o My cute Black girl, boy
Nalgona, nalgón Big butt				El nalguero The big butt ¡qué nalguero! What a big butt!
Betún Black as shoe polish				
Voluntariosa, -o She/he acts like she/he is free!	Negra, -o acomplejá, -o Black person with a complex			
Parejera, -o Sassy or cocky				

We have presented an analysis of how Puertorriqueños use language to construct a discourse that denies race and anti-Black racism. It is important to also call attention to people who question these practices and reappropriate language to ascribe positive characteristics to Blackness in Puerto Rico. Activists suggest new ways to address Blackness: *prietagonismo* (centering Blackness), use of the phrase *Blanca Maldad* (whiteness as bad) in the patriotic song "Preciosa"; eliminating the word *negroide* (Negroid, a term describing race as biological) to describe Black literature and other Black cultural expressions. They use *blancoide* to racialize white cultural expressions, question the need to talk about Black literature unless it is used to visibilize *literatura negrista* o *literatura negra*, not the racializing designation *literatura negroide*. In a recent (2020) panel presentation for the Universidad de Puerto Rico in Carolina, the writer Yolanda Arroyo Pizarro argued for replacing expressions like *pelo malo* with phrases that promote Black pride: *Mi pelo malo se porta bien; no hace travesuras. No se porta mal.* Translated, this means: my "bad" hair behaves just fine, it is not misbehaving, there is nothing wrong with it.

Conclusion

We have demonstrated that everyday discourse in Puerto Rico is complex, fraught with imprecision and "slippery semantics" wherein explicit renunciations of racism are silenced. Puerto Rico is presented as a racially harmonious and blended society and identities are presented as "mixed" and multiple—trigueño–or white, but seldom Black. Yet, as we have also shown, the language of everyday speakers is weaponized against Black people and Blackness. Language overtly and covertly attacks Blackness within a discourse that allows Puerto Ricans to deny everyday racist ideologies while upholding notions that only lazy people are poor and that a social welfare system to alleviate poverty only makes them more lazy. Our work calls attention to these linguistic practices that erase and degrade Blacks and Blackness in Puerto Rican society, reproducing ideologies that support structural racism and rationalize the place of Afropuertorriqueños at the bottom of society in wealth, power, status, and well-being. We hope that by calling attention to the ways language and everyday discourses reproduce and construct anti-Black racism, we can amplify awareness and resistance.

If ever there was a time to thrust aside notions of being post-racial that were elevated and rationalized with the Obama election, this is it! No more denials of racism here, there, everywhere as the recent police lynching of George Floyd fuels the Black Lives Matter Movement and the movement goes global; systemic racism and anti-Black racism are exposed. White supremacy and systemic racism function best amidst silence on race; hence the taboo against a racial discourse retards the struggle for racial justice and Black upliftment. To proclaim and contest white supremacy is "speaking truth to power;" this is calling out the naked emperor, this is resurrecting our African ancestry and DuBois' pan Africanism. Even in Puerto Rico, the whitest of the Antilles, where so many dreams, claim, and chase whiteness and mythologize the island as yielding hybrid identities and racial harmony, it is time to recognize. It is time to be boldly Black, to listen to the drum, to "call out" the police, to bring your grandmother out of the kitchen and stand her on the balcony for everyone to see your connection to Blackness. For too long, Puerto Ricans have been chasing blanqueamiento, insistent on a trigueño identity that denies the specificity of Black identity, culture, and social conditions.

References

Alim, H. Samy. 2016. "Introducing Raciolinguistics: Racing Language and Languaging Race in Hyperracial Times." In: H. Samy Alim, John R. Rickford, Arnetha F. Ball (eds). *Raciolinguistics. How Language Shapes our Ideas about Race.* Oxford, New York pp. 7–8.

Bell, Lee Anne. 2003. "Telling Tales: What Stories Can Teach Us About Racism." *Race Ethnicity and Education*, Vol. 6, No. 1: 3–28.

Bonilla-Silva, Eduardo. 1997. "Rethinking Racism: Toward a Structural Interpretation." *American Sociological Review*, Vol. 62: 465–480.

Bonilla-Silva, Eduardo. 2010. *Racism without Racists: Color-Blind Racism and the Persistence of Racial Inequality in the United States.* New York: Rowman and Littlefield Publishers, Inc., Third Edition.

Collins, Patricia Hill. 1990. *Black Feminist Thought: Knowledge, Consciousness, and the Politics of Empowerment.* Boston: Unwin Hyman.

Crenshaw, Kimberle. 1989. "Demarginalizing the Intersection of Race and Sex: A Black Feminist Critique of Antidiscrimination Doctrine, Feminist Theory and Antiracist Politics." *University of Chicago Legal Forum,* Vol. 1989, No. 1: 8.

Godreau, Isar. 2008. "Slippery Semantics: Race Talk and Everyday Uses of Racial Terminology in Puerto Rico. *Centro Journal,* Vol. 20: 5–33.

Grice, H.P. 1975. "Logic and Conversation," In: P. Cole and J. Morgan (eds). *Syntax and Semantics: Speech Acts 3.* New York: Academic Press.

Grice, H.P. 1989. *Studies in the Way of Words.* Cambridge, MA: Harvard University Press.

Hill, Jane. 2008.*The Everyday Language of White Racism.* Malden, MA: Wiley Blackwell.

Hudley, Anne H. Charity, Christine Mallinson, and Mary Bucholtz. 2018. "Toward Racial Justice in Linguistics: Interdisciplinary Insights into Theorizing Race in the Discipline and Diversifying the Profession" *Proceedings of the Linguistics Society of America.* Retrieved June 20, 2020. https://www.linguisticsociety.org/news/2018/03/07/third-volume-proceedings-lsa-published

Leandra, Victoria. 2020. "How Loiza, Puerto Rico Became One of the First Latin American Cities to Join the George Floyd Protests," *Remezcla.com* 6.03.2020. https://remezcla.com/culture/puerto-rico-protests-loiza-george-floyd-black-lives-matter/

Leech, G. 1983. *Principles of Pragmatics.* London: Longman.

Mintz, Sidney. 1956. "Cañamela: The Subculture of a Rural Sugar Plantation Proletariat," In: Julian H. Steward et al. (eds). *The People of Puerto Rico: A Study in Social Anthropology.* Urbana: University of Illinois.

Reinat-Pumarejo, María. 2013. "El querer queriendo del racism lingüístico." Colectivo Ilé. http://colectivo-ile.org/?p=486

Rosa, Jonathan. 2019. *Looking like a Language, Sounding like a Race. Raciolinguistic Ideologies and the Learning of Latinidad*. New York: Oxford University Press.

Rosa, Jonathan, and Flores, Nelson. 2017. "Unsettling race and language. Towards a raciolinguistic perspective." *Language in Society*, Vol. 46, No. 5: November 2017.

Santa Ana, Otto. 2002. *Brown Tide Rising: Metaphors of Latinos in Contemporary American Public Discourse*. Austin: University of Texas Press.

Urciuoli, Bonnie. 1996. *Exposing Prejudice: Puerto Rican Experiences of Language, Race, and Class*. Boulder, CO: Westview.

Wheeler, Eva Michelle. 2015. (Re)Framing Raza: Language as a Lens for Examining Race and Skin Color Categories in the Dominican Republic. (Unpublished doctoral dissertation). University of California Santa Barbara.

Zentella, Ana Celia. 1997. *Growing Up Bilingual: Puerto Rican Children in New York*. Oxford And Malden, MA: Blackwell.

Section IV

Resistance

Chapter 8

The Enchantment of Language Resistance in Puerto Rico

Kevin Alejandrez and Ana S.Q. Liberato

"English has to be the principal language. There are other states with more than one language such as Hawaii but to be a state of the United States, English has to be the principal language"

(Former U.S. Senator and Republican
U.S. presidential candidate Rick Santorum, 2012)

Introduction

Puerto Rico, known as La Isla del Encanto (The Island of Enchantment), is a predominantly Spanish-speaking Caribbean island and an unincorporated commonwealth of the United States. The island has been the subject of repeated subordination since being colonized by Spain at the start of the sixteenth century. The United States still holds some level of control over the island, but it has not been without a challenge. The political project of control has always involved ideological and social policy struggles over language. The pronouncement expressed by Senator Rick Santorum in the quote above reflects a thought shared by many in American society, and also reflects the continuing political relevance of these struggles even in this early stage of the twenty-first century. This line of thought was prevalent among many American politicians throughout the twentieth century. And, given that American society has interpreted learning English as a sign of loyalty, English acquisition will continue to be taken as proof of Puerto Rican loyalty to the United States. Only then would the federal government be willing to consider granting statehood to the island and full citizenship rights to its people (Velez, 1986; Pousada, 1996; Barreto, 2000; Nickels, 2005; DuBord, 2007).

This makes clear that the linguistic social sphere represents one of the most fruitful platforms from where to gauge the nature and impacts of the United States' colonial intervention in Puerto Rico. The meaning Puerto Ricans assign to language, what they do with language, and the fact that there also is a Puerto Rican diasporic linguistic sphere are all part of the historical processes unleashed by U.S. domination. The language sphere also reveals a great deal about the construction of the self and national identity among Puerto Ricans.

DOI: 10.4324/9781003257509-13

This chapter examines past and present issues associated with linguistic struggles in the context of the island's 122 years old relationship with the United States. The chapter explores both ideological and policy dimensions of linguistic domination and resistance, particularly in the field of education. It also provides important historical background and discussions that are relevant to the topic. Our main argument is that the U.S. government systematically used Anglo-centric and ethnocentric language ideologies and policies during the first half of the twentieth century as a method of maintaining control of the colonial frontier. However, the island thwarted Americanization efforts that pushed for English-language acquisition through the preservation of its Spanish-speaking identity. While we emphasize the resistance efforts, we argue for critical explorations of the role language plays in the production and reproduction of socioeconomic inequalities on the island and the Puerto Rican diasporic sphere. Also, although we present general statements about educators, political parties, working and business class people's stances within the language debate, we do so to give the reader an idea of some of the groups that are usually emphasized in the literature. There is much nuance in the perspectives and positions of different groups of Puerto Ricans concerning English language acquisition and the meaning of language practices. We do not discuss the language ideologies and practices of Puerto Ricans outside the island (see Urciuoli, 2013 for a case study of New York bilinguals).

Language Policy: Establishing U.S. Domination

The United States established a military government in Puerto Rico on October 18, 1898, following the Spanish American War (Barreto, 2000). The federal government immediately sought "to remold Puerto Rico in its own image" based on notions of Anglo-American superiority (Barreto, 2000:5). American policymakers copied past efforts directed toward Indigenous and immigrant peoples elsewhere and imposed a heavy-handed Americanization plan aimed at indoctrinating the island's people into U.S. dominant culture (Zentella, 1982; Barreto, 2000; Mazak, 2012). The initiative included fierce political and economic policies as well as the introduction of English language policy. This policy is still affecting the island today (Language Policy Task Force, 1978; Mazak, 2012).

The Foraker Act of 1900 took political autonomy away from Puerto Rico by establishing a civilian regime overseen by the federal government. The Act gave the U.S. president the power to appoint all major government officials on the island (Language Policy Task Force, 1978; Burrows, 2014). The act's stipulations established the foundation under which economic transformation would take place. For instance, the Act enabled total U.S. control of the markets and tariffs, as well as the appropriation of land by U.S. corporations. As a result, local merchants and landowners faced restricted production and overall loss of economic power (Clachar, 1997a). The federal government actively attempted to eliminate Spanish and Anglicize the island's population between 1898 and 1900 (Clachar, 1997b:464). While such efforts were short-lived, English was declared an official language alongside Spanish in 1902 (Barreto, 2000; Nickels, 2005; Mazak, 2012). It was then that English was also mandated as the language of instruction within public schools. Between 1900 and 1949, the imposition of English was packaged as an endeavor to create a bilingual citizenry, but the ultimate aim behind its incorporation was to root the English language on the island (Clachar, 1997b; Zentella, 1982). Such policy was not up for debate. In the eyes of the federal government, it was imperative that Puerto Ricans learn English whether they wanted to or not. Indeed, constant grievances raised by Puerto Ricans resulted in multiple shifts within English language policies, but English was, nonetheless, persistently, and forcefully implemented.

Whether the United States ever had any real intention of fully integrating the island into the country is uncertain. What is clear is that the U.S. government viewed Puerto Rican assimilation into U.S. dominant culture as a beneficial way to maintain command of the territory. Control of the island has always implied economic benefits from industrial expansion, economic invest-ment, potential resource extraction, and greater access to an exploitable labor force (Meléndez, 2017). By the late 1940s, the U.S. government and American corporations began to create policies to bring Puerto Rican workers to the United States for the benefit of U.S. agriculture. The Puerto Rican govern-ment also advocated the use of Puerto Rican labor in the mainland under the argument they represented domestic rather than migrant labor (Meléndez, 2017). Symbolically, such paternalistic domination serves to uphold the ideol-ogy of American superiority, recycled to justify other manifestations of U.S. domination elsewhere. The United States actively refused the island's political autonomy and ignored its peoples' culture. Instead, the federal government used language policy to guide assimilation efforts and uphold Puerto Rican subordination. It systematically used legislation to forcefully impose English on the island insistent on creating a colony loyal to the United States. Despite such subordination, however, language policies attempting to convert Puerto Ricans into bilingual English speakers ultimately failed.

Language Ideology and Resistance in Puerto Rico

Language ideology points to the meanings attached to language and people's understandings and use of it. Language ideology influences people's sense of identity, nationality, and belonging. Because of this, language policy can operate as an identity-shaping socio-structural tool. If language policies are perceived to be legitimate, then they "can serve as a symbol of national unity, cohesion, and ideology, and as an aid to nation-state organization. Otherwise, language uniformity-driven policies may be perceived as an imposition of the norm of one class or national sector upon the others" (Language Policy Task Force, 1978:3).

Consequently, in the context of U.S. domination and English assimilation failures, what exactly do English (and Spanish for that matter) mean to Puerto Ricans? Which are their most common perspectives and beliefs? These questions fall into the language ideology realm, and their exploration leads to the understanding of Puerto Ricans' language use and collective action toward language policies.

Language Policies and Resistance in the Education Sector

Many Puerto Ricans took 50 years of imposed English promotion as illegitimate and resulted in resistance to perceived Anglo invasion. Early on, educators, politicians, and members of the upper class advocated for the dismissal of the English language (Clachar, 1997b; Nickels, 2005). The U.S. government did not take such opposition lightly and insisted on English assimilation. The persistent push of English quickly led to it becoming a symbol of U.S. imperialism. It also became a symbol of antagonism to Spanish, which increasingly grew to symbolize Puerto Rican nationalism and ethnicity. Consequently, instead of Americanizing Puerto Ricans, English helped strengthen the attachment that many Puerto Ricans had to the Spanish language (Barreto, 2000; DuBord, 2007; Mazak, 2012).

Particularly, the local elite and other social, cultural, and political social actors viewed English's seemingly antagonistic relation to Spanish as a threat to Puerto Rico's cultural identity and national integrity. They continuously challenged English language policy implemented throughout the public-school system. This made it impossible for any U.S.-appointed commissioner of education to uphold any English-only instructional policy (Velez, 1986; Pousada, 1996; Kerkhof, 2001). Programs constantly had to be restructured and no English-only instructional policy ever lasted long in the school system (Language Policy Task Force, 1978; Zentella, 1982).

Still, the United States was persistent in its efforts. For instance, Commissioner of Education, Jose Padín, was forced to resign in 1937 after designating Spanish as the medium of instruction within public schools. President Roosevelt appointed Dr. Jose M. Gallardo as the new Commissioner of Education and insisted that Puerto Rico needed to be an English-speaking territory. In 1942, the federal government declared that the island would not receive any federal aid unless Puerto Ricans used English throughout their daily lives and as the medium of instruction within the public schools (Clachar, 1997b).

One example in which educators actively defied U.S. language policy comes from the Chavez Committee. At the start of World War Two, Dennis Chavez, Senator of New Mexico, advocated for the strengthening of relationships between the United States and Latin America (Lozano 2018). Chavez along with U.S. senators Homer Bone, Allen Ellandar, Robert Taft, and Ralph Brewster conducted hearings in 1943 to examine the island's relationship with the United States. The hearings paid particular attention to English instruction in public schools. The committee insisted on English-language instruction regardless of how unpopular or unrealistic English-only instruction was (DuBord, 2007; Lozano, 2018). Educators pushed back, citing empirical evidence in favor of teaching students English through Spanish instruction. Educators also argued that public education suffered when an enormous amount of time and resources were directed toward English acquisition given that "the most critical issue in Puerto Rico was the lack of access to education" (DuBord, 2007:249).

The Chavez committee put aside the access issue and instead focused on critiquing Puerto Rican educators for not doing sufficient English instruction. The committee warned educators that the island would never achieve statehood without English acquisition. Pedro A. Cebollero, former Subcommissioner of Education, responded by stating that if maintaining Puerto Rican culture would prevent them from being integrated into the United States, then "perhaps it was necessary to pursue other political options" (DuBord, 2007:250). The committee's actions helped cement the view among educators that U.S. ideals were antagonistic to their own goals and identities. As a result, they continued to ignore the committee's recommendations and continued to instruct in Spanish (Clachar, 1997b; DuBord, 2007; Lozano, 2018).

The Truman's Veto of 1946 provided another context for further resistance. In 1945, the Puerto Rican legislature made Spanish the medium of instruction throughout public schools under Law 51, better known as *el Proyecto del Idioma*. The law, however, was vetoed by two U.S.-appointed governors. After being overturned by the legislature, it was vetoed by President Harry Truman as well. For many, the Veto was a blatant act of U.S. domination that ignored the authority of the Puerto Rican legislature (DuBord, 2007). In the short term, organized protests challenged the president's actions. There were long-held public debates on the Veto in the island. Activists used the Veto incident to spark national conversations about Puerto Rico's relationship with the United States.

The situations surrounding the Chavez Committee of 1943 and the Truman Veto of 1945 help illustrate the tribulations of the language debate in Puerto Rico. These two examples highlight ways in which the United States repeatedly utilized English language policy as a method of creating an Americanized colony compliant to its own subordination. They show constant resistance to English that led to continued policy changes and the iterative increased use of Spanish in public schools (Language Policy Task Force, 1978). By 1948, it was clear that Americanization efforts had failed, and the United States granted Puerto Rico the right to elect its own governor. In 1949, Luis Muñoz Marín, founder of the *Partido Popular Democrático* (PPD), which had been in power since 1940, became Puerto Rico's first elected governor.

As governor, Muñoz Marín appointed Mariano Villaronga as Secretary of Public Instruction on August 10, 1949. Villaronga "immediately instituted

Spanish as the medium of instruction at all levels with English taught as [a preferred subject]" (Carroll, 2016:178). The decisions made under the PPD reflected its position of embracing the supremacy of Spanish as a symbol of Puerto Rican identity while holding on to English and U.S. citizenship. In doing so, the party's ideology was nestled between a push for independence and a continued relationship with the United States (Kerkhof, 2001; DuBord, 2007).

It may seem odd to think that Puerto Ricans would elect a party that was supportive of both Spanish *and* English – a language so vehemently resisted just years earlier. However, this shows that the story of language policy in Puerto Rico – in the education sector and beyond – is much more complex than simply being about defying English as a symbolic way of resisting colonization. The history of English resistance and its connection to U.S. domination should not be downplayed. At the same time, it would be a mistake to imply that English has only been viewed negatively and always contested by the Puerto Rican people. The perspective presented thus far is simply one piece of a greater political and socioeconomic puzzle. Hence, we discuss how economic policies and political struggle have impacted distinct groups in the island to better understand the nuances of language policy.

The Complexity of Language Resistance in Puerto Rico

Class and geographic inequalities are important in understanding how Puerto Ricans made sense of and reacted to language policy. The inequality lens helps illuminate differences in their rationale for resistance. Important, too, is to remember that despite substantial gains in the expansion of education service, the U.S. political project in Puerto Rico was not successful in improving the education access problem (Angrist, Chin, and Godoy 2008:108–109):

> One American goal was to expand the public-school system [...]. The American administration set up a U.S.-style school system providing free education through 12th grade. Schooling was compulsory for those aged 8-14, though in practice the compulsory schooling law was of little consequence since many rural communities had no school offering grades beyond 4th. To increase access, spending on public education was increased from half a million to 21.4 million dollars between 1900 and 1948, while the number of public-school teachers increased from 897 to 9101. These efforts generated sizable gains in educational attainment. Individuals born 1914-23 had an average of 6.4 years of schooling, but those born 10, 20 and 30 years later had 7.9, 9.3 and 10.7 years of schooling, respectively. Much of the increase in attainment came from a shift in the distribution of years of schooling from four or fewer to more than four years. Forty-two percent of those born 1914-23 had zero to four years of schooling, compared with 29% of those born 1924-33, 16% of those born 1934-43, and 8% of those

born 1944-53. The effort to increase English proficiency proved to be at least as much of a challenge as increasing access to public education.

Puerto Ricans of rural and working-class backgrounds were already at a great disadvantage when the United States implemented these policies. They did not have access to good education to begin with, and this became a barrier to their becoming proficient in the new language being imposed upon them in public schools.

In contrast, those with class privilege were able to acquire – and in some cases expand English proficiency in their private or Catholic schools while still adopting a resistant stance. Resisting English did not mean they did not learn it or benefit from it. They were able to create linguistic boundaries around working-class Puerto Ricans who, according to elite views, were both unable and unwilling to cognitively manage bilingualism; poor Puerto Ricans could not think straight in either Spanish or English. This linguistic stigma failed to acknowledge that poor Puerto Ricans were fully proficient in the Spanish language. Indeed, the local Puerto Rican elites have historically sought English education while simultaneously opposing the English language in public schools. In fact, as English language instruction decreased in public schools, private and Catholic schools teaching English began springing up. Given the costs associated with private schools, this has mostly benefited the elite while poor and working-class students miss out on such opportunities (Kerkhof, 2001; Carroll, 2016). Migration to the United States eventually became the way to learn English for the working class.

Historical Roots of Language Resistance

At the end of the nineteenth century, agricultural and light industrial production made up a large sector of Puerto Rico's economy. Sugar, tobacco, coffee, and needlework made up the island's top four export industries (San Miguel, 2008; Burrows, 2014). Landed *hacendados* and merchant capitalists possessed significant political and economic power when the United States invaded in 1898. At the start of the twentieth century, economic policy under the Foraker Act led to greater integration of U.S. corporations on the island and transformed its economic structure into a more liberal capitalist economy. This resulted in land loss to corporate takeover (Santiago-Valles, 2007), urban growth with an increasingly proletarianized population, and a loss of power among Puerto Rican merchants and *hacendados*.

These shifts were influential in forming different stances concerning language policy. The United States, of course, favored English as a symbol of U.S. loyalty. Wanting to retain power, members of the Puerto Rican middle-class and local elite sided with the intelligentsia and adamantly opposed U.S. colonization and English language policy. The working class, however, has never held significant political or economic power, held a different position than much of the island's middle- and upper-class. On the one hand, turbulent waves in the economy led to unemployment crises among peasants and laborers. On the other hand, the working-class had also organized itself and sought economic assistance from the United States (Language Policy Task Force, 1978; Burrows, 2014). To be clear, between 1898 and the 1940s, the people of Puerto Rico carried a predominantly "nationalist, anti-colonial stance that projected both the Spanish language and Hispanic culture as the main fronts of anti-American struggle" (Language Policy Task Force, 1978:6). Still, the pro-statehood stance held by a significant segment of the island's people should not be ignored. Their political objectives, along with the fact that English has become increasingly entangled with social mobility, have made English difficult to dismiss. It becomes clear that the language debate goes beyond resistance to U.S. Americanization efforts. How people view and engage with English is also political and heavily influenced by peoples' historical socioeconomic positioning.

As mentioned earlier, educators and many middle-class and local elites believed that the imposition of English symbolized colonial domination. Possessing social and economic privilege themselves, they were against the idea of assimilating to U.S. dominant culture and becoming second-class subjects under a colonial context. In the end, educators and local elites joined other anti-imperialist groups in fighting for local autonomy. They took anything American to be anti-Puerto Rican and continuously rejected English policies. Even after obtaining commonwealth status and enjoying its own constitution in 1952, they pointed out the fact that Puerto Rican "statutes were [and are] restricted by both the U.S. Constitution and the Federal Relations Act. Despite being American citizens since 1917, they are not allowed to vote for the nation's president as long as they reside on the island. They cannot elect representatives to Congress except a resident commissioner who has no voting power on issues directly affecting the island. Puerto Ricans on the island are, therefore, strapped with all the duties of citizenship, but they are not given all the benefits of citizenship" (Clachar, 1997b:461–462).

Within this context, members of the middle and upper class have long favored complete separation from the United States and supported Spanish-only instruction. They have argued that teaching English only produces a populace that is neither fluent in English nor Spanish (Pousada 1996). But the increased integration of U.S. corporations persists, and economic shifts more broadly have made English a valuable asset in Puerto Rico. The wealthy have always been able to acquire such assets through English education, but broad English language policy threatened their monopoly of the English language. While their class standing has never been seriously threatened by poor and working-class Puerto Ricans, they may have believed otherwise. At the very least, they seem to have been concerned with maintaining a distinction between themselves and lower social classes. It could be argued that the true intentions of the local elite regarding language policy are questionable. Here, a difference arises between the defensive elite who initially lost power because of U.S. policies and those who never had any significant amount of power to begin with.

Working-Class Resistance and Political Parties

At the start of the twentieth century, the Puerto Rican working-class organized itself in connection with the American Federation of Laborers (AFL). By the 1930s, they formed the *Partido Socialista* (Socialist Party). Given their connection to the AFL, they hoped working-class Puerto Ricans would benefit from U.S. resources. They were not threatened by English language policy. The *Partido Republicano* (Republican Party), generally representing business interests, was also not concerned with fighting imperialism. Instead, their connection to landowners allowed them to benefit from U.S. economic and political policies resulting in their advocacy for statehood. In other words, the Socialist Party wanted to use the state to improve working-class livelihoods while the wealthy in the Republican Party took advantage of its positioning to systematically profit from corporate dominance. Interestingly, although they originated from different social and economic positions, and although the Socialist Party opposed corporate dominance in Puerto Rico, both had a positive view of the United States and English language policy (Gatell, 1958; Burrows, 2014).

Taking on a different angle, the *Partido Liberal* (Liberal Party) of Puerto Rico and the *Partido Nacionalista* (Puerto Rican Nationalist Party) argued against statehood, advocated for independence, and were both initially opposed to English language policy. Both parties attacked colonial oppression and regarded English language policy as a vessel for the preservation of subordination (Burrows, 2014). The Liberal Party, stemming from the *Alianza*, a faction of the Republican Party, did not oppose English per se. Rather, it tentatively advocated for independence, seeking greater autonomy, and supporting Spanish instruction while recognizing English as a beneficial resource. Unlike the Liberal Party, the Nationalist Party had absolutely no love for the United States or its language policies. It unapologetically fought for complete independence, blaming poor social and economic conditions experienced on the island on U.S. corporate interests (Pantojas-Garcia, 1989). While the Liberal Party had the most popular support, in 1932, the Socialist Party and the Republican Party formed a coalition deliberately set around combatting the independence movement and, together, successfully came into power later that year (Burrows, 2014).

Although the Socialist and Republican Parties were sympathetic to the United States, under their coalition, they represented corporate interests on the island and were against the New Deal's welfare programs of the 1930s. The Liberal Party – less critical of the United States than the Nationalist Party – took responsibility for initiating the Reconstruction of Puerto Rico Project in

1935 under the New Deal (Burrows, 2014). Worried that it would strip Puerto Rico of its natural resources, Pedro Albizu Campos, leader of the Nationalist Party, opposed the project. On October 20, 1935, he publicly denounced the Liberal Party as traitors for complying in Americanization efforts within the university system. Things escalated quickly and on October 24, 1935 four Nationalist Party supporters were killed in what is now known as the Rio Piedras Massacre (Villanueva, 2009). The event sparked outrage throughout the island, including among statehood supporters who agreed that the killings were uncalled for. Many took the Nationalist Party as too radical but, in many ways, understood its stance. Two years later, the murder of U.S. Army Colonel Riggs resulted in increased repression from the state (Barreto, 2000). This caused more and more people to shift toward greater autonomy. The Liberal Party garnered increasing support from middle-class educators, family farmers, politicians, and others, while the Socialist and Republican parties continued to lose support. By 1940, the coalition fell out of power (Burrows, 2014).

The 1940s was a period of transition. The old parties had fractured, died, or evolved and new parties emerged. Among them was the *Partido Popular Democrático-Popular Democratic Party* (PPD) stemming from the Liberal Party and the *Partido Independentista Puertorriqueño-Puerto Rican Independent Party* (PIP), a new iteration of the Nationalist Party. Though segments of the population continued to support statehood, many Puerto Ricans increasingly supported the PPD and greater autonomy for Puerto Rico overall. While the PPD was initially deliberate in taking a pro-autonomy attitude between independence and statehood, by the end of the century, the PPD and the PIP were unanimous in their pro-Spanish, anti-English stance. However, the language debate is no longer about Spanish versus English (although some would argue otherwise). The island is still predominantly Spanish-speaking and will continue to be so for the foreseeable future. The use of Spanish is not questioned on the island. The debate then, is about whether people should be learning English in addition to Spanish (i.e. become bilingual). A great example of the Spanish versus bilingual debate comes from the two language laws implemented in the 1990s.

The Current Language Debate

Spanish versus Bilingualism

In 1991, the PPD government announced that Spanish would be the sole official language of Puerto Rico, replacing the 1902 law that had designated both English and Spanish as the official languages. The bill was an anti-imperialist move set to denounce English and U.S. domination. It was supported by the PIP. The bill equates Puerto Rican identity with the Spanish language. It was meant to protect Puerto Rican ethnic and cultural pride by protecting the maintenance of Spanish. Interestingly, most Puerto Ricans opposed the highly controversial law (Velez and Schweers, 1993).

The bill was opposed on two grounds. The first comes from statehood supporters who feared that the policy would not sit well with the United States and would, therefore, hurt their chances of obtaining statehood. Despite arguments stating that English was hurting the Spanish language, statehood advocates believed that such claims were invalid. To them, people could learn English while also adequately learning Spanish. Statehood advocates saw no threat or shortcomings in English skills acquisition, and believed their position was supported by the language and identity scholarship. Instead, they viewed English proficiency as an instrumental prerequisite for achieving statehood (Language Policy Task Force, 1978; DuBord, 2007).

The second stream of opposition to the law stemmed from the internalization of English as a superior, or at least beneficial, language. Within this view, English represents increased opportunities and social mobility for those who are proficient. English facilitates access to multinationals and commercial enterprises in the island and economic and cultural adaptation for those who migrate to the U.S. mainland. As Clachar (1997b) states, whether people like it or not, "knowledge of English is synonymous with prestige, power, and social opportunities, and economic rewards" (461). While the government in power, the elite, and separatists all favored Spanish as the only official language, they completely misinterpreted how crucial most Puerto Ricans now perceive bilingualism to be. Those who are fluent in both English and Spanish tend to come from middle- and upper-class backgrounds. They tend to be in business, science, technology, or education and learn English through their access to costly private schools. Recognizing that wealthy families would continue to obtain educational instruction in English, regardless of the language policies implemented in public schools, people wanted and fought for the same opportunities for all (Velez and Schweers 1993). Thus, in 1993, the law was abolished directly after the 1992 victory of the rival PNP that reinstated English as an official language alongside Spanish (Kerkhof, 2001; Nickels, 2005; Carroll, 2016).

The PNP had a pro-bilingual position in the 1990s. One of its major goals at the time was to reestablish English as an official language after Spanish had been made the only official language by the PPD. In general, the PNP did not view English as a threat to Puerto Rican identity but rather as a part of its complex identity (Kerkhof, 2001; Nickels, 2005; Carroll, 2016).

Language Today

Language reflects the important social and historical transformations that have taken place in the island over time. Today, the positions that Puerto Ricans take within the language debate have been influenced by the island's relationship with Spain and the United States. For one, Spain virtually eliminated Indigenous languages from Puerto Rico, creating a predominantly

Spanish-speaking colony (with African and Indigenous influences). Language domination was widespread, and resistance was crushed. Over time, positions of power were overwhelmingly taken up by Hispanic elites who were descendants of white Spaniards. Other people were not so fortunate. Within this context, English as a secondary language is a constant reminder of the United States' continued imperialist domination of Puerto Rico. Rejection of English reaffirms a distinct Puerto Rican identity influenced by Spanish, African, and Indigenous cultures separate from U.S. dominant culture. Such rejection of English throughout the twentieth century has resulted in the maintenance of Spanish on the island with only about 20% of the population speaking English (Kerkhof, 2001). However, this demonstrates the resilience of Puerto Ricans in the face of attempted assimilation and the lack of funding within its education system. English is both an imposition and an asset given the United States' ever-adapting capitalist hand in Puerto Rico, increased access to English media, and increasingly circular migration between the island and the U.S. mainland. Most Puerto Ricans currently view English favorably on the basis of its connections to opportunity and social mobility (DuBord, 2007; Mazak, 2012; Carroll, 2015, 2016). With that said, because of limited access to English, it also continues to serve as a marker of class differences. Given that the middle- and upper-class have greater access to English instruction, it is those who have been the most historically oppressed that now find themselves fighting for their right to English. They are not alone as this is the result of the long-standing inequalities that persist today.

Conclusion

Tackling the language debate in Puerto Rico and the inequalities embedded within it is not an easy task. When we look at the historical control of the island by the United States, we see that the federal government initially implemented a heavy-handing Americanization plan attempting to use language as a tool of domination. The people of Puerto Rico impressively used language to resist the policies imposed on them. Maintenance of the Spanish language, however, is also the result of Spanish domination on the island, inadequate funding in the school system, and other persisting inequalities stemming from the island's history.

Here, it is important to make one thing clear. Although the initial argument of this paper is that the United States systematically attempted to use language in its domination of Puerto Rico, the broader argument is that language can be used as a tool in the systematic maintenance of subordination on behalf of the state, or as a tool of resistance on behalf of the people. Language and domination are also embedded in discussions of national identity. Language in Puerto Rico is the outcome and multifaceted response to domination from, and resistance to, two separate states in two different periods of time. This is apparent in the positions taken by different sectors of the population within the various political parties. Those that believed they had something to gain from being under the reign of the United States generally favored English. Those that believed their positions were threatened generally opposed it. Those able to learn English, regardless of their initial beliefs, find themselves privileged in a society in which English is a marker of class differences (Clachar, 1997b). Limiting access to English in the name of cultural preservation without advocating against social, political, and economic inequality, helps the state uphold social stratification based on class, race, and place. Sadly, many of those without access to English, who did not benefit from U.S. colonial rule, and continue to experience inequalities, still find themselves fighting for a piece of the pie they have been so long denied. Many of these are dark-skinned Puerto Ricans.

What then, can we expect moving forward? Unfortunately, the forces that have produced and help maintain the oppression and inequalities presented in this chapter do not seem to be disappearing anytime soon. Still, the people of Puerto Rico have proven that they can stand up to colonial and neocolonial domination. Doing so, however, requires a collective front. This is the case regardless if the goal is independence, statehood, or increased resources under a continued commonwealth status. What that front should look like, and with what goals, is up to the people of Puerto Rico to decide. What is known, however, is that without widespread systemic change, the inequalities currently underlying the language debate in the unincorporated commonwealth are likely to persist.

References

Angrist, Joshua, Aimee Chin, and Ricardo Godoy. 2008. "Is Spanish-only Schooling Responsible for the Puerto Rican Language Gap?" *Journal of Development Economics* 85: 105–112.

Barreto, Amilcar Antonio. 2000. "Speaking English in Puerto Rico: The Impact of Affluence, Education and Return Migration." *CENTRO Journal* 12: 5–16.

Burrows, Geoff G. 2014. *"The New Deal in Puerto Rico: Public Works, Public Health, and the Puerto Rico Reconstruction Administration, 1935–1955."* Dissertation submitted to the History Department, The City University of New York.

Carroll, Kevin S. 2015. "Language Maintenance in the Caribbean: Examining Perceptions of Threat in Aruba and Puerto Rico." *Language Problems and Language Planning* 39: 115–135.

_____. 2016. "Understanding Perceptions of Language Threat: The Case of Puerto Rico." *Caribbean Studies* 44: 167–186.

Clachar, Arlene. 1997a. "Ethnolinguistic Identity and Spanish Proficiency in a Paradoxical Situation: The Case of Puerto Rican Return Migrants." *Journal of Multilingual and Multicultural Development* 18: 107–124.

_____ 1997b. "Students' Reflections on the Social, Political, an Ideological Role of English in Puerto Rico." *Hispanic Journal of Behavioral Sciences* 19: 461–478.

DuBord, Elise M. 2007. "La Mancha del Plátano: Language Policy and the Construction of Puerto Rican National Identity in the 1940s." *Spanish in Context* 4: 241–262.

Gatell, Frank Otto. 1958. "Independence Rejected: Puerto Rico and the Tydings Bill of 1936." *The Hispanic American Journal Review* 38: 25–44.

Kerkhof, Erna. 2001. "The Myth of the Dumb Puerto Rican: Circular Migration and Language Struggle in Puerto Rico." *New West Indian Guide* 75: 257–288.

Language Policy Task Force. 1978. "Language Policy and the Puerto Rican Community." *La Revista Bilingüe* 5: 1–39.

Lozano, Rosina. 2018. *An American Language: The History of Spanish in the United States.* Berkeley: University of California Press.

Mazak, Catherine M. 2012. "My Cousin Talks Bad Like You: Relationships Between Language and Identity in a Rural Puerto Rican Community." *Journal of Language, Identity, and Education* 11: 35–51.

Meléndez, Edgardo. 2017. *The State and Puerto Rican Postwar Migration to the United States.* Columbus: The Ohio State University Press.

Nickels, Edelmira L. 2005. "English in Puerto Rico." *World Englishes* 24: 227–237.

Pantojas-Garcia, Emilio. 1989. "Puerto Rican Populism Revisited: The PPD during the 1940s." *Journal of Latin American Studies* 21: 521–557.

Pousada, Alicia. 1996. "Puerto Rico: On the Horns of a Language Planning Dilemma." *Teachers of English to Speakers of Other Languages (TESOL) Quarterly* 30: 499–510.

———1999. "The Singularly Strange Story of the English Language in Puerto Rico." *Milenio* 3: 33–60.

Ramirez, Rafael L. 1976. "National Culture in Puerto Rico." *Latin American Perspectives* 3: 109–116.

San Miguel, Pedro L. 2008. "Reseña de 'Puerto Rico in the American Century: A History since 1898' de Cesár J. Ayala y Rafael Bernabe." *Centro Journal*, 20(1): 259–264.

Santiago-Valles, Kelvin. 2007. "Our Race Today [Is] the Only Hope for the World': An African Spaniard as Chieftain of the Struggle against 'Sugar Slavery' in Puerto Rico, 1926–1934." *Caribbean Studies* 35: 107–140.

Urciuoli, Bonnie. 2013. *Exposing Prejudice: Puerto Rican Experiences of Language, Race, and Class.* Long Grove: Waveland Press.

Velez, Diana L. 1986. "Aspects of the Debate on Language in Puerto Rico." *La Revista Bilingüe* 13: 3–12.

Velez, Jorge A., and C. William Schweers. 1993. "A U.S. Colony at a Linguistic Crossroads: The Decision to Make Spanish the Official Language of Puerto Rico." *Language Problems and Language Planning* 17: 117–139.

Villanueva, Victor. 2009. "Colonial Memory and the Crime of Rhetoric: Pedro Albizu Campos." *College English* 71: 630–638.

Zentella, Ana Celia. 1982. "Spanish and English in Contact in the United States: The Puerto Rican Experience." *Word* 33: 41–57.

Chapter 9

Subtracting Spanish and Forcing English

My Lived Experience in Texas Public Schools

José Angel Gutiérrez

My rearview mirror on life shows me many amazing interventions in my public education. In 2020, I see that the ultimate purpose of my education in Texas public schools imposed by whites was to make an Anglo out of me as my father said they would. This is also what other nation-states do around the world: through imposed education and socialization make a replica generation of the conquering group. In France, centuries past and now, they make and socialize the next generation of French residents via public schools. Spain does the same, as do Germany and China. The United States is no exception, with its Anglo-centric pre-K to 12 and higher education curriculum and literature based on English-only books written by them.

In our case, we do have the Spanish legacy from the late 1490s, but physically, given our geographic location, the Anglo conquest and domination has been our reality. The British and their successors in the United States, the Anglos, stole all our lands in Spanish America, which existed years before Jamestown colonists began the genocide against Native Americans. I got in trouble in the fourth grade by asking why if the United States was started with Fort James, later to become Jamestown, in 1607; there already was a *San Augustine, Florida*, in 1565. My mother had ordered an encyclopedia for us and I used to read about such things. It was not until 2014 that I re-read most of this again in Felipe Fernandez Armesto's (2014) book on the history of Spanish America. White people do not know this history, and unfortunately, neither do our own. By 1863, Mexico had lost more than half of her original territory obtained during the independence movements against Spain of the early 1810s. We became Occupied Mexico within the United States, a little nation within a bigger nation.

In 2020, we were replicas of Anglo *Americanos*; they have monopolized the term American since about 1820 and our public education.

Not many of us managed to enter public schools, which were segregated until after 1957–58. A handful of us were able to graduate from high school back then. San Miguel Jr. tells us that by the 1940s more than 122 school

DOI: 10.4324/9781003257509-14

districts in 59 counties had segregated schools for Mexican American children. I was a student in one of those. Some of our schools for Mexicans were former concentration camps for Japanese Americans (Gutierrez, 1998).

Crystal City, Texas, was one of many detention centers for U.S. Japanese citizens and lawful residents were ordered to be rounded up shortly after the Japanese attack on Pearl Harbor. President F. D. Roosevelt believed those of Japanese blood may not be loyal to the United States and issued Executive Order 9066 in 1942 to arrest, remove, and detain 120,000 Japanese ancestry people living in the United States and another 150,000 living in Hawaii. The Crystal City detention center also held a few others, mainly German and Italian persons, suspected of espionage and threats to U.S. security from South America. The detention center, more aptly termed a concentration camp for Japanese families, opened in December 1943 and closed in February 1948. Within a few months, the camp was somewhat remodeled and converted into a Mexican school for kids living in the *Avispero Barrio*, one of four such barrios in *Cristal*, as we called our hometown. By the time I reached middle school years the school, named *El Campo* by us, was a Junior High School and later a Migrant School for late arrivals from working in the agricultural fields of northern states; this was in 1956. But two other happenings occurred in my hometown and a few other places affecting the education of Mexican children.

The biggest disaster was reassigning the very same people who had been guards and administrators of the Japanese concentration camp as administrators, teachers, support, and other personnel staff. That was who was in charge at *El Campo* Junior High School. The classrooms were former housing rooms of Japanese families and barracks, the gym was the former assembly hall, we had no sports other than what we made up on our own outside in the dirt fields, and the non-existent heating during the winter was ineffective. The buildings were not insulated nor built to be air-tight. Cracks in the walls were prevalent and there were no heaters other than those in the administrator's offices and teacher's break room. The toilets seldom functioned or were cleaned, nor was there a cafeteria.

The second disaster was the delay in obeying the U.S. Supreme Court order to integrate the schools. *Cristal* did not integrate schools until spring 1957, which is when I was transferred to Sterling Fly Junior High, next to Crystal City High School. Related to this event was the death of my father that same year but in October, days before my birthday. I was 12 going on 13. Overnight, my mother and I were in poverty and had to turn to migrant labor like all other Mexicans to survive. My half-brother, Horacio Gutierrez, stole all our properties and bank accounts and even took equipment from my father's medical practice. My father had been the Mexican doctor in town and somewhat in the middle class economically. Overnight my mother and I had to become seasonal migrant workers like all other Mexicans in *Cristal*.

Growing Up

I like boxing because my father liked boxing. He often took me to see live box-ing matches in *Cristal*, what we called our hometown in Spanish, San Antonio, and *Piedras Negras* in Mexico, but not wrestling. He did wait until I was about seven years old to begin taking me with him to these events and other more violent events like cockfights and bullfights.

A lesson learned, or rather reinforced, was to deal with blood. I saw plenty of blood at home, where my father had to have his medical office, examining, and treatment rooms. The segregationist environment of the time did not allow him hospital privileges nor professional relations with local or Anglo doctors and nurses despite his certification from the state of being a licensed medical doctor. The nearest medical care option, the public hospital, was too far away in San Antonio, Texas, and nearer was *Piedras Negras, Coahuila, Mexico*, which he preferred in emergencies.

At these boxing matches we usually had front-row seats next to the judges, bell ringers, radio announcers, and fighters' corners. My father was often hired to be the ringside physician, a critical person to prevent the unnecessary muti-lation and death of the fighters. The fights took place just above our heads at ringside, especially mine, given my size then. Blood, sweat, yelling, and pro-fanity coming our way were always part of each fight. My father never made an issue of any of that as he was used to all of that. I guess he assumed that I was also or that it did not matter. He was right because I would soon learn the profanity part in Spanish soon in the streets. I also guess that was part of the "becoming a man" mode he was in for me. He did point out repeatedly, for example, the type of blows being thrown and finding their mark or missing. I soon knew the difference in Spanish between a jab, hook, body punch, upper-cut, overhand right or left, and, of course, a counter punch, a clinch, a slip, referee signals and count, and significance of the bell. What my dad wanted me to observe besides the punches were the knockdowns.

He explained how some fighters fake a low blow to get a few minutes rest to recover, how some fighters when knocked down take the referee's count to near end but get up at eight or nine just before the ten-count allowed and losing the fight. What excited him the most was to see an early knockdown of a fighter and then have that same fighter weather the follow-up storm of punches from the other fighter trying to capitalize on that vulnerable moment without suc-cess. He would cheer on the seemingly vulnerable fighter's stamina and desire to win. Sometimes that fighter would turn the tables on the other one who had knocked him down by getting up and beating up the other fighter. There were reasons for this unexpected result, he would explain to me in Spanish. He only spoke to me in Spanish. "Fighters know they are going to get hit, to hurt, to be cut, to bleed and to get knocked down." The first thing to learn in boxing, he said, is to get used to the noise of the blow. The second thing is the hurt. "Getting hit hurts. Learn to move out of the way." And, the most important thing is the knockdown, he explained. "The better fighters tell themselves; telling their championship soul, to overcome the moment. Get up. Get back to your fight plan."

My father would say out loud, "The other fighter may have tried too hard to knock you out. He may be arm weary. He may be tired. He may be afraid he could not knock you. Now, he could very well believe you are too much for him." My dad never stopped looking at the fight as he said all this. It was hard for me to digest all these seemingly contradictory statements while listening, looking at him, and looking at the fight.

The Lessons Learned

As a Mexican child, however, I knew my role was to listen and not ask; to be talked to and not with; and to figure out the meaning behind the words. Many times, he would admonish me to hear what was not said; see what was not apparent; and focus on the big picture as much as on the details. He used to say, "Think you are at the movies. You see the big screen and at the same time you do see all the details. You do not look at a corner, the top, the center. You look all over the screen. You see it all. You have trained yourself to see all and even anticipate what is about to happen next or be said." That is exactly what helped me learn to speed read, see the whole page, not read word by word, line by line. The whole thing at once. At the Anglo-centric school they do not teach this speed-reading method. They are still stuck on word by word, line by line. Later in life, you must pay someone else to teach you to speed read.

The boxing matches I soon realized were to teach me vicariously how to fight, but more importantly, to get up from being knocked down, an alternative, a switching instead of derailment.

By age 9, I was already getting into fights with other kids for name-calling and just for looking at me—eventually over girls became the main reason. When I was an altar boy, I got into fights every Saturday morning with other boys after the training session with the priest on how to serve during the Mass and funeral services. That is how I not only learned about fighting my way but also that a separate Mass in English was held for whites and that they had a separate cemetery in our town and in La Pryor and Batesville, neighboring towns.

My First Fight

My first lesson in personal power was over the pronunciation of my middle name, *Ángel*. Douglas Cook, a second-grade classmate, at afternoon recess began making fun of my name pronouncing in it in drawn-out Texas English: "Hay N Gel" and "Oh Aaayn Gel" and "Angle" not the Spanish version of *"An Hel."* I put the accent on *Ángel* to draw attention that it does have that emphasis but not when it is capitalized. Exception here to make a point about the pronunciation.

Douglas also added at times, "Joe Hay N Gel" for the full name. Everyone knew I went by *José Angel,* certainly not Joe or Angel. He was just harassing me. He was sore I had beat him at a marble game during morning recess. I first told him to shut up and got close enough to push him. At the next "Oh Aaayn Gel" I jab punched him right on the nose, which began to bleed before he hit the ground. I jumped on him, grabbed his hair, and started knocking his head on the hard dirt as I said, "Shut up. My name is *"An Hel."* Stop making fun of my name!"

Needless to say, I was pulled off Douglas and taken to the principal's office for an explanation of my assault while my parents were summoned. My mother came and assured Principal Darrell Ray that it would never happen again and that she would punish me, not him. She and I both knew the punishment would be three "licks" with the big bat–size wood paddle and three days suspension. But Ray also knew it was best not to take on my mother or my father. He just ordered her to take me home and do what she had to do "so this does not happen again."

I learned four lessons from this. I had physical power over Douglas. My mother had some sort of power over the principal. I was not sure what. Now I had reputational power over my schoolmates who feared I might punch them. Lastly, my father was proud I won my first fight and argued with my mother about that. The point is, I realized that you could make others do what they do not necessarily want to do. I also realized that most things happen because someone makes another do what they do not want to do. Much of this I began to glean from what I read in the English-only textbooks and heard the Anglo-only teachers say to us as the "lesson."

Another interesting aspect of this first fight was that it was over the use of English and Spanish at the school. In a way, Douglas was right. My name was Joe Angel in English, and speaking of Spanish at school, regardless of whether it was the playground, restroom, hallway, or classroom, was strictly prohibited. No. *José Angel.* I began to understand there was not only personal power but also bigger powers like my teachers, Principal Ray, the Catholic priest, the local police, my father, and my mothers, and so on.

From Being to Becoming a Mexican

My father, Angel Gutierrez Crespo, and mother, Concepcion Fuentes Casas, were tremendous assets as teachers and parents when it came to preparing me for the world experience. My father, a Mexican revolutionary exile from the 1910 Revolution along with about a million others who fled that civil war between 1901 and 1930, as cited by Roger Daniels (2004) in his book on U.S. immigration policy since 1882. During this time, 1924 specifically, the U.S. Congress passed a quota bill on immigration favoring white Europeans and limiting non-white immigrants except Mexicans. As Daniels states it, Mexican labor was needed by U.S. agricultural interests; and that is still the case. They

want our labor but not us. They want our consumption and spending, not us.
That is why the U.S. Border Patrol was established then to patrol the Mexican
border and not the Canadian. By the late 1940's President Truman noticed
more Jews were emigrating to the United States, passing as white Europeans.
By the 1960s clearly there were fewer Europeans coming to the United States
than from Asia, other parts of the Americas. The subsequent U.S. wars in
Korea and Vietnam and the military operations directed by the Central
Intelligence Agency (CIA) in Guatemala, Santo Domingo, Cuba, and Chile
led to the almost open-door immigration policy adopted by President Ronald
Reagan. This brief period brought us our cultural cousins from the Caribbean
and Central America to live among us. Their presence caused our national
political identity as a group away from Mexican to Hispanic in the 1970s.
The push back by other ignorants was to want Latino as our group identity
and name, not knowing they were just trading one European colonizer of the
Americas; pick a King from Carlos V to Fernando VII, or Napoleon III's hand-
picked emperor for Mexico, *Maximilliano* and his Queen, *Carlota.* Napoleon
III was also responsible for the huge land transfer known as the Louisiana
Purchase to the United States by his deals with U.S. leaders and the actions of
his brother José whom he placed as King of Spain in 1808 to settle the matter.
But all we know is that we are to hate being *Gachupin* or Spanish or French
and proud to be Mexican. Most whites think *Cinco de Mayo* it is about Mexican
Independence from Spain.

My dad was a traditional Mexican who made sure I also became one. I had
to learn Spanish—read, write, speak—and discuss *en Español* astronomy, philosophy, history, current events, politics, and literature with him during the
evenings. He was a learned man who spoke Spanish, Latin, German, English,
and Italian, a real pentalingual. He used to kid me by asking this question:
"How many languages do you speak?" I would answer two plus a little Latin
from being an altar boy. He would laugh and say, "they do not teach you much
about our history and heritage in school, do they?" From time to time, he
would give me a lesson on this, starting with making me pronounce *"etimolo-
gia."* I would often have to ask my mother what some of his words in Spanish
meant. Together we would look them up in our household Spanish-English
dictionary, which even the school libraries did not have such a dictionary, only
Webster's. My father would ask me, "Why do you say *Adios,* To God, and the
Gringos say Goodbye?" He would not provide answers to his many questions. As
a traditional Mexican kid, I long had learned not to ask questions of my elders,
just listen, and learn. He would tease me to find the origins of such Spanish
words ending in "te." He would ask me are those words from *Castellaño.* It was
not until the tenth grade in high school Spanish II class with one of the few
Mexican teachers hired by Crystal City Independent School District (CCISD),
Diamantina Rodriguez, that I found an answer when she discussed word origins of Spanish and told us that *Nahuatl,* the language of the *Meshicas* also
called Aztecs was the basis for many of our contemporary words like *aguacate,*

chocolate, mesquite, tomate and so on. Later, I found out that Arabic words also are a large part of the so-called "Castellano" and our contemporary Spanish. Words that begin with "al" such as *"alfombra, algodon, almohada, alambre,"* and so on, are from the Arabic language. So, my father was correct, I actually am pentalingual, as we all are, not just a B3 person. It is our ignorant monolingual English-only teachers who have misled us and erased this heritage. Today, their "students" who now teach at community colleges, colleges, and universities so-called Chicano/Latino/Hispanic/Latinx studies also do not know or teach this heritage. They forgot or never learned that language transmits culture.

My mother, Concepcion Fuentes Casas, born in San Antonio, Texas, was a Chicana. She came at me and my education from the other angle—teaching me English— to become a B3 person, bilingual, bicultural, biliterate, which I did. The pre-kinder classes I also had to take with a private teacher ensured I was fully functional in either language. My mother was pushed out during her eighth-grade year because a bus driver took the liberty of feeling her booty as she boarded the bus. She slapped him and promptly was not only put off the bus but also out of school. My grandparents, the Fuentes clan, lived in an unincorporated area of *Cristal* called *"El Swiche"* because it was literally a switching point for the rail cars loaded with harvested vegetables from that area to hook up with the mainline about a mile down the tracks. This was an all-Mexican *barrio* right next to the Nueces River, about 7 miles from the south side of *Cristal*. Mom, however, did not let this incident deter her from an education. Once married to my father she made it a habit to enroll in correspondence courses on many topics. I recall seeing the booklets arrive via the postal service and her pouring over them every chance she had. She took courses on book-keeping and accounting; aspects of nursing; medical terminology; and basic laboratory procedures to help my father with his medical practice. She ran his laboratory, X-ray machine, blood tests, pharmacy dispensary, and assisted in medical care. She also took courses in English, Spanish, and music appreciation. As I moved up in grade levels she would ask me for opinions on what she was reading, so I also became somewhat learned in medical practice and procedures. Between her and my father also asking me for help with some medical procedures, I learned one major thing: Never become a medical doctor. After I helped deliver a baby on the couch in the waiting room of his office, which was halfway to our home and saw a man die from bleeding also on our front steps of the office as he held his stomach and intestines in his hands. This was all on one day. The local police had a bad habit of leaving wounded and bleeding Mexican men from their own violence or of others on our doorstep as if it was my father's responsibility to provide care. In a way, they were correct because Mexicans were not taken to the local hospital and my father was not extended medical privileges. Everything he did was at our home or the patient's home.

My maternal grandmother, Maria del Refugio Casas Fuentes, added to the learning of *dichos,* folk sayings, which are the soul of Spanish. *Dichos* contain moral lessons, values, philosophy, ethics, and guides for the life experience.

Grandma, who I spend lots of time with because I was the only grandson left in *Cristal* who had to do her errands and some house chores, basically talked to me in *dichos*, not normal conversation, and always in Spanish. She would just spout something like, "*dime con quien andas y te dire quien eres*" or "*dos agujas no se pican*" or "*no hay mal que por bien no venga*," for example.

Also Becoming Me, Myself, and I

More importantly and often overlooked by most is that our parents and environment teach us to become several personalities. I became three persons—Me, Myself, and I—the Mexican, the Anglo, and the Chicano. All of us in this environment have to learn to be three people at once and know which hat to wear when if you were going to make the world work for you. My father made me the Mexican I still am. My mother, the Anglo teachers and peers, and television which is all about white life, made me an Anglo. Out in the streets and with my buddies, I learned to be a Chicano. Each personality has its own rules of behavior, word choice and language, values, and ethics, and one ugly aspect: the dumb Down syndrome. If you were Chicano you did not answer teacher questions in class; you did not show you knew anything; and you did not snitch. Anyone who violated these basic rules was labeled a Gringo-wanna-be or just "*muy agrabachado*." The reproach from a Chicano peer was not long in coming: "*Cres que sabes mas que yo?*" or "*Te cres muy chingon?*" I explain this 3-person phenomenon in greater detail in my book for middle school readers, *The Making of A Civil Rights Leader, José Angel Gutiérrez,* and for the adult reader I wrote another one, *The Making of a Chicano Militant: Lessons from Cristal,* which is a political autobiography.

Back to subtractive education, as first explained by Angela Valenzuela (1999) in her book. Chicano kids and now immigrants arrive at the public-school door somewhat complete. They have their Spanish names, rudiments of language, some knowledge of their culture—music, art, cuentos, dichos, and oral family history. But from day one at the public school, their names are changed from Pedro to Pete, Domingo to Sunday, Valentina to Vicky, for example. English-only becomes the rule and severe punishment awaits those who violate the rule. I was paddle spanked twice for this and suspended from school for three days for speaking Spanish and being in a fight. The family oral history goes out the window. Back then we were children of *Braceros* or Wetbacks, and today, they are children of illegal aliens; everyone is an immigrant. We had to unlearn that the *Dia de La Raza*, October 12, was now Columbus Day. Later we had to drop using the phrase *La Raza* because whites claimed it meant we were exalting our race over all others, and hence we were racists in reverse. I am sure you have heard this nonsense before. White lore tells us *Cristoforo Colon*, an Italian but navigating under the Spanish empire flag, discovered the *Americas*, not that they had been here forever and inhabited by our indigenous ancestors for centuries. In fact, these First Nations or Indians were also the first migrants walking across the then frozen ice cap known now as the Bering Strait. They just kept walking south to find more food and warmer climates. This has been known for years but not taught as official history, rather the lie perpetuated is that the Spanish killed the Indians who have always been in what is now the United States. Perhaps, everyone should read a recent article by Brian Handwerk (2019) on this point in the *Smithsonian* magazine or even the U.S. government's National Park Service posting of Scott Elias' (2020) article on the same topic of migrations across Beringia.

The LULAC "Little School of 400 Words" in English

In *Cristal* somebody began two pre-kindergarten schools for Mexican kids sometime in the 1950s. They were run by Hortencia Sifuentes and Azusana Salazar, respectively, for profit. They charged a minimal weekly tuition and sold us snacks, fees for ViewFinder slide shows, and ice cube size popsicles. I attended the one led by Ms. "Suse" Salazar over in the *Mexico Grande Barrio* almost next door to Canela's Panaderia, which was about a six-block walk from my house. My parents, as did a few others, believed if we were taught some rudimentary English, math, reading, and vocabulary, success in the English-only segregated schools could be had. They were right. Later in 1957, this idea of a private Mexican school to teach kids how to navigate the Anglo school became a project of Felix Tijerina, the National President of the League of United Latin American Citizens (LULAC). He called his project the Little School of 400. Basically, it was the teaching of 400 basic words in English, later expanded to 500 words. Much later, in the 1960s President Lyndon B. Johnson made this LULAC program the foundation for his Head Strat War on Poverty initiative. This history has been recovered by Thomas Kreneck (2001) in his biography on Felix Tijerina.

I was one of those unfortunate ones who was not seven years old on the first day of school in 1950. My birthday, October 25, was still many weeks away. I had to sit out that year. Fortunately, I did get promoted ahead of time from third to fourth grade. I made up that delay and graduated from high school at age 17 in May 1962. The year before, 1961, I won the state championship in Declamation, an Interscholastic League competition back then, for my size school district, 28-AA, the first Chicano to do so. That same year, Richard Gallegos, my classmate, won another state championship in the mile run. He also was the first Chicano to win that competition for our size school district. A couple of other mentions of my high school career. I was not only class president my junior and senior year but also student body president my last year. My cumulative grades were above average, but I still did not get selected to be part of the National Honor Society by half a point, I was told.

First, from 1947 to 1964, millions of Mexicans from the mother country, Mexico (we live in Occupied Mexico), crossed over as *Braceros,* lawful contracted labor, plus a few million more via illegal entry. These Mexicans often jumped their labor contracts over how they were treated and simply moved into the nearest town with a Mexican American population, like mine, Crystal City, Texas. We had a huge Bracero labor camp about 10 miles from town operated by the California Packing Corporation, which is now Del Monte. I worked there since age nine as a dishwasher because my father decided it was time for me to learn to work like a man. Our across-the-street neighbor, Armandina Galvan, had the contract to feed the hundreds of men working and housed at the farm labor camp. These Braceros who jumped contracts soon made new families with local Mexican American women and their children became U.S. citizens and our classmates.

Second, the population of Mexican ancestry school children in segregated Texas public schools in the 1950s was about half of all such kids, maybe two-thirds, according to Dr. Guadalupe San Miguel, Jr.'s (2020) posting for the Texas State Historical Association (TSHA). Access to educational opportunity was one of the major civil rights planks of civil rights groups then, not retention, much less graduation. In 1950, the median educational attainment of Mexicans in my home county of Zavala, Texas was only 1.8 years and up by 1960 to 2.3 years, according to John Shockley (1974), who did a study of our Chicano revolts in the county seat, Crystal City in 1963 and 1969. And San Miguel, Jr. (2020) adds that a majority of Mexican ancestry students dropped out of school between the third and sixth grades. Why leave school in the third, fourth, fifth, and sixth grades. I have one answer as part of my lived experience in my hometown.

Across the street from our home was the De Zavala Elementary School, the one for Mexicans. The assumption made by our Anglo educational leaders from the state level to the local school district and made policy was that Spanish speakers held back English speakers and learners if in the same classrooms and school. The curriculum and pedagogy were English only.

De Zavala Elementary actually placed Mexican students in the Low-Zero grade, then if progress was made they passed to Zero, then low-first followed by first, then low-second and then second, and so on. Factoring in age, assuming the Mexican pupil entered at age seven, he or she would be 10 by the time he or she reached the first grade and 13 by the time they reached the low third. Most boys by then had mustache and beard fuzz while the girls began to menstruate. Their families did not lose sight of the slow progress and began asking when their daughters would marry, their sons get a job, and both genders work to help the family.

My mother made such a stink at the prospect of my being assigned this school at the De Zavala's principal's office, and at a school board meeting, I was not assigned to De Zavala. Actually, I was allowed to enroll at Grammar School, the Anglo one. My mother had challenged the principal in his office, the superintendent in his office, and school board members at a public meeting to test me right then and there in English. Instead, I was tested over my English proficiency by Ms. Reed, the first-grade teacher. She recommended I be moved up to third- or fourth-grade level, which simply could not be permitted. My move up was not done until the third grade to the fourth grade. After the fifth grade, I was reassigned back to the segregated middle school at *El Campo*.

Third, panic was the name of every summer day in June 1954 because President Dwight D. "Ike" Eisenhower initiated his ethnic cleansing campaign against Mexicans. It was called Operation Wetback. I wrote a chapter on this in my 2020 book working with FBI files (Gutierrez 2020). Purpose was to remove all unlawful entry and Braceros who had jumped contracts from the United States. I recall my teachers handing out "I Like Ike" political buttons for us to wear like they were doing. I did it. When I got home my father gave me one of his superb tongue lashings on Gringo Racists. We never really knew who was deported because Mexicans and Mexican Americans in *Cristal* often never returned after summer/early fall. They were seasonal, migrant, agricultural workers, and many settled out or moved elsewhere.

In charge of the massive round-up of Mexicans in South Texas during Operation Wetback was Harlon Carter. That summer, when he was a 17-year-old teen in Laredo, Texas, he killed Ramiro Casiano, 15 years old, with a shotgun blast. Casiano was unarmed and innocent of any wrongdoing. Carter's conviction was overturned on appeal. Like his father, he joined the U.S. Border Patrol and took charge of Operation Wetback in South Texas, later he became the Southwest regional head of the Immigration and Naturalization Service (INS) until 1970. During this same time, he joined the National Rifle Association (NRA), became its leader in 1965, and its head of NRA lobbying in 1975.

In the third grade, I was given, as we all were, a comic booklet on Texas It was awful, and if you were Mexican you wanted to crawl under your chair or better yet run away from the school building. The caricature of Mexicans in the booklet was viciously stereotypical and racist. Mexicans all wore big hats and beard stubble, were dirty, and had flies flying around them. Blacks had huge lips and wide noses, were also dirty, and usually had a hat in their hand as they stooped I deference to whites. This booklet was first introduced in 1932 by the Dallas Independent School District Superintendent as a way to teach history easily using comic book features. He was able to convince the Magnolia Petroleum Company to print him all the booklets he needed, which they did. Within a few years, all school districts in Texas were receiving these booklets free courtesy of the corporate successor, Mobil Oil which is now the Exxon Corporation. The booklet, now titled "Texas History History Movies," (Markstein, 2020) was used in Texas schools until 1959. I still have a copy and you can preview some of this at the website for toonopedia.com. My father saw it once among my school things and hit the roof. He told me that he knew I had to use this for school but not rely on it as truth. He also said I was not to bring this trash into the family home. From then on, I seldom brought home books and was so happy for lockers to be assigned to us in the new Fly Junior High School.

By fifth grade, I was introduced to my "new" history written by Ralph W. Steen (1942), which we all had to read and learn to score well on exams and pass to the next grade level. I was handed *Texas: A Story of Progress*, first published and adopted in the state in 1942. The first page of the Preface put out the Anglo-centric message:

> More than four centuries have passed since the first Spaniard visited the shores of the land we know as Texas. Since that visit of long ago, six flags have flown over Texas (*see the frontis-piece*). French traders and settlers earned a few brief pages in its history. Spanish explorers, settlers, and churchmen accomplished much more. Anglo-Americans, led by Stephen F. Austin, began moving into Texas in 1821. Since that date, the state had made remarkable progress
>
> (Steen 1942: iii).

The Steen book detailed several aspects of Texas history that simply are not true but that we had to learn as such. For example, it dismisses the fact that slavery was prohibited in Texas after Mexican President Vicente Guerrero outlawed the practice in the country in 1829. Texas was a Mexican state under the name of *Tejas/Coahuila*. It dismisses the fact that most Anglos coming into Texas were illegal aliens from Kentucky, Tennessee, Virginia, Georgia, North Carolina, and other states including some aliens from Scotland, England, and Canada. They wanted free land. It was not free. Earlier settlers like Stephen F. Austin's father, Moses, to get Mexican land, had to sign pledges to be loyal to Mexico, become Catholic, and not bring slaves. These first lawful settlers lied and committed perjury in signing such an official document transferring Mexican land to their names. The illegal aliens coming after 1821 did not bother to ask, sign, or pay for land; they just stole it by illegal means, usually terrorizing the owners or killing the head of the family and negotiating with the widow. Others like Mifflin Kenedy of King Ranch fame just married Mexican women who owned land such as Petra Vela a widow with eight children. Read about it her biography, titled *Petra's Legacy* (Monday and ick, 2007). One of the most violent campaigns by these illegal aliens was over the land covering most of what is now Victoria, Texas, and first settled and owned by Martin De Leon in 1803 when Texas the state much less Republic as such did not legally exist and was part of Spain. This story was first told in *The Empresario Don Martin De Leon* and is not taught in the Victoria public schools or any other public school in Texas or the United States, not even in colleges and universities (Hammett 1973). This sordid and violent Anglo history toward Mexicans is not taught because the ignorants passing as Professors of various ranks and even Emeriti do not know it or chose to ignore it and those who graduate from such institutions of higher learning do not either. No small wonder we are ignorant of our own history. To be fair, the Mexican government's *Secretaria de Educacion Publica*, does not impose that type of information in their curriculum or mandated books either. They choose to have self-imposed amnesia on this era of history and loss of more than half its territory beginning with Florida, the Louisiana Purchase, then Texas.

Even while taking my first doctoral courses at the University of Texas at Austin in 1968 did the Anglo ignorance about our history and heritage continue to plague me. I had to read a chapter on Leander Perez of Louisiana in *Gothic Politics in the Deep South* for a class on regional politics in the South (Sherill 1968). There was no chapter on Texas in this book. I got in trouble on two counts because I asked if Perez was a Mexican, Spanish, or of what ancestral nationality, given that the surname was not from any Anglo or British derivation. The professor dismissed me with, "that is not important." Secondly, I asked why a chapter on Texas was not included only to be told emphatically that everyone knows Texas is part of the Southwest, not the South. I did not know that and later found it to not be true. Texas is more southern than part of the Southwest. The illegal alien Anglos targeted Texas in the 1820s to make it a slave state before going after the southwestern states in 1846.

Chicano Power

A few years later armed with a PhD, I sought to repeat the electoral victory Chicanos had in 1963. I was part of the Mexican American Youth Organization (MAYO) and head of the Winter Garden Project aimed at organizing four counties in southwest Texas: Frio, La Salle, Dimmit, and Zavala. First, we pulled off a walkout followed by electoral victories in 15 races in those counties. Second, we created a political party that I became its national president with a presence in 17 states plus the District of Columbia. The election involving the Crystal City Independent School District got me on the school board and its president. After a few tumultuous meetings, it was clear I knew how to use power and was unafraid to use it. When we hired our first Chicano superintendent, Angel Noe Gonzalez, we asked him to plan and propose a bilingual program. He did incrementally but by 1973, my last year on the board, he proposed, and we adopted by a vote of 4-3 his 22 Recommendations for a Bilingual and Bicultural Program. It was the birth of our B3 commitment and is completely laid out in *The Politics of Bilingual Education: A Study of Four Southwest Texas Communities*. Item 9 reads in part:

> The historical contributions and cultural characteristics identified with the Mexican American will become an integral part of the total program (Pre-K to 12). This will ensure all students to understand and appreciate, in a positive sense, historical contributions and the rich culture of the Mexican and the Mexican American"
>
> (Hardgrave and Hinojosa 1975:62).

As a practicing attorney, I once had a public fight on a Jerry Springer television show over our ethnic identity and ancestry. There were four of us on the program, a white Aryan brotherhood male and young white girl, a Nation of

Islam representative, and me as supposedly the Chicano nationalist. The Black guy, sitting next to my right, made the claim that Mexicans were the progeny of Africans and showed a photo of the Olmec head figure everyone has seen with the big flat nose, big lips, and clearly other African phenotypical features but for the hair covered with what looks like a football helmet. He nearly shoved it on my face after showing it to the camera. I elbowed him in the face, and we went to a commercial break.

Being a B3 person has given me stature and respect I never imagined. When as head of La Raza Unida Party I opened dialogue with the Mexican President in the 1970s and continued into the early 2000s, I usually was the one to be the lead speaker at those first meetings with public officials and dignitaries, the Mexican press, and other interested persons in our cause. The same thing happened to me in 1992 when I took a huge delegation to Spain in what we called "The Trip Back" to re-introduce Spaniards to their orphaned progeny. I addressed the nation on a government television station only because I spoke Spanish better than others. The most important aspect of knowing Spanish, however, has been the ability to have spent time talking to my father and grandmother as well as many other elders who only speak Spanish. I realize now that this was the utmost respect for our culture and family relationships. But the most important question in 2020 is that given that students in the public schools of Texas and other southwestern states are the majority of pupils are of Mexican origin and other Hispanic ancestries, why do we keep an Anglo-centric curriculum? Is it not time for the discipline of Mexican origin and Hispanic studies to move front and center and teach the majority?

References

Armesto, Felipe Fernandez. 2014. *Our America: A Hispanic History of the US*. New York: W.W. Norton.

Daniels, Roger. 2004. *Guarding the Golden Door: American Immigration Policy and Immigration since 1882*. New York: Hill and Wang.

Elias, Scott. 2020. "Beringia's Lost World of the Ice Age," at https://www.nps.gov/articles/nps-v12-i12-c8-htm/. Retrieved September 13, 2020.

Gutierrez, Jose Angel. 1998. *The Making of a Chicano Militant: Lessons from Cristal*. Madison, WI: University of Wisconsin Press.

————. 2020, "Chapter Eight: Operation Wetback: The "Ike" Eisenhower's Ethnic Cleansing Program," in *FBI Surveillance of Mexicans and Chicanos, 1920–1980*. Lanham, MD: Lexington Books.

————.2020. *FBI Surveillance of Mexican and Chicanos, 1920–1980*. Lanham, MD: Lexington Books.

Hammett, A. B. J. 1973. *The Empresario Don Martin De Leon*. Austin, TX: Texian Press.

Handwerk, Brian. June 5, 2019. "Ancient DNA Reveals Complex Story of Human Migration, Beringia Siberia and North America." *Smithsonian* Magazine, July/August 2020.

Hardgrave, Jr., Robert L., and Santiago Hinojosa. 1975. *The Politics of Bilingual Education: A Study of Four Southwest Texas Communities*. Manchaca, TX: Sterling Swift Publishing Company.

Kreneck, Thomas H. 2001. *Mexican American Odyssey: Felix Tijerina: Entrepreneur and Civic Leader, 1905–1965*. College Station, TX: Texas A&M University Press.

Markstein, Don. 2020. "Texas History Movies" at www.toonopedia.com/texhist.htm/. Retrieved September 14, 2020.

Monday, Jane Clements, and Frances Brannen Vick. 2007. *Petra's Legacy: The South Texas Ranching Empire of Petra Vela and Mifflin Kenedy*. College Station, TX: Texas A&M University Press.

San Miguel, Jr., Guadalupe. 2020. "Mexican Americans and Education" at https:www/tshaonline.org/handbook/entries/mexican-americans-and-education/. Retrieved September 11, 2020.

Sherill, Robert. 1968. *Gothic Politics in the Deep South*. New York: Ballantine Books.

Shockley, John Stapes. 1974. *Chicano Revolt in a Texas Town*. Notre Dame, IN: University of Notre Dame Press.

Steen, Ralph W. 1942. *Texas: A Story of Progress*. Austin, TX: The Steck Company.

Valenzuela, Angela. 1999. *Subtractive Schooling: US-Mexican Youth and the Politics of Caring*. Albany, NY: State University of New York Press.

Index